The New Europe

The New Europe:
Revolution in East-West Relations

Proceedings of
The Academy of
Political Science

Volume 38
Number 1

ISSN 0065-0684

Edited by Nils H. Wessell

New York, 1991

Copyright © 1991 by The Academy of Political Science

All rights reserved

Library of Congress Catalog Card Number 90-84819

Cover design by Cynthia Brady

Printed by Capital City Press, Montpelier, Vermont

Contents

Preface

The Academy originally proposed this volume in response to the historic changes contemplated by the countries of Western Europe. Since then the volume — much like Europe itself — had to be continually reappraised as virtually every day brought new surprises with profound consequences. Even as this preface is being written, Margaret Thatcher — the one constant factor in European politics since 1979 — has been forced to resign as prime minister of Great Britain.

With Europe undergoing such change, today's astute analysis is often outdated tomorrow. Thus, for the contributors to this volume, writing about a changing Europe has truly been a Sisyphean task. No matter how frequently they rethought and revised their manuscripts, events in Europe outpaced them. It was therefore with courage that they reduced a moving picture to a snapshot in an attempt to describe some of the recent events and lend historical and political perspective to emerging realities that constitute the new Europe.

The "new Europe" suggests that established orders and their protective institutions have crumbled and that formation is taking place. People create institutions, but these institutions generally shape the quality and direction of human experience. Europe, both east and west of what was the Berlin Wall, is engaged in an effort to create a new set of institutions that will consequently establish a new order. It is this process of change that serves as the subject of this volume.

Although the title *The New Europe* represents the currents of change sweeping over Europe, it might be more accurate to speak of the new Europes. While nothing remains of the Berlin Wall except memories, and Germany is once again a united country, the two halves of Europe are still divided and headed in virtually opposite directions.

In Western Europe, the trend is toward integration and consolidation, quite possibly the most significant ceding of power from sovereign states to central authority since the ratification of the United States Constitution in 1787. It is primarily a tribute to the West's political stability and the strength of the desire for economic expansion that these nations have decided to overcome their nationalistic differences and move toward an economic and political union more reminiscent of confederated states than sovereign nations.

In Eastern Europe, on the other hand, the immediate trend points toward disintegration rather than integration. In Czechoslovakia, Poland, Romania, Bulgaria, Hungary, Yugoslavia, and the USSR itself, a new nationalism — or as some have defined it, tribalism — is threatening the effort to build up strong and radically different political and economic institutions that seek to guarantee democracy and political freedoms. This tribalism, which is marked by virulent racism and intolerance, thrives in the nearly bankrupt political and economic cultures that the demise of Eastern European tyranny has exposed.

Whether the incipient political and economic institutions in both the East and the West will succeed is still open to question. This volume is intended to further the understanding of the changes sweeping Europe and thus contribute to the ongoing dialogue that is trying to build new understandings and to redefine conceptions of the world order. The Academy believes that this volume is an important contribution to the contemporary literature on Europe. Indeed, given the rapidity of change, there is nothing like it.

The views expressed in *The New Europe* are those of the individual authors and are not necessarily those of any organizations with which they are associated. The Academy of Political Science, founded in 1880, serves as a forum for the development and dissemination of opinion on public-policy questions. It is a nonpartisan, not-for-profit organization, and it does not make recommendations on political and social issues.

Robert H. Connery, who was president of the Academy for many years and is now an honorary member, suggested that the Academy undertake the project, and the Academy is indebted to him for his encouragement and support. We are pleased, moreover, that Nils H. Wessell agreed to edit the volume.

The Academy was able to complete the project because of generous contributions from its members. We thank them.

Finally, the Academy is grateful to William V. Farr for his editorial direction of this project and to Stephen H. Weinstein, Rob Mitchell, and Roger Berkowitz for their editorial assistance.

FRANK J. MACCHIAROLA
President

Contributors

MADELEINE ALBRIGHT is president, Center for National Policy, and Donner Professor of International Affairs and director, Women in Foreign Service Program, School of Foreign Service, Georgetown University. She is the author of *Czechoslovakia 1968: The Role of the Press* and *Poland: The Role of the Press in Political Change*.

JOHN A. COLEMAN, S.J., is professor of religion and society, Graduate Theological Union, Berkeley, California. He is coauthor, with Gregory Baum, of *The Church and Christian Democracy*.

STEPHEN COONEY is director, International Investment and Finance, National Association of Manufacturers. He is the author of *EC-92 and U.S. Industry: An N.A.M. Report on the Major Issues for U.S. Manufacturers in the European Community's Internal Market Program*.

DAVID GRESS is a historian and senior research fellow, Hoover Institution, Stanford University. He is the author of many works on European history and politics, most recently, with Dennis L. Bark, of the two-volume *History of West Germany 1945–1988*.

ROBBIN LAIRD, director, European and Soviet Studies, Institute for Defense Analyses, is the author of *The Future of the Alliance: The Europeanization Challenge* (forthcoming).

F. STEPHEN LARRABEE is senior staff member, RAND Corporation. Formerly vice president and director of studies, Institute for East-West Security Studies, he is the author of *The Two German States and East-West Security*.

FRANK J. MACCHIAROLA, formerly chancellor of the New York City school system, is president and executive director, the Academy of Political Science, and professor of business, Columbia University.

KENNETH MAXWELL is senior fellow, Council on Foreign Relations, and director, Camões Center for the Study of the Portuguese-Speaking World, Columbia University. His most recent books are *Democracy and Foreign Policy in the New Spain* and *Portugal: Ancient Country, Young Democracy*.

PHILLIP A. PETERSEN, formerly senior Sovietologist for Soviet military and external affairs, Office of the Secretary of Defense, is senior fellow, Strategic Concepts Development Center, Institute for Strategic Studies, National Defense University. He is the author of sixty works on security and the Soviet military, including his March 1990 study, "The Emerging Soviet Vision of European Security."

ROBERT L. PFALTZGRAFF, JR., is president, Institute for Foreign Policy Analysis, and Shelby Cullom Davis Professor of International Security Studies, Fletcher School of Law and Diplomacy, Tufts University. He has written and lectured widely on NATO policies and strategy.

DAVID ROBERTSON, official fellow, St. Hugh's College, Oxford University, is Krupp Senior Associate, Institute for East-West Security Studies. He is the author of *Enhancing European Security*.

ALLEN L. SPRINGER is associate professor of government and legal studies, Bowdoin College. He is the author of *The International Law of Pollution: Protecting the Global Environment in a World of Sovereign States*.

ROBERT STRAUSZ-HUPE is a distinguished fellow, the Heritage Foundation. Formerly ambassador to NATO and Turkey, he is the author of *In My Time* and *Protracted Conflict*.

STEPHEN F. SZABO is associate dean for academic affairs, the Paul H. Nitze School of Advanced International Studies, Johns Hopkins University. He is the author of *The Changing Politics of German Security*.

VLADIMIR TISMANEANU is assistant professor, Department of Government and Politics, University of Maryland. He is the author of *In Search of Civil Society: Independent Peace Movements in the Soviet Bloc* and *The Crisis of Marxist Ideology in Eastern Europe: The Poverty of Utopia*.

MICHAEL VLAHOS, formerly director, Center for the Study of Foreign Affairs, United States Department of State, has also been director, Security Studies Program, School of Advanced International Studies, Johns Hopkins University. He is the author of *Thinking about World Change* and *Strategic Defense & the American Ethos*.

NILS H. WESSELL is head, Department of Humanities, and associate professor of government, the U.S. Coast Guard Academy. Formerly director of the Office of Research, U.S. Information Agency, he is coauthor, with Joane Gowa, of *Ground Rules for Soviet and American Involvement in Regional Conflicts* and coeditor, with Grayson Kirk, of *The Soviet Threat: Myths and Realities*.

The New Soviet Approach to Europe

F. STEPHEN LARRABEE

Under Mikhail S. Gorbachev, Soviet policy toward Europe has undergone the most dramatic changes since the end of World War II. Soon after coming to power, Gorbachev embarked on a policy designed to strengthen ties with Western Europe and exploit transatlantic differences. At the same time, he tried to redefine relations with Eastern Europe, putting greater emphasis on "freedom of choice" and economic efficiency.

Gorbachev's policy was predicated on a gradual evolution of the bipolar security system in Europe and the continued existence of two German states. His initiatives, however, unleashed forces that took on a dynamic of their own and resulted in the collapse of communism in Eastern Europe and the destruction of the bipolar security order based on the division of Europe into two opposing political-ideological blocs. As a result, the Soviet leadership is now faced with the need to construct a new policy not only toward Eastern Europe but toward Europe as a whole. Moreover, it must do so at a time when the Soviet Union faces major internal difficulties that could severely limit its capacity to pursue a vigorous and coherent European policy.

Brezhnev's Legacy

Soviet policy in Europe under Gorbachev must be seen against the background of the policy that he inherited from his predecessors, especially Leonid I. Brezhnev. Brezhnev's policy during his latter years was characterized by two principal features. The first was the USSR's isolation in Western Europe. Brezhnev's military buildup, especially the development of the SS-20 medium-range missile, proved

This essay was written while the author was Distinguished Scholar-in-Residence at the Institute for East-West Security Studies in New York City and was supported by a grant from the Ford Foundation, whose financial assistance is gratefully acknowledged. The author is a senior staff member at the RAND Corporation in Santa Monica, California, but the essay reflects his personal views and not those of the RAND Corporation or any of its sponsors.

to be a major strategic blunder and had a negative impact on Soviet relations with Western Europe. Rather than weakening Western cohesion and providing the USSR with important military advantages — as was its apparent intention — the buildup had the opposite effect, strengthening the cohesion of the North Atlantic Treaty Organization (NATO) and leading to a counterdeployment of United States missiles on European soil.

This miscalculation was compounded by a serious tactical error: the decision to walk out of the intermediate-range nuclear forces (INF) talks in Geneva in November 1983. This walkout made the Soviet Union appear to be the main obstacle to arms control, further tarnishing its image in Western Europe. As a result, by the time Gorbachev assumed power in March 1985 the Soviet Union had become seriously isolated.

The second feature of Brezhnev's policy was a visible erosion of Soviet hegemony in Eastern Europe. On the economic side, progress toward integration within the Council for Mutual Economic Assistance (CMEA) had virtually ground to a halt. On the political side, the Soviet effort to freeze East-West relations after the collapse of the INF talks upset the USSR's East European allies and accentuated differences within the Warsaw Pact, particularly with Hungary and East Germany, both of which had developed a strong vested stake in East-West détente. These problems were compounded by the impact of the succession issue, which increasingly preoccupied the Soviet leadership, deflecting attention away from pressing international problems, including those in Eastern Europe. As a result, Soviet policy toward Eastern Europe was increasingly characterized by drift and stagnation.

In short, by the mid-1980s the Soviet empire, as Charles Gati aptly put it, was "alive but not well."[1] The once monolithic bloc had become not only more diverse but also more fragmented. Stability had been bought at the price of stagnation, and ideological corrosion had replaced ideological cohesion as the hallmark of Soviet policy toward Eastern Europe.

New Thinking and Western Europe

When Gorbachev assumed power in March 1985, he inherited a European policy in deep crisis. In Western Europe, the Soviet Union was isolated, its policy stalled as a result of the INF debacle. In Eastern Europe, the USSR found itself at odds with its allies, many of which increasingly sought to exploit the Soviet preoccupation with internal problems — particularly the succession issue — to expand their room for maneuver. At the same time, Gorbachev was confronted with a mounting economic crisis that threatened to undermine the Soviet Union's ability to remain a major military and political power.

These developments required changes in Soviet policy toward Europe. Moreover, they coincided with a shift in Soviet perspectives on Western Europe and NATO. In the 1950s and 1960s the Soviet Union had seen Western Europe (with the exception of France) largely as a pliant tool in the United States global strategy. While the Soviets realized that West European interests were not always identical with those of the United States, they thought that American economic and military power ensured that American interests would largely prevail.

In the 1970s and 1980s, however, there was a growing recognition of the importance of Western Europe as an independent "power center" within the capitalist world. As Alexander Yakovlev, one of Gorbachev's closest advisers, noted in 1985: "The distancing of Western Europe, Japan, and other capitalist countries from U.S. strategic military plans in the near future is neither an excessively rash fantasy nor a nebulous prospect. It is dictated by objective factors having to do with the rational guarantee of all of their political and economic interests, including security."[2]

Gorbachev's report to the Twenty-seventh Party Congress reflected some of these insights. He noted that the economic, financial, and technological superiority that the United States had exercised in the past had been "put to a serious test" and that Western Europe and Japan were challenging the United States even in areas where it had traditionally exerted undisputed hegemony, such as high technology. Many sectors of West European public opinion, he claimed, "had begun to openly discuss whether US policy coincides with Western Europe's notions about its own security and whether the US was going too far in its claims to leadership." While admitting that the economic, political, military, and other common interests of the three centers of power (the United States, Japan, and Western Europe) could not be expected to break up in the near future, he warned that the United States "should not expect unquestioning obedience of its allies" and predicted that "contradictions" within the capitalist camp were likely to increase as a result of the emergence of new centers of power.[3]

Gorbachev's early statements clearly suggested that he intended to take a more differentiated approach to relations with the West, according greater importance to Western Europe. Soon after coming to power, for instance, he acknowledged the importance of relations with the United States but noted: "We do not view the world solely through the prism of these relationships. We understand the importance of other countries."[4] In effect, this represented an upgrading of the role of other areas, especially Western Europe, in Soviet policy.

There were other signs that the USSR was according Western Europe greater priority. One of the most important was the creation in late 1987 of the Institute on Europe, headed by a highly respected academic, Vitali Zhurkin, former deputy director of the Institute of USA and Canada. The establishment of the new institute reflected the Kremlin's growing appreciation of the importance and autonomy of Western Europe. At the same time, it provided the Soviet leadership with an important additional source of information and informed analyses on current developments in Europe.

This is not to argue, as some observers have, that Gorbachev has adopted a "Europe first" strategy.[5] Indeed, one of the striking features of Gorbachev's first years in power was his high priority on obtaining an accommodation with the United States. Relations with Western Europe, though accorded a higher priority than in the past, were still regarded as secondary to the improvement of relations with the United States.

Some Soviet officials, in fact, openly complained that this preoccupation with the United States had blinded the USSR to trends toward greater political and military self-assertion on the part of Western Europe:

> US monopoly on engaging in dialogue with the USSR consolidates American leadership in the West, leaving Western Europe a secondary role in world politics. In our view, we largely facilitated this ourselves. Bewitched by the industrial and military might of the United States, we failed to notice, or—to be more precise—did not take fully into account, the fact that Pax Americana was shaking and had begun to crumble, while other imperialist centres, including Western Europe, were becoming more active in world affairs.[6]

Soviet policy, they charged, had failed to pay sufficient attention to these changes. They pointed in particular to the intensification of European military integration, which "had picked up speed since Reykjavik," warning that "passivity" and attempts to ignore the creation of a European defense "will inescapably lead to a situation where this defense will be fashioned according to American formulas, to the prejudice of the USSR." As a result, the Soviet Union would be forced to deal with a joint NATO position, in this case a United States position, just as it was increasingly forced to deal with a joint European position of the European Community (EC). These officials called for "new approaches" that would take due account of the European desire for greater independence in security matters.

These remarks, though hardly typical, reflected a growing debate about the implications of European defense. On this issue, as on others, there was no consensus. One school of thought saw the prospects for serious cooperation as largely ephemeral; a second, taking the trend more seriously, argued that the intensification of economic integration was providing the basis for much closer security and military cooperation.

The key issue, in Moscow's view, was the impact of these developments on East-West relations. Were they an effort to develop Western Europe into a truly independent power center or simply an attempt to strengthen the European pillar of NATO and influence Western Europe's voice in the shaping of NATO military policy? Again, there were different views. However, the dominant one—at least within the Soviet Foreign Ministry—tended to regard the trend toward closer military cooperation as a potential threat to East-West détente and an effort to strengthen the European pillar of NATO. Writing in *International Affairs*, the journal of the Soviet Foreign Ministry, V. Stupishin, a high-ranking Foreign Ministry official, concluded:

> The growth of military integration in Western Europe and creation of some new organizational forms of a "European buttress" of NATO may provide Western Europe with yet another instrument for influencing the USA. But a far more essential and really negative result of this will be that the split of Europe into opposed blocs will be consolidated and new obstacles will be put up in the general European process and the construction of a common European home will be impeded, to the detriment of our interests as well. That is why we are so concerned over the military-integration tendencies in Western Europe.[7]

The debate over European defense reflected a broader shift in Soviet attitudes in the late 1980s regarding developments in Western Europe. In the 1970s and early 1980s the greater self-confidence and assertiveness of Western Europe had generally been welcomed and seen as undermining United States influence within NATO. Gorbachev's remarks at the Twenty-seventh Party Congress had largely reflected this perspective. By the late 1980s, however, Soviet officials and analysts were beginning to take a more differentiated view of these developments. The critical West European reaction to the Reykjavik summit and the fears of "denuclearization" prompted by the INF treaty, especially in France and Great Britain, contributed to a growing recognition that this new West European self-assertiveness might not always work to Soviet advantage.

These growing doubts were also visible in the shift in Soviet attitudes and policy toward France. When Gorbachev came to power in 1985 he tried to make France the centerpiece of his West European policy. This effort, however, produced few positive results. Soviet commentary on France after 1986 reflected growing disappointment with the course of French policy. France's adherence to nuclear deterrence and its plans to modernize its strategic nuclear arsenal caused particular concern. France was also seen as the spearhead behind the intensification of military and security cooperation in Western Europe, which, Soviet officials charged, was designed to justify France's adherence to nuclear deterrence: "The revival of the military articles of the 1963 Elysée Treaty with the FRG [Federal Republic of Germany], the stepped-up military cooperation with Britain, Italy and Spain, the reanimation of Western European Union, the Platform for European Security Interests adopted in the Hague — all these and other integrational processes in Western Europe have been inspired and organized mainly by Paris, which clearly is looking for a 'European' political justification of its policy of perpetuating 'nuclear deterrence.'"[8]

The intensification of French military ties with West Germany also provoked concern. "What and whom are these ties directed against?" asked Soviet officials.[9] Such questions reflected the USSR's fear that French-German military cooperation might provide the basis for broader West European cooperation in the military area and possibly even help West Germany acquire nuclear weapons through the back door. Thus, after 1986, Soviet enthusiasm for France's "Europeanism" was largely overshadowed by a concern that the emerging military cooperation with West Germany would strengthen NATO and tip the military balance in Europe against the Soviet Union.

The European Community

Concern with the implications of West European military integration has been one aspect of the broader Soviet concern with the process of West European integration generally. For many years the USSR regarded the EC as little more than an instrument to strengthen the European pillar of NATO. Soviet attitudes toward the EC, however, have undergone a significant evolution under Gorbachev. Since the mid-1980s, Soviet analysts have shown an increasing appreciation of the growing role of the EC as an economic and political actor in international affairs. In particular, analysts have pointed to a marked evolution toward formulating common EC positions on foreign policy.[10]

Soviet analysts see the EC decision to create a single internal market by 1992 as "a qualitatively new stage" in the integration process, which will have major implications for East-West relations.[11] This, they argue, will accelerate integration — including foreign policy and military — and encourage closer cooperation in other areas. In the 1990s the United States (and, by implication, the Soviet Union) will have to deal with a Western Europe that is economically and technologically stronger as well as politically and militarily more cohesive.

The emergence of the EC as a new power center has required the Soviet Union to adopt a new approach toward the organization. This new approach began to manifest itself soon after Gorbachev assumed power. During Italian Prime Minister Bettino Craxi's visit to Moscow in May 1985, the new Soviet leader announced the USSR's willingness to recognize the EC as a "political entity" and to resume negotiations regulating relations between the EC and the CMEA, which had been broken off in the spring of 1980.[12] These negotiations led to the signing of a "Common Declaration" between the EC and the CMEA on 25 June 1988, which provided the framework for the establishment of diplomatic relations and the conclusion of trade agreements between the EC and individual members of the CMEA.

The 1988 Common Declaration was primarily motivated by economic concerns, particularly the USSR's desire for access to West European trade and technology. But it also reflected the Soviet leadership's growing appreciation of the important political role that the EC had begun to play in East-West relations. Soviet officials and analysts have increasingly pointed to the long-term political implications of accelerated integration, which is seen as laying the groundwork for closer cooperation in other areas, including foreign policy and the military.

From the Soviet Union's perspective, the main danger is that West European integration will solidify the division of Europe into blocs, erecting new barriers to East-West trade, and deepening the economic and technological gap between the two parts of Europe. Gorbachev's emphasis on the "common European home" has thus partly been aimed at preventing the creation of new impediments to Soviet access to West European research and development programs and ensuring that the USSR will benefit from new technology as West European integration intensifies.

Eastern Europe

Gorbachev does not appear to have had a "grand design" for Eastern Europe. Rather, his policy emerged gradually as a result of incremental changes and adjustments. The cumulative effect of these changes, however, has been seriously to erode Soviet influence in Eastern Europe.

Initially, Gorbachev's policy differed little from that of his predecessors. Its emphasis was on increasing political, economic, and military integration — albeit on a more consultative basis. In effect, Gorbachev tried to strike a balance between the legitimization of "national interests" and the promotion of "international obligations" and between the demands of diversity and the desire for unity. The greater weight, however, was clearly on the side of closer unity.

Gorbachev's statements during 1986 and 1987 continued to reflect this uneasy balance between the demands of diversity and the desire for unity. The sense of continuity in Soviet policy in this period was reinforced by the appearance of authoritative articles by top Soviet officials in the Soviet press stressing the importance of "proletarian internationalism" (a code word for Soviet hegemony) and attacking market-oriented policies and other steps that violated "general laws of socialist construction."[13] Such articles were counterbalanced, however, by others representing a more open and flexible policy, suggesting the lack of a firm line on Soviet policy toward Eastern Europe.[14]

During late 1987 and early 1988, however, the outlines of a new policy toward Eastern Europe — a "Gorbachev doctrine" began to emerge. In essence, this doctrine represented an effort to extend the principles of perestroika and "new thinking" to relations with the USSR's East European allies. It was designed to eliminate "distortions" that had inhibited socioeconomic development of the bloc countries in the past — many of them rooted in the Stalinist system imposed on these countries in the late 1940s and early 1950s — and to create a more balanced relationship based on true partnership and mutual respect for national differences.

In the political arena, Gorbachev showed a willingness to grant East European leaders greater flexibility and freedom to decide their own affairs — as long as their efforts did not directly contradict or undercut Soviet interests. Allies were allowed greater initiative, especially in disarmament matters and relations with Western Europe. Consultation between the Soviet Union and its allies became more regularized and more genuine. While the Soviet Union continued to set the agenda for bloc relations, especially on military matters, the views of the East European allies were more frequently solicited.

There was also greater recognition — and tolerance — of diversity within the bloc. As Gorbachev stressed in a speech in Prague in April 1987: "We are far from calling on anyone to copy us. Every socialist country has its specific features, and the fraternal parties determine their political line with a view to the national conditions. . . . No one has the right to claim a special status in the socialist world. The independence of every party, its responsibility to its people, and its right to resolve problems of the country's development in a sovereign way — these are indisputable principles for us."[15] He reiterated this point in his speech commemorating the seventieth anniversary of the Bolshevik Revolution on 2 November 1987, noting: "Unity does not mean identity or uniformity."[16] In short, the Soviet Union no longer claimed that there was a single path to socialism or that only one model is universally valid. Each national party had the right to decide how socialism should best be developed in its own country, taking into account its own circumstances as well as its obligations to the socialist community as a whole.

The most important shift, however, was Gorbachev's willingness to repudiate the Brezhnev doctrine. Initially, Gorbachev showed a reluctance to face the issue squarely, in part because he did not want to destabilize the Gustáv Husák/Milos Jakes regime in Prague, which was closely associated with the period of "normalization" following the Soviet-led invasion in 1968. Soviet domestic considerations — above all, resistance from the conservatives within the Communist Party of the Soviet Union (CPSU) — also probably played a role.

Beginning in 1988, however, Gorbachev began step by step to move closer to repudiating the doctrine. The communiqué issued at the end of the Gorbachev trip to Yugoslavia in March 1988, for example, expressed "respect for different paths to socialism and stressed the right of all countries to unimpeded independence and equal rights" regardless of their sociopolitical system.[17] In his speech to the Council of Europe in Strasbourg in July 1989 Gorbachev was even more explicit, stating that "any interference in internal affairs, any attempts to limit the sovereignty of states — both friends and allies or anyone else — is inadmissible."[18]

Finally, during his visit to Finland in October 1989, Gorbachev openly repudiated the Brezhnev doctrine. The doctrine, Soviet Foreign Ministry spokesman Gennadi Gerasimov stressed, was "dead." It had been replaced by what he termed the "Sinatra doctrine," referring to Frank Sinatra's popular song entitled "My Way." This implied, as Gerasimov put it, that each East European country was free to carry out political and social changes "their way" without interference from the USSR. At the Warsaw Pact meeting in Moscow in December 1989 the 1968 invasion of Czechoslovakia was formally condemned as "illegal," and the member states committed themselves to following a policy of strict noninterference in each other's internal affairs.

These measures were accompanied by a strong emphasis on the need for economic reform. While Gorbachev did not force the Soviet model of reform on his East European allies, he made it clear that the East European economies had to be restructured to make them more efficient and competitive. On the one hand, he stepped up the pressure on his East European allies to increase the quality of their manufactured goods exported to the Soviet Union; on the other, he indicated that the USSR was no longer willing to provide Eastern Europe with raw materials and energy at previous levels.

Rather than creating greater cohesion within the bloc, however, Gorbachev's emphasis on reform accentuated the divisions among the Soviet Union's East European allies. Within Hungary and Poland, his calls for reform legitimized the reformers' calls for more radical, more rapid change. At the same time, these calls indirectly increased the pressure on the remaining bloc members to embrace reform more seriously.

By 1988 the bloc had in effect split into two camps. On one side was a reformist group composed of the USSR, Hungary, and Poland. On the other was a "rejectionist front" consisting of Czechoslovakia, East Germany, and Romania, which either rejected reforms outright or were less than enthusiastic about implementing them. Bulgaria was somewhere in between: General Secretary Todor Zhivkov paid lip service to reform, but he dragged his feet in actually implementing them.

To be sure, Gorbachev did not directly demand that his allies adopt the Soviet model of reform. However, by way of example and word he indirectly increased the pressure on the orthodox members of the bloc to embrace reform more seriously. Perhaps most important, he increased popular expectations and pressures for change from below. In many East European countries, such as East Germany and Bulgaria, Gorbachev became a symbol of reform and a rallying point for discontent, especially among intellectuals.

In several instances, moreover, Gorbachev directly intervened to accelerate the process of change. In Poland, for example, Mieczyslaw Rakowski, the party leader, reportedly agreed to the creation of a Solidarity-led government in August 1989 after a telephone call from Gorbachev. In Bulgaria, Foreign Minister Petar Mladenov apparently received a green light to oust Zhivkov during a stopover in Moscow just before the critical Central Committee meeting that led to Zhivkov's removal on 10 November 1989. And, in Czechoslovakia, Soviet officials reportedly worked behind the scenes in November 1989 to undermine the Jakes government.

Gorbachev's role in initiating the transition in East Germany was also critical. He did not stop Hungary from opening its borders and allowing the East German refugees camped in Budapest to emigrate to West Germany — the move that touched off the crisis in East Germany — and he intervened to press the East German leadership to allow the East German refugees in the West German embassy in Prague to emigrate to the Federal Republic. Moreover, in the crucial period in August and September 1989 the Soviets appear to have encouraged the efforts by Egon Krenz and some of his close associates to depose Erich Honecker.[19]

Finally, during his visit to East Berlin in early October 1989, Gorbachev made it clear to the East German leadership that in case of any turmoil the Soviet troops in East Germany would stay in their barracks. Thus, effectively withdrawing his support of Honecker, Gorbachev accelerated the crisis in East Germany (and indirectly the entire bloc). In the past the East German leaders had assumed that in case of major unrest they could count on Soviet "fraternal assistance." Gorbachev's remarks, however, made it clear that the East German leaders could no longer count on Moscow to intervene to save them if things got out of hand.

The unrest in East Germany had an important "demonstration effect" throughout Eastern Europe: it provided concrete proof that the Brezhnev doctrine was really dead. Once this became clear, the other regimes fell in rapid succession. Bulgarian leader Todor Zhivkov was ousted on 10 November 1989; Czechoslovak leader Milos Jakes stepped down in early December; and Nicolae Ceausescu was forced to flee on 22 December and was executed a few days later. By Christmas the spasm of revolt was over and the transition process had begun in all the former Communist countries of the Soviet bloc.

This is not to argue that Gorbachev consciously sought to introduce Western-style democracy in Eastern Europe. Clearly, he did not. What he hoped for was to replace orthodox Communists with more reform-minded ones. However, the legitimacy of the Communist parties in Eastern Europe was so weak that the process of change, once initiated, was impossible to control from above. Even in Hungary, where the party had begun the transition and carefully sought to stage-manage the process, the changes soon took on a momentum of their own, eroding support for the party and eventually sweeping it from power in the March 1990 elections.

The German Question

Soviet policy toward West Germany—and the German Question—also underwent a major, far-reaching shift under Gorbachev. Gorbachev's German policy, however, was not animated by any sort of grand design to resolve the German Question. Rather, it emerged incrementally, largely in reaction to events that Gorbachev unleashed but then proved powerless to control.

Gorbachev did not set out to unify Germany. On the contrary, he initially saw its division as a key element of a new European security order. However, he recognized the need for a new policy and saw that Andrey Gromyko's effort to isolate and "punish" West Germany after the collapse of the INF talks had largely backfired, resulting instead in the Soviet Union's self-isolation. Soon after coming to power, therefore, Gorbachev gradually began to abandon the policy of isolation and to cultivate more cordial and cooperative relations with West Germany.

This shift in policy did not manifest itself immediately. During the first year and a half after Gorbachev assumed power, West Germany continued to be the subject of constant vituperation for its "revanchist" policy. Gorbachev made highly visible visits to Paris and London in 1985 and 1986 but bypassed Bonn. Indeed, Gorbachev's policy during this period bears striking similarities to Soviet Westpolitik in the late 1960s, when the Soviet Union sought to make France the centerpiece of its détente efforts and at the same time tried to isolate West Germany.

By 1986, however, the Soviet attitude showed signs of softening. The campaign against German "revanchism" initiated in the spring of 1984 gradually began to abate. During Foreign Minister Hans-Dietrich Genscher's visit to Moscow in July 1986, Gorbachev offered to open a "new page" in relations; a number of important bilateral agreements were initiated or signed, including a long-delayed framework agreement on scientific and technological cooperation.

Genscher's visit was followed by other small but important signs that the Soviet attitude toward West Germany was softening: a visible increase in the number of high-level visits, an increase in the number of ethnic Germans allowed to emigrate to West Germany, and a more cooperative attitude toward Berlin. These changes contributed to an improvement in relations and paved the way for Chancellor Helmut Kohl's visit to Moscow in October 1988.

Kohl's visit was a watershed in relations. The visit essentially ended the quarantine that had been imposed on West Germany in the aftermath of the Soviet walkout from INF talks. During the visit, six new governmental agreements were signed in areas ranging from environmental protection to nuclear and maritime safety. In addition, more than thirty new contracts with West German firms were signed, including a major deal for the sale of a high-temperature nuclear reactor.

The Kohl visit was the culmination of the shift in Soviet policy that had begun soon after Gorbachev assumed power. In effect, it represented the Soviet Union's effort to bring its policy toward West Germany into harmony with its policy toward the rest of Western Europe. Given West Germany's key role in Europe and within the Western alliance, any détente policy that excluded it had little chance of success.

The reassessment of policy toward West Germany also reflected a disappointment with French policy. Initially, Gorbachev seemed to have had hopes of reviving the Soviet Union's special relationship with France and making France the centerpiece of Soviet policy toward Western Europe. The progressive hardening of French policy during President François Mitterrand's first term, however, and France's reserved attitude toward arms control — especially the INF agreement — dashed whatever hopes Gorbachev may have had in this regard and made rapprochement with West Germany more attractive. At the same time, West Germany's favorable attitude toward perestroika and arms control, embodied particularly in Foreign Minister Genscher's Davos speech in February 1989, undoubtedly encouraged Gorbachev to seek closer ties to West Germany.[20]

Economic factors also played an important role. West Germany was the Soviet Union's largest trading partner in the West. If Gorbachev's policy of perestroika were to succeed, the USSR would require financial assistance from the West. Since West Germany was the most likely source of both credits and technology, the Soviets had an additional incentive to improve their ties.

This rapprochement, however, did not imply a shift in the Soviet approach to German unification or Berlin. During Kohl's visit, Gorbachev emphasized that Germany's division was the result of a specific historical development. Any attempt to change the situation or pursue "unrealistic policies," he said, would be "an unpredictable and even dangerous business."[21] Similarly, he warned that efforts to seek improvements in the status of West Berlin contradicted the 1971 Four Power Agreement on Berlin as well as the Helsinki Accord. In other words, limited "reassociation" between the two German states was one thing, unification quite another.

Gorbachev's remarks during Kohl's 1988 visit, however, were made within the context of a relatively stable Eastern bloc. This situation changed dramatically in the latter half of 1989, after the Hungarian government allowed East German refugees camped in Budapest to emigrate to West Germany. This move precipitated a mass exodus of refugees from East Germany and contributed to Honecker's fall and to the collapse of the German Democratic Republic (GDR).

In sanctioning — or at least not stopping — the opening of the Hungarian borders, Gorbachev clearly did not intend to precipitate the collapse of the GDR. Rather, he apparently hoped to encourage the removal of Honecker and the installation of a more reform-oriented leader who would be more flexible but could still be counted on to maintain firm control of the reform process. Wittingly or not, however, Gorbachev's actions did contribute to the collapse of the GDR and the growth of pressure for unification. Once it was clear that the Soviets would not intervene militarily, the demands for reform took on a momentum of their own, sweeping first Honecker, then his successor Egon Krenz, and finally the whole Socialist Unity Party (SED) from power.

Gorbachev seems to have been caught off balance by the dynamism and rapidity of events in East Germany. From the onset of the crisis and throughout the spring of 1990, Soviet policy toward East Germany was largely reactive, and Gorbachev was more a prisoner of events than their master. Once the Berlin Wall fell, events took on a momentum of their own and Gorbachev was largely forced to react to fast-changing developments that neither he nor the Western allies proved capable of controlling. While he expressed a willingness to allow German unification during Chancellor Kohl's visit to Moscow in February 1990, he insisted that a united Germany could not be a member of NATO. Indeed, Soviet policy during the first months of 1990 was remarkably rigid and inflexible.

The reasons for this have both psychological and political roots. The division of Germany was regarded as the main prize of World War II. For many Soviets, especially those in the top ranks of the military and the party, it was inconceivable that a united Germany would be allowed to enter NATO, which they regarded as an "anti-Soviet" alliance. In their minds, this would suggest that World War II had been fought in vain.

Moreover, many of these officials failed to grasp how significantly Soviet political influence in Eastern Europe had eroded as a result of the collapse of communism in the area. They continued to act as if the Soviet Union still had more political leverage than it actually had. In addition, few Soviet officials had foreseen that pressures for unification would emerge so rapidly or so soon. Moscow thus had no contingency plans on which it could draw. As a result, the Soviet leadership was ill-prepared to deal with the growing pressure for unification and its policy had an ad hoc and inconsistent character.

Domestic factors also influenced Soviet policy calculations. Indeed, they may have been decisive. Before the Twenty-eighth Party Congress in July 1990, Gorbachev faced mounting criticism of his policies on a wide variety of issues. At a time when perestroika was under fire for having shown few concrete results and he was being attacked for having "sold out" Eastern Europe, Gorbachev could ill-afford to give his domestic critics another weapon to use against him. The military in particular was strongly opposed to a united Germany's membership in NATO. But it was not alone. Party conservatives also warned of a "new German danger."

As a consequence, Gorbachev put forward a variety of schemes designed to forestall or prevent the integration of a united Germany in NATO: neutrality, a continuation of four-power rights for an extended duration after unification, the integration of Germany into both alliances, a pan-European security system based on the Conference on Security and Cooperation in Europe (CSCE), and finally a "French" solution in which Germany would be a member of the alliance but not of its military command. None of these proposals, however, were acceptable to West Germany or the other Western powers. Moreover, the USSR found itself isolated within its own alliance: the majority of the East European members of the Warsaw Pact, including Poland, favored a united Germany integrated into NATO.

By the time of the Washington summit with President George Bush in June 1990 there were signs that Gorbachev was looking for a face-saving mechanism that would allow him to accept a united Germany's incorporation into NATO but which could be portrayed in such a way that it did not look like a Soviet defeat and capitulation to a Western ultimatum. The main elements of such a package were contained in the nine-point plan that Bush presented at the Washington summit. The package was designed to make German membership in NATO more palatable and involved, inter alia, a gradual and phased withdrawal of Soviet troops, no forward deployment of NATO troops on East German territory, and economic assistance and compensation to the Soviet Union.

For domestic reasons, however, Gorbachev was unwilling to agree to final terms until after the Twenty-eighth Party Congress. As noted earlier, he apparently feared that his critics would use any concession on the German issue against him. The defeat of Egor K. Ligachev and the conservative faction at the congress, however, removed this danger. At the same time, the shift in NATO strategy announced at the NATO summit in London in early July 1990, together with promises by West German Chancellor Helmut Kohl of economic assistance and a reduction of the united Germany's armed forces to 370,000 men made it easier for Gorbachev to argue that Germany's entry into NATO would benefit the Soviet Union.

West Germany's agreement to reduce the size of its army was particularly important. This demonstrated that West Germany was willing to make a concrete contribution to military détente and paved the way for Gorbachev's formal agreement to the membership of a united Germany in NATO, which was announced at a joint press conference during Chancellor Kohl's visit to the Soviet Union in mid-July. In order to provide Moscow with further assurance, this commitment to reduce the size of the armed forces of a united Germany to 370,000 men was explicitly incorporated in article 3 of the "Final Settlement" of the "two plus four talks" regulating the external aspects of German unification, signed in Moscow on 12 September 1990.

In addition, in September, West Germany and the USSR signed a separate treaty of Good-neighborliness, Partnership and Cooperation, designed to expand and update the Renunciation of Force Agreement signed by the two countries in August 1970. Like the 1970 treaty, the new agreement emphasizes that the two sides will refrain from using force to resolve their differences. However, it goes considerably further than the 1970 treaty and contains a controversial nonaggression pledge (article 3). Although the new treaty specifically states that it does not infringe on rights and obligations arising from other bilateral and multilateral agreements signed by the two parties (article 19), the nonaggression clause has raised concerns in some Western capitals that it could lead to a weakening of Germany's commitment to Western defense.

As part of the overall settlement of German unification, Bonn also agreed to provide a 12 billion DM (about $8 billion) package to help underwrite the cost of the housing and withdrawal of the 380,000 Soviet troops stationed in East Germany. This package also included a 3 billion DM interest-free credit to aid the ailing Soviet economy.

Despite these "sweeteners," the unification of Germany, particularly a united Germany's membership in NATO, is a bitter pill for the Soviets to swallow. It effectively means the Soviet Union's military expulsion from Europe and a dramatic shift in the balance of power in favor of the West. More fundamentally, it represents the collapse of the USSR's postwar strategy toward Europe, which at least since 1955 has been aimed at maintaining two separate German states. Thus the USSR is now faced with the need to construct a new policy not just toward Germany but toward Europe as a whole.

Arms Control

In contrast to his predecessors, especially Leonid I. Brezhnev, Gorbachev has seen arms control as the primary means of enhancing Soviet security and reducing East-West confrontation. Moreover, he has been willing to adopt more flexible positions than his predecessors, especially regarding verification, in order to obtain agreements. He has also shown a much greater appreciation of the political impact of such agreements.

This change is well illustrated by Gorbachev's approach to limitations on intermediate-range nuclear forces (INF). Leonid I. Brezhnev and Yuri V. Andropov had consistently rejected President Ronald Reagan's proposal to eliminate all INF systems (the "zero option"). Instead, they tried to maintain Soviet superiority in this category of weapons, arguing that they wanted only "equal security," which in reality meant that the USSR should be allowed to maintain intermediate-range weapons equal to all those possessed by the United States and its European allies. This refusal led to the breakup of the negotiations and the American counter-deployment of American cruise and Pershing II missiles in later 1983.

In contrast to Brezhnev and Andropov, however, Gorbachev — after some hesitation — agreed to the total elimination of all Soviet medium-range missiles, including those based in Asia. Moreover, during United States Secretary of State George Schultz's visit to Moscow in April 1987, Gorbachev proposed eliminating not only all intermediate-range missiles but also all shorter-range missiles (with ranges from 500 km to 1,000 km) — the "double zero" option. This proposal caused considerable consternation within NATO, especially in West Germany, because it meant that the West would be left with only short-range missiles and nuclear artillery with ranges below 500 km for defense against a Soviet conventional attack. Many Europeans thought the proposal was a dangerous step toward the "denuclearization" of Europe. Once the United States had signaled its willingness to accept the offer, however, the West European countries, especially West Germany, had little choice but to accept the decision and put the best face on it.

Gorbachev's willingness to agree to eliminate all intermediate- and shorter-range missiles appears to have had several motives. First, in contrast to his predecessors,

Gorbachev thought that Soviet security could be better ensured by "political means"—i.e., arms control—than through a continued military buildup. Second, Gorbachev needed to break the general deadlock in arms control in the wake of the collapse of the Reykjavik summit in October 1988. The West saw the INF issue as the main obstacle to improved East-West relations. Thus, Gorbachev apparently hoped that the INF agreement would have a positive impact on East-West relations and break the logjam in other areas, especially the Strategic Arms Reduction Talks (START).

Third, there were sound military reasons for agreeing to the zero option. While the accord required the Soviet Union to scrap its entire SS-20 force as well as its remaining SS-4s and SS-5s, it eliminated an important nuclear threat to Soviet territory—particularly from the Pershing II, which has a short flight time of twelve to fourteen minutes. Moreover, the Soviet Union could still cover many of the same targets in Europe by redirecting some of its strategic forces—a fact that may well have helped convince the Soviet military to go along with the decision.

Finally, the agreement threatened further to erode the credibility of the American nuclear deterrent and to increase fissures within NATO. As Western analysts and officials pointed out, the elimination of all INF and shorter-range nuclear missiles in Europe would make the strategy of flexible response much more difficult and probably require some changes in Western strategy. The pressure for further reductions was bound to increase, especially from West Germany, where most of the remaining short-range nuclear systems were deployed. Thus the long-term political benefits may have seemed worth the short-term military costs.

The INF accord also had important advantages for the West. First, it eliminated an important military threat to Western Europe. Second, it required the Soviet Union to make large asymmetrical reductions and set an important precedent for other negotiations, especially those related to conventional arms. Third, the agreement contained stringent verification provisions, including on-site inspection. This represented a significant shift in the Soviet position and set another important precedent for other negotiations.

In the field of conventional arms control, however, Gorbachev has shown the greatest inclination to depart from past Soviet policy. Gorbachev's predecessors, especially Brezhnev, showed little inclination to take conventional arms control seriously. Brezhnev gave top priority to strategic nuclear arms control. Moreover, he feared the consequences of any large-scale withdrawal of Soviet forces on the political stability within the bloc.

Gorbachev, by contrast, seems to believe that Soviet political and military objectives can be furthered by progress in conventional arms control. His interest in conventional arms control has probably been influenced by several factors. First, on the broadest political level, it had become increasingly clear that a major improvement in Soviet relations with Western Europe was impossible without seriously addressing West European concerns about Soviet conventional preponderance. This was the main source of West European insecurity and the main rationale for NATO's existence and its reliance on nuclear weapons for defense. Second, a major reduction of conventional forces promised substantial economic savings over the long run. Third, on the military level, there was increasing concern that Western advances in high-tech conventional weapons, especially precision-guided missiles, would erode traditional Soviet advantages in tanks and manpower.

Gorbachev's "new thinking" provided an important framework for the shift in the Soviet approach to conventional arms control. The concept of "reasonable sufficiency" was applied not only to strategic weapons but also to conventional arms. This meant, in effect, that the USSR could afford to reduce some conventional forces, since it only needed enough forces to repel an aggressor rather than to conduct an offensive on his territory.

Similarly, the shift in Soviet doctrine toward an increasing emphasis on defense and war prevention pointed in the same direction.[22] In the past, Soviet conventional forces had been configured and trained to conduct a rapid offensive designed to seize and hold Western territory if a conflict in Europe broke out. This required large-scale conventional superiority in order to overrun Western defenses. Under the new doctrine, however, Soviet forces were to be trained to fight defensively in the initial period of a conflict and then to reestablish the status quo ante rather than seek to carry the war immediately over to Western territory.

This new doctrine permitted a gradual reduction and restructuring of Soviet conventional forces in a less offensive and threatening posture. Under the new doctrine the Soviet Union no longer needed great numerical superiority in tanks and manpower. Nor did it need large quantities of offensively oriented materials, such as bridge-building equipment, which was primarily designed to enhance its capacity to conduct large-scale offensives. Long-range offensive aircraft could also be reduced.

Gorbachev's approach to conventional arms control reflected these new realities. Beginning in 1986 the Soviet Union began to adopt a more flexible approach to conventional arms control. The most important shifts in the Soviet position included: Gorbachev's willingness to extend the negotiating zone to admit Soviet territory up to the Ural Mountains, a long-standing Western demand; his open acknowledgment that asymmetries existed — which his predecessors had implicitly denied — and his commitment to eliminate them; the adoption of a more flexible position on verification, especially on-site inspection; a more forthcoming attitude toward the release of data; and a shift, noted above, in Soviet doctrine, putting greater emphasis on defense.

The latter shift was codified in a new Warsaw Pact Doctrine, announced at the meeting of the Warsaw Treaty Organization (WTO) Political Consultative Committee in East Berlin at the end of May 1987. The communiqué issued at the end of the meeting specifically stated that the doctrine of the WTO was defensive.[23] In addition, it asserted that the goals of the Vienna negotiations on Conventional Forces in Europe (CFE) should be guided by the principle of "reasonable sufficiency" and that the negotiations should seek to eliminate the capability for surprise attack and large-scale offensive action. These goals had long been espoused by the

West, and the public commitment to them by the Warsaw Pact implied a significant rapprochement between the two alliances.

The most important indication of Gorbachev's seriousness about conventional arms control, however, came in his speech to the United Nations General Assembly in December 1988. Gorbachev promised unilaterally to withdraw 50,000 Soviet troops and 5,000 Soviet tanks from Hungary, Czechoslovakia, and East Germany; reduce the Soviet armed forces by 500,000 men by 1990; withdraw from Eastern Europe assault-landing troops and other offensively oriented accessories, such as bridge-crossing equipment; cut Soviet forces in the Atlantic-to-the-Urals area by 10,000 tanks, 8,500 artillery systems, and 800 combat aircraft; and restructure Soviet forces in Eastern Europe along "clearly defensive" lines. Although the initiative still left the Soviet Union with substantial advantages in a number of important areas, it significantly undercut the Soviet capability to launch a short-warning attack — a long-standing Western concern.

Few Western officials or analysts had expected Gorbachev to make such a dramatic gesture. Moreover, in taking the initiative, Gorbachev seems to have overridden objections by the military, including those of the chief of the General Staff, Marshal Sergei Akhromeyev, whose removal was announced the same day. Indeed, the initiative was evidently the result of a prolonged debate between those favoring unilateral measures (located primarily in several Soviet think-tanks and in key positions in Foreign Ministry) and those opposed (located mostly in the Ministry of Defense and General Staff.)[24] In the end, Gorbachev was apparently persuaded that a dramatic political gesture was needed to convince the West of his seriousness and to give new momentum to the conventional arms control talks in Vienna due to begin a few months hence. Gorbachev may have also hoped that the unilateral cuts would have a favorable impact on Western public opinion and stimulate pressure in the West to make a reciprocal gesture.

While the West did not respond with a reciprocal reduction, the initiative did have an important political impact on the general climate surrounding the opening of the CFE negotiations in Vienna in March 1989. In fact, by the time that negotiations opened, the Western and Soviet approaches were relatively close. The Soviet proposal presented at the opening round of the talks on 6 March by Foreign Minister Eduard A. Shevardnadze provided for a three-stage process:

• Both NATO and the WTO would reduce their armed forces and conventional armaments 10 to 15 percent below their current levels.

• Troop levels and armaments would be reduced by 25 percent.

• Each side's armed forces would be reduced in all categories of arms, including naval forces.

Shevardnadze also called for strict verification provisions and the immediate initiation of separate negotiations on short-range nuclear systems.

The Soviet proposal was in broad accord with NATO's proposal on several important points: equal limits on important weapons systems; the general magnitude of reductions (the WTO proposed cuts 10 to 15 percent below current levels, the West 5 to 10 percent), and the need for extensive verification measures. Moreover, both sides agreed that the overall goal of the talks should be to eliminate the capacity for surprise attack and large-scale offensive action.

Important differences, however, remained on whether to include aircraft and troops — the United States wanted to focus solely on tanks and offensive armor — and on short-range nuclear weapons. These differences were narrowed by the USSR's proposal at the end of May, which suggested geographic ceilings on weapons and essentially accepted the basic Western framework for cutting tanks, artillery, and armored troop carriers. The differences were further reduced by President George Bush's proposals at the NATO summit a few days later. The president agreed to include combat aircraft and attack helicopters in the negotiations. He also proposed that each side reduce its armed forces to 275,000 soldiers — a move that would require the United States to withdraw 30,000 and the Soviets 350,000 soldiers. Finally, he agreed that talks on short-range nuclear forces (SNF) could be initiated once the CFE negotiations had been concluded. Bush insisted, however, that the SNF talks should be designed to lead to a "partial reduction" of SNF, not their total elimination. And in deference to West German concerns, a decision regarding the modernization of 88 Lance short-range missiles (FOTL) was postponed.[25]

These two moves significantly reduced the gap between the two sides and contributed to rapid progress in the talks. The negotiations were given new impetus in March by the agreement in Ottawa to limit each side to 195,000 soldiers in the central zone. The United States, however, was allowed to maintain 225,000 overall in Europe. The latter agreement marked an important compromise by Gorbachev in that it codified unequal ceilings — a major American goal.[26] The Soviets, by contrast, were given no right to deploy troops outside the central zone.

However, Soviet interest in a rapid conclusion of the talks waned visibly in the spring of 1989, slowing their momentum. The deadlock appears to have been related to Soviet concerns about the process of German unification. The Soviet Union was apparently unwilling to move forward in Vienna to reduce its own forces substantially until there was greater clarity about the size and configuration of the military forces of a united Germany, as well as the future nature of NATO strategy. The changes in NATO nuclear strategy announced at the NATO summit in July, together with Chancellor Helmut Kohl's public assurances shortly thereafter that the forces of a united Germany would be reduced to around 370,000 men (less than half the current total of the two armies combined), appear to have allayed the most important Soviet concerns. Thereafter, rapid progress was made in resolving the remaining major outstanding issues — limits on weapon holdings by individual nations (the "sufficiency rule"), limitations on naval aircraft, and limitations on weapons in specific subzones. In early October the two sides agreed in principle on the outlines of a draft treaty. The final breakthrough in the negotiations was the result of an important Soviet concession: Moscow agreed to include land-based naval aircraft in the final agreement — a long-standing United States goal — without insisting that the same apply to carrier-based aircraft, which the United States wanted excluded. This concession removed the last major obstacle to an agreement.

The CFE treaty, which was officially signed at the thirty-four-nation CSCE Summit in Paris in November 1990, is the most important arms-control treaty signed in the postwar period. The treaty codifies a fundamental change in the balance of power in Europe by establishing equal ceilings on major categories of equipment, including tanks, artillery, and personnel carriers, thereby eliminating major Soviet advantages in these weapons systems. As a result of the treaty, the Warsaw Pact will have to destroy about 19,000 tanks, while NATO will have to destroy only about 4,000 tanks. The treaty will require no substantial cuts in NATO's armored troop carriers and no cuts in its artillery or combat aircraft. The Warsaw Pact, by contrast, will have to destroy thousands of these weapons.

The signing of the CFE treaty is likely to be followed by a new set of negotiations (CFE-IB) designed to establish national ceilings on the forces of individual countries. In these talks the Soviet Union's main goal will probably be low ceilings on the military forces of a united Germany. It is also likely to try to obtain treaty-related restrictions on NATO and German forces stationed in the former territory of East Germany.

The conclusion of a CFE I agreement will also open the way for negotiations on short-range nuclear forces (SNF). Such talks have long been a Soviet goal, but there has been a visible shift in the Soviet position on SNF negotiations since mid-1989. Originally, the Soviets seemed intent on pressing for total elimination of all short-range systems (the "third zero"). However, Gorbachev spoke of the creation of a "minimum nuclear deterrent" in his speech in Strasbourg in July 1989.[27] Similarly, during a visit to NATO headquarters in Brussels, Soviet Foreign Minister Shevardnadze suggested a two-stage process for SNF negotiations. In the first stage, SNF would be reduced to low common ceilings, and in the second stage they would be eliminated entirely. Leading Soviet analysts have also referred to such a two-stage process.[28]

The shift in the Soviet position appears to have several motivations. First, the Soviet Union seems to recognize that there is strong resistance in Western Europe, especially in France and Britain, to the total denuclearization of Western Europe and that pressing for such a goal at this point would be counterproductive, stiffening Western resistance to reductions and possibly inhibiting further progress in conventional arms control. Second, with the loss of Soviet conventional superiority, which will be codified in a CFE I agreement, the Soviets may feel a greater need to retain some nuclear weapons as a hedge against NATO's technological superiority. Finally, eliminating all tactical nuclear weapons could precipitate a withdrawal of American troops from Western Europe, thereby increasing instability during the transition period.

Thus, unless the West European countries, particularly Germany, press for a total elimination of short-range systems, the USSR is likely to accept the continued presence of some nuclear weapons on West European soil at least for an interim period. The first phase of the SNF negotiations will probably be directed at establishing equal but lower ceilings on land-based nuclear systems. Nevertheless, despite what appears to be an emerging consensus on the basic goals of the negotiations, substantial technical problems remain. There is no agreement, for instance, on the "unit of account"—warheads, launchers, or delivery vehicles—or the geographic scope of the negotiations. Moreover, the verification problems are formidable. Finally, the question of whether to include French and British nuclear systems remains unresolved.

The political evolution in Europe, however, may make the resolution of some of these problems easier. It is increasingly likely that the United States will unilaterally withdraw most, if not all, ground-based tactical nuclear weapons from Europe, leaving air- and sea-based nuclear weapons as the backbone of its deterrent strategy. Moreover, from the Soviets' perspective, the change in NATO strategy announced at the NATO summit in London in July 1990—whereby nuclear weapons will only be used as a "last resort"—diminishes the threat posed by the remaining weapons on European soil. At the same time, the withdrawal of Soviet troops and military equipment from Eastern Europe will significantly reduce the Soviet short-range nuclear threat to Western Europe.

These developments have somewhat diminished the importance of the SNF negotiations. Nevertheless, since such weapons can be easily moved back into the negotiating zone, it will be useful to have agreed, verifiable constraints on them. For political reasons, moreover, the Soviet Union is likely to press for the rapid commencement of negotiations. They strengthen the impression, both at home and in Europe, that Europe is entering a new era of reduced confrontation, thereby legitimizing the Soviet push for a greater reliance on pan-European security structures. In addition, negotiations offer an important means to try to block the modernization of NATO's air-based component, particularly plans to develop a new tactical air-to-surface missile (TASM). Thus, in future talks, the Soviets are likely to press for deep cuts in nuclear-capable aircraft as well as restrictive provisions on air-to-surface missiles. Initially, the USSR may also try to link the negotiations to the question of tactical nuclear weapons at sea, though it seems likely that this issue will be dealt with in separate talks on naval arms control.

The USSR and the Future European Security Order

The collapse of communism and the unification of Germany have shattered the foundations of the USSR's postwar policy toward Europe. This policy was based on three pillars: (1) Soviet hegemony in Eastern Europe; (2) the division of Germany; and (3) the bipolar political division of Europe. All three pillars are now destroyed beyond repair. The USSR is thus faced with the task of constructing a new policy not only toward Eastern Europe but toward Europe as a whole.

Originally, Gorbachev appears to have envisaged a gradual process of change in Europe during which both alliances would continue to exist but would lose their predominately military character and take on increasingly political functions. The alliances, including the Warsaw Pact, were seen as stabilizing mechanisms. Soviet analysts argued, for instance, that the Warsaw Pact could play a useful role as an instrument for the "controlled and orderly transition" of the two blocs to a lower level of military confrontation and as a means for conducting arms-control negotiations.[29] Others argued that the pact should be maintained, but that it should be transformed into a "mature political partnership" in which all parties enjoyed equal rights.[30] They suggested that the East European role be expanded and that a permanent secretariat be set up in one of the East European countries.

The idea of a prolonged transition based on the continued existence of the two alliances, however, seems increasingly unrealistic. As a result of the rapid changes in Eastern Europe, the Warsaw Pact has become a hollow shell. It may continue to exist for several more years but as an effective military alliance it is clinically dead. The unification of Germany deprives the pact of its most important military asset. At the same time, the withdrawal of Soviet forces from Hungary and Czechoslovakia — scheduled to be completed by the end of 1991 — severely weakens the USSR's ability to conduct coalitional warfare. Hungary, moreover, has announced that it will formally withdraw from the pact in 1991, which could lead to the formal disbanding of the Warsaw Pact.

As the pact has disintegrated, the Soviet Union has begun to push more forcefully for strengthening pan-European structures as an alternative to the two alliances. Some Soviet analysts, for instance, have suggested a two-phase approach. The first phase (1990–91) would begin with the creation of all-European centers for the prevention of crisis and arms-control verification. This phase would be followed by a second stage in which a permanent secretariat and agencies on ecology, migration, and economic cooperation would be set up.[31] Soviet analysts have also suggested that the Council of Europe could be expanded to take on a pan-European character.

There have also been hints that the USSR may favor setting up a two-tier security structure with a permanent council, composed of the USSR, the United States, France, Britain, and Germany, which would become the core of a new security system and report back to the 35. Such ideas, moreover, dovetail closely with those put forward by Moscow's former East European allies. The foreign minister of Czechoslovakia, Jiri Dienstbier, for example, has proposed that a European Security Commission be formed with headquarters in Prague. This commission would act as an executive organ of a pan-European system of collective security.

In the future the Soviets can be expected to push such pan-European schemes more vigorously. They are one of the few ways that the USSR can be assured of exerting influence in Europe. In addition, such schemes could contain the growth of instability and nationalism in Eastern Europe, which many Soviet analysts see as a growing threat to European security. To counteract this danger, some Soviet analysts have called for the intensification of ties to Western countries and the "accelerated construction of a new security system, particularly the creation of permanent institutions for all-European control of political processes."[32] Such a system is also seen as providing a "corset" to ensure that German unification evolves peacefully and does not pose a threat to the general trend toward increased East-West cooperation.

The Soviets recognize, of course, that NATO is unlikely to fade away immediately, but they hope that the general political climate of East-West détente will make it increasingly less relevant and that its military functions will gradually atrophy. Thus they can be expected to put intensified emphasis on disarmament proposals that will weaken NATO's military potential, especially its nuclear capability. As noted earlier, one of the USSR's prime goals will probably be eliminating land-based missiles and nuclear artillery and preventing any modernization of NATO's air-delivered nuclear component. Soviet negotiators are also likely to press for significant reductions of United States combat aircraft and troop levels in any follow-on negotiation to CFE.

This does not mean, however, that the Soviet Union wishes to see the United States withdraw from Europe. The USSR recognizes that it will take some time to create a new security order in Europe and that the transition period could be destabilizing. Thus, it has come to see the presence of American troops — albeit at significantly reduced levels — as a factor of stability, at least for the short to medium term.[33] In addition, it seems willing temporarily to accept some stationing of American nuclear weapons on European soil.

This shift has been part of a general evolution of the Soviet attitude toward the American role in the construction of the "common European home." Initially, the concept had a strongly anti–United States edge and Soviet officials were ambiguous about the American role. Recently, however, Soviet officials and analysts have stressed that the United States has an important place in the European home. In his speech before the Council of Europe in Strasbourg, for instance, Gorbachev noted that the United States and the Soviet Union were a "natural part of the European international-political structure" and that their participation was "not only justified but historically qualified."[34] Soviet analysts, echoing this line, have argued that without the participation of the United States, construction of the common European home would be more difficult.

The process of German unification, moreover, is likely to reinforce the Soviets' predisposition to keep the United States involved in Europe. Although Gorbachev has accepted German unification as well as German membership in NATO, the USSR cannot be sure about the long-term direction of political developments in Germany. The United States remains an important constraint on German freedom of action, especially regarding nuclear weapons. A total withdrawal of American forces might reopen the nuclear question in Germany — something the Soviet Union strongly wishes to avoid. This concern gives the USSR an added incentive to keep the United States engaged in Europe rather than to encourage its total withdrawal.

At the same time, Germany's importance in the Soviet Union's European policy is likely to increase. Germany is the USSR's largest Western trading partner and its main source of technology and credits, which will be important for the modernization of the Soviet economy. Moreover, Germany will be the most important political actor in Europe. Thus, if the Soviet Union wishes to pursue an active policy toward Europe, it will have little choice but to strengthen its ties with Germany. Indeed, Gorbachev's invitation to Kohl to visit his hometown of Stavropol during the chancellor's visit to the USSR in July 1990 – an honor accorded no other Western leader to date – seemed designed to initiate a new era of more cooperative relations with a united Germany.

The unification of Germany, moreover, is likely to give a new push to the process of European unification. Over the long term, unification may lead to a weakening of Atlanticism and United States influence in Western Europe, but it will also pose serious dilemmas for the USSR. For one thing, it will increase the attractiveness of the EC to the countries of Eastern Europe, making any efforts by the Soviet Union to transform the CMEA or keep it alive more difficult. For another, it will make the export of Soviet industrial products and other commercial transactions to Western Europe more difficult.

On the political level, the process of integration is likely to foster a more cohesive foreign policy on the part of Western Europe, allowing EC members to speak more forcefully with one voice on international issues. Internally, moreover, it will accelerate a shift in the locus of decision-making power on many issues from national capitals to Brussels and Strasbourg. Thus, if the Soviet Union wishes to pursue an active European policy, it will have to develop stronger ties to the EC and its associated institutions rather than simply concentrating on expanding ties to individual West European countries.

The CMEA, however, is not likely to disappear, at least not immediately. The countries of Eastern Europe conduct 40 to 80 percent of their trade within the CMEA. If it were to be disbanded, they would have to redirect their trade toward new markets. Replacing the Soviet market quickly would be difficult – and costly – since many East European goods are not internationally competitive. Thus the CMEA will probably continue to exist in some form for the next few years, at least as a means of facilitating bilateral trade. It is likely, however, to become much more of an "information gathering agency" like the Organization for Economic Cooperation and Development (OECD) in Paris than a mechanism for promoting close economic cooperation between the Soviet Union and its former East-European allies. Moreover, given the Soviet Union's own growing economic difficulties, the USSR is likely to reduce its delivery of energy and raw materials to Eastern Europe. This will exacerbate these countries' economic problems as they attempt to transform their economies along market lines.

Conclusion

The Soviet Union will face a substantially changed security environment in Europe in the 1990s. In order to adapt to this environment, major adjustments in Soviet policy will be necessary. These adjustments will have to be made at a time when the Soviet Union is undergoing profound change. How this process evolves will have a major influence on the Soviet Union's role in Europe in the coming decade.

Indeed, the disintegration of the Soviet internal empire is likely to be one of the most important factors affecting the future of Europe in the 1990s. It is highly questionable whether the Soviet Union will remain an integral multinational state. As centrifugal pressures increase, some of the republics, such as the Russian Federation and the Ukraine, are likely to seek greater autonomy — even independence — and may begin to pursue their own "European" policies, especially in the economic area. The growing political fragmentation of the USSR could be a major source of instability in Europe and make the integration of the Soviet Union — or major remnants of it — into a broader European framework more difficult.

It would be short-sighted, however, for the West to exploit this period of convulsion and weakness to exclude the Soviet Union from Europe. That would only strengthen the more radical nationalist and exclusionist forces in Soviet society. Rather, Western policy should encourage a gradual evolution toward greater internal democracy, a greater reform of the Soviet economy, and its integration into the world economy. A less inward-looking, more democratic Soviet Union integrated into a broader European security order in which it has a strong but not dominant voice is more likely to guarantee peace and stability than a frustrated but still militarily powerful empire that feels isolated and excluded from Europe.

NOTES

1. Charles Gati, "Soviet Empire: Alive But Not Well," *Problems of Communism*, March-April 1985, 73–86.

2. Interview in *La Repubblica*, 21 May 1985 (reprinted in Foreign Broadcast Information Service, *Daily Report: Soviet Union*, 24 May 1985, CCI).

3. *Pravda*, 26 Feb. 1986.

4. Ibid., 8 Apr. 1985.

5. Jerry Hough, "Gorbachev's Strategy," *Foreign Affairs* 63 (Fall 1985): 33–55.

6. S. Vybornov, A. Gusenkov, and V. Leontiev, "Nothing Is Simple in Europe," *International Affairs*, no. 3 (March 1988), 35.

7. V. Stupishin, "Indeed, Nothing in Europe Is Simple," *International Affairs*, no. 5 (May 1988), 73. This article was essentially a reply to the Vybornov, Gusenkov, and Leontief article cited in n. 6.

8. Ibid., 72.

9. Nikolai Afanasyevsky, Eduard Tarasinkevich, and Andrei Shvedov, "Between Yesterday and Today," *International Affairs*, no. 5 (May 1988), 27.

10. See the report on the EC prepared by the Institute of World Economy and International Relations (IMEMO), in Moscow, "Europeiskoe soobshchestvo segodnia. Tezisy Instituty mirovoi ekonomiki i mezhdunarodnykh otnoshenii AN SSSR," *Mirovaia ekonomika i mezhdunarodnye otnosheniia*, no. 12, April 1988, 8–9.

11. See the material prepared by the West European Research Department of IMEMO on the implications of the formation of the internal market of the EC, "Posledstviia formiro-vaniia edinogo rynka Evropeiskogo soobshchestva material podgotovien otdelom zapadnoevropeiskikh issledovanii IMEMO," *Mirovaia ekonomika i mezhdunarodnye otnosheniia*, no. 4, April 1989, 40.

12. On the background to the Gorbachev Initiative and the development of relations between the EC and the CMEA before 1985, see Christian Meier, "Die Gorbachev-Initiative vom 29 Mai 1985-vor

neuen Verhandlungen zwischen RGW und EG," *Aktuelle Analysen*, Bundesinstitut fuer ost-wissenschaftliche und internationale Studien, 20 Aug. 1985; and Bernhard May, "Normalizierung der Beziehungen zwischen der EG und den RGW," *Aus Politik und Zeitgeschichte* B 3/89, 13 Jan. 1989, 44–54.

13. See in particular O. Vladimirov, "Vedushchii faktor mirovogo revolyutsionnogo protsessa," *Pravda*, 21 June 1985. The article was reportedly written by Oleg Rakhmanin, the hard-line deputy chief of the Department for the Liaison with Socialist Countries within the International Department of the Central Committee. In the fall of 1986, Rakhmanin was replaced by Georgi Shakhnazarov, a prominent supporter of reform. Rakhmanin's removal and Shakhnazarov's ascendancy were important signs that the reformist line was beginning to gain ground.

14. See in particular Oleg T. Bogomolov, "Soglasovanie ekonomicheskikh interesovi i politiki pri sotsialisme," *Kommunist*, no. 10, July 1985, 82–95.

15. *Pravda*, 11 Apr. 1987.

16. Ibid., 3 Nov. 1989.

17. Ibid., 19 Mar. 1988.

18. Ibid., 7 July 1989.

19. David B. Ottoway, *Washington Post*, 11 Nov. 1989.

20. "Nehmen wir Gorbatschow's 'Neue Politik' beim Wort" (Bonn: Auswaertiges Amt und Presse und Informationsamt der Bundesregierung, March 1987).

21. *Izvestiia*, 26 Oct. 1988. See also Gorbachev's assessment in his book *Perestroika: New Thinking in Our Country and the World* (New York: Harper and Row, 1987), 200, where he notes the "reality" of the German states with different political systems and asserts that "what there will be in 100 years is for history to decide." This became the standard Soviet line regarding unification up until the fall of the Berlin Wall in November 1989.

22. For a detailed discussion of the shift in Soviet doctrine, see William Odom, "Soviet Military Doctrine," *Foreign Affairs* 67 (Fall 1988): 114–34; and Edward L. Warner III, "Soviet Military Doctrine: New Thinking and Old Realities in Soviet Defense Policy," *Survival* 30 (January-February 1989): 13–33.

23. See *Pravda*, 30 May 1987.

24. See Roy Allison, "Gorbachev's New Program for Conventional Arms Control in Europe," in *Gorbachev's Agenda Changes in Domestic and Foreign Policy*, ed. Susan L. Clark (Boulder: Westview Press, 1989), 5–13.

25. In May 1990 the Bush administration quietly shelved the idea of Lance modernization altogether after it became apparent that there was no support for the program in Europe. For a good discussion of the Lance modernization issue, see Hans Binnendijk, "NATO's Nuclear Modernization Dilemma," *Survival* 30 (March–April 1989): 137–55.

26. The United States was eager to avoid equating American troops in Europe with Soviet troops. Hence, it pressed for unequal ceilings in order to avoid the appearance of parity. See R. Jeffrey Smith, "U.S., Soviets Reach Troops Cut Accord," *Washington Post*, 14 Feb. 1990.

27. *Pravda*, 7 July 1989.

28. See Paval Bayev et al., *Tactical Nuclear Weapons in Europe* (Moscow: Novosti Press Agency Publishing House, 1990), 14, 40–46.

29. Andrei Kokoshin, "Konturi peremen," *SShA: Ekonomika, Politika, Ideologiya*, no. 2, February 1990, 31–33.

30. Mikhail Bezrukov and Andrei Kortunov, "What Kind of an Alliance Do We Need?," *New Times*, no. 41, 10–16 Oct. 1989, 7–9; and idem, "Nuzhna Reforma OVD," ibid., no. 3, March 1990, 30–35.

31. Sergei Karaganov, "Architecture for Europe to Ensure the Transition Periods Safely," *Moscow News*, 21–27 May 1990, 12.

32. Sergei Karaganov, "Problemi evropeiskoy politiki SSSR," *Mezhdunarodnaya Zhizn*, July 1990, 93.

33. As the study *Tactical Nuclear Weapons in Europe* by Bayev et al. noted, "Despite all its negative features, the US military presence is a major stabilizing element in relations among Western nations, and to some degree, in the entire system of East-West relations," 12.

34. *Pravda*, 7 July 1989.

The New Europeans: Beyond the Balance of Power

STEPHEN F. SZABO

Europe enters the 1990s reunited, no longer as Western and Eastern Europe. This historic transformation of the Continent has thrown into doubt all the assumptions and verities accumulated over the preceding forty years. The contours of the new Europe will be molded by new generations of Europeans; born after the end of that great caesura, World War II, they are already a majority of the population and will provide the leaders who will refashion the Continent in the 1990s.

This essay will outline the worldview of these new Europeans and the kind of Europe they would like to build. While they will have to react to many factors beyond their control, a sense of what they would like to create will be an important, perhaps decisive, factor in the development of a new Europe.

Their work will be more landscaping than architecture. Unlike Jean Monnet, Konrad Adenauer, Alcide de Gasperi, and others of the generation that rebuilt postwar Europe, the Europeans of the 1990s are not faced with the task of total reconstruction. They will build on the solid foundations laid in 1945 in Western Europe as they reconstruct the Continent. While they confront an Eastern Europe devastated by two generations of communism, they can approach their mission from a restored Western Europe that is increasingly self-confident and assertive.

Now that the economic and political framework of the new Europe seems clear, the focus here will be on the broad security structure that the new Europeans are likely to prefer. Eastern Europe wishes to adopt what has been developed in Western Europe: the European Community (EC), parliamentary multiparty democracy, and a social-market economy. The security framework, though not so clear, will be crucial in providing the stability and confidence needed for the political and economic structures to prosper.

Defense against What?

Since the end of World War II, Europe has suffered from the common fear that the Soviet Union would use its military preponderance on the Continent to impose its will on its neighbors in Europe. The nations of the eastern part of Europe have directly experienced the consequences of Soviet military power. With the exception of Yugoslavia and Albania, they have had a Stalinist system imposed on them by the Soviet Union. These countries were never allies, only satellites.

The result of this domination has been a strong revulsion by the people of Eastern Europe to the presence of Soviet military forces and of Soviet-style regimes in their countries, tempered by an appreciation for Mikhail S. Gorbachev and his policies toward Eastern Europe. One of the first acts of the newly independent governments in Czechoslovakia and Hungary was a request that the Soviets leave as soon as possible. Poland is likely to follow suit once the border issue with Germany is settled. Germans in the former East Germany are likely to sense a Soviet threat more strongly than those in the West.

The emerging leaders in this part of Europe along with vast majorities of their publics are likely to be primarily concerned about the possibility of the reemergence of a Soviet threat to their independence. This fear, combined with a strong revulsion against communism and the old ruling Communist parties, will favor Christian Democratic, Conservative, Peasant, and Social Democratic parties. The leaders of these parties will do all they can to exit the Warsaw Pact gracefully or at least to pretend to belong and allow the Soviets to pretend to believe it.

With the unlamented demise of the Warsaw Pact, however, comes a series of potential national threats to security. The revival of ethnic rivalries in Bulgaria, Transylvania, and Yugoslavia as well as the dispute over the German-Polish border that flared in early 1990 may become important security concerns for many in these regions. These concerns are unlikely to turn into a new Sarejevo, however, because they are not linked to broader alliance rivalries. But they could threaten to transform parts of central and Balkan Europe into Beirut-like areas. Not much reliable survey data are available on the importance of ethnic nationalism to the people in these regions. Yet it seems likely that the postwar generations are less preoccupied with these traditional conflicts and are more concerned with rebuilding their own polities and economies within a new European framework.[1] This is especially true among the better educated people who are likely to lead in the next decades.

Because of Soviet hegemony, institutionalized by the Warsaw Pact, central Europeans of the postwar generations have not experienced nationalist conflict to the same extent as earlier generations. Many have developed a shared sense of a common destiny with their neighbors, as indicated by their discussions over the renewal of *Mitteleuropa* and by their common struggles against communism and the Soviet Union.

It is fair to conclude that the revolutions of 1989 were patriotic but not nationalist revolutions.[2] There has been a revival of nations and also of Europeanism. If central Europe and the Balkans fall into deep economic recessions, the nationalist temptation may grow — especially among desperate politicians. Yet, as a starting point, the political culture of the postwar generations offers hope that Europe will not repeat the mistakes of the first half of the century.

Evidence for this is already present in attitudes toward German unification.

With the exception of Poland, most publics in both central and Western Europe are overwhelmingly in favor of German unification and believe it will benefit rather than harm Europe.[3] Again, the postwar generations are the most open to this development. With regard to Germany, they tend to look to the future rather than to the past: they think of Mercedes rather than the Wehrmacht, of the Federal Republic more than the Third Reich.

In Western Europe, views of the threat are changing. The fear of a Soviet military threat receded over the two decades leading up to 1989. The concern over the Soviet Union as a political or revolutionary threat, a concern that was central to European leaders in the first decade of the cold war, also disappeared as the USSR became an ideological antimodel even for the left in the 1970s. What remained was a residual concern that unbalanced Soviet military power could be used for political intimidation.

These trends were most intense among the postwar generations. Having come of age during the era of détente followed by the decline and collapse of communism, Western Europeans under the age of forty have little sense of a real Soviet threat. Soviet President Mikhail S. Gorbachev—the leader with whom this new generation associates the USSR—remains the most popular world leader, not only for this group but for most Europeans. Even in relatively hard-line France, the number of those believing that the Soviet Union respects the independence of the Eastern European countries has increased from 7 percent in 1982 to 40 percent in 1989.[4]

In contrast, the new Europeans have viewed America as less of a protector than a threat or at best as part of the landscape. Part of this generation was socialized in the 1960s and formed their views of America during the Vietnam War. Another group, which came of age in the 1980s, has been simultaneously repelled by the militarism of the Reagan administration and attracted by the continuing dynamism of the American economy and of its popular culture.

These new generations, no longer concerned about an invasion from the East, now fear a nuclear war precipitated by both superpowers. The debate over the Euromissiles in the 1980s was seen by many—especially in the university-educated group—as being dangerously irrelevant, fostering an arms race and raising the prospect of conflict while ignoring more pressing issues, such as environmental threats and the problems of economic underdevelopment.

With the moderation of American policies during the last years of the Reagan administration and the early Bush administration, European confidence in American leadership has been largely restored. Yet as the perceived need for the American security umbrella has declined, so has the willingness to follow the American lead.

The fear of the Soviet threat or of a superpower war in Europe has been replaced by concerns over environmental problems, the North-South relationship, and the growing prospect of instability in the Soviet Union and Eastern Europe. The new Europeans in the West now worry about the implications of the implosion of the Soviet Union rather than its expansion. They are concerned about the dangers of economic collapse on the eastern side of the Continent and about the problems that immigration and demands for economic assistance could create for them.

The new generation of leaders coming to power in the West view Germany with more optimism than do those who lived through World War II. Like their counterparts in Eastern Europe, they have not experienced Germany as an invader or occupier but as a country of good democrats and good Europeans. They seem less worried that the new Germany will pose a security threat to them or anyone else in Europe. While a good deal of concern can be found among the current generation of leaders about possible instability resulting from German unification and the upheavals in the East, few postwar Europeans seem to share these concerns.

In short, the 1990s are likely to produce leaders in the West who will be relatively sanguine about their security and devalue the utility of military force in Europe. These leaders are likely to see threats as nonmilitary in nature and requiring nonmilitary solutions. The leaders of the new democracies in the East will be more pessimistic about the Soviet Union but will be preoccupied with the problems of building democracies and market economies and therefore unlikely to have so much influence on the broader shape of European security policy as those in the West.

With the Soviets out of central Europe militarily and overwhelmed by their internal problems for some time, Europeans, like Americans, wish to maximize their peace dividend and to turn to the great challenge of building a European architecture as well as dealing with their own domestic problems.[5] If ethnic violence breaks out in central Europe or the Balkans, they will try to mediate the disputes but are unlikely to organize any military response.

How these new leaders confront threats to European interests outside Europe will be a key test for the future of their security policies. Europe will continue to remain far more dependent than the United States on the developing world for its raw materials. In addition, the proliferation of chemical and nuclear threats from non-European countries could pose a serious problem for Europe in the 1990s. The decline of dependence on the United States for military protection may produce a European assertiveness in defending interests in the Middle East and other vital areas. The Europeans may repeat their actions in the Persian Gulf during the Iran-Iraq War and begin to deploy their forces outside the context of the North Atlantic Treaty Organization (NATO) and separate from American control, possibly offering key Arab and other states an alternative to the American protectorate.

To this point, European leaders and publics alike have preferred to deal with regional problems through diplomatic and economic instruments of policy. With the exceptions of France in Africa and Britain in the Falkland Islands, Europe has relied on the United States military, while often criticizing it. This could begin to change with a more assertive Europe. European publics have been less critical of European military actions outside Europe than they have of American operations. Terrorism, both international and domestic, is more than an abstract threat in Western Europe, and public concerns combined with a growing gap with the United States over the Middle East may make counterterrorism an important European security matter. This could continue to foster a Euro-American divergence.

In Search of a New Collective Security

European leaders in the 1990s will respond to an environment with a residual Soviet threat and a more palpable nationalist one. They will also have to be more responsive to instability and military contingencies in the developing world, especially in the Middle East. Their former ally, the United States, will be less essential for security and possibly a greater adversary in economic conflict.

Faced with this new context, Europeans have a number of security options: they can continue to rely on NATO, though in a restructured form; they can push forward with a European defense community separate from the United States; or they can move toward a pan-European security arrangement. At the beginning of 1990, NATO remained the popular choice for most Europeans. Support for membership in NATO was higher in most European countries in the 1980s than at any other time in the postwar period.[6] A survey conducted by the Gallup organization in October 1989 found that majorities in all NATO countries except Denmark, Spain, and Portugal still believed that NATO should be maintained; only in Spain was there a plurality agreeing that it was not necessary.[7] It seems that acceptance of NATO is not directly related to the Soviet threat, for while the perception of that threat has fallen steadily, support for NATO has not. To the younger generations, the alliance — like the European Economic Community (EEC) — has always been part of the European landscape. It has become associated with the stability of the postwar period and remains a valuable insurance policy to many, yet one on which the premiums may now be substantially lowered.

To many, NATO also has an important dimension for Europe (as it has for Spain) or may be seen as useful to small states (as it is to the Netherlands, Belgium, and Luxembourg) or as an instrument of conflict management (as it is in Greece and Turkey). Most important, NATO remains identified with the American connection to European security, a connection that still seems to be prudent.

With the end of the Eastern bloc, NATO will be pressured either to diminish its military role or eventually to allow itself to be replaced by a more European organization. This pressure will be due to a combination of interacting factors, including the lowered sense of threat from the East, a growing Europeanism that is likely to include defense, and a reduced desire on the part of the United States to play the military role it has in Europe since 1945. European defense is therefore likely to be Europeanized by the end of the century.

There will be a debate within Europe in the 1990s over the institutional form of collective security and the role of deterrence within it. The nuclear powers, Britain and France, will retain and expand their nuclear forces. The publics in those countries have continued to support their national deterrents, although they have increasing doubts about the desirability of American nuclear weapons in their countries. The new leaders of Britain and France are also likely to wish to maintain these forces because they convey a special power status that nonnuclear states lack, because nuclear deterrence is still viewed as more effective than conventional deterrence, because nuclear weapons are cheaper than conventional forces (a consideration of growing importance in a decade of peace dividends), and because the American presence in Europe looks more questionable than at any other time in the postwar period.[8] They may also be more concerned about the dangers of chemical and nuclear proliferation to smaller and less stable states and will see their deterrents as insurance policies against blackmail from these new nuclear and chemical powers.

The key debate will be within nonnuclear Europe, and Germany is especially crucial. The German public remains divided on the need for nuclear deterrence, but antinuclear sentiments, which grew in the 1980s, will continue to strengthen as the Soviet Union withdraws from the eastern portion of the Continent. The partisan dissensus on nuclear questions remains deep, and the pronuclear Christian Democrats are increasingly on the defensive on this issue.

While pressure to eliminate all short-range nuclear forces in Germany will undoubtedly succeed, a residual longer-range nuclear deterrent could be politically sustainable. Germany will not have the independent deterrent option because of both external and internal resistance. The German military and the Christian Democrats are likely to continue to believe in the necessity of nuclear deterrence and to remain hostile to an exclusive reliance on conventional deterrence. The highest-ranking Bundeswehr officer, Admiral Dieter Wellershoff, said in April 1988 that "the history of war is . . . the history of the failure of purely conventional deterrence."[9] This sentiment continues to be repeated by key civilian and military officials in the Ministry of Defense.

The Social Democrats have moved away from the concept of deterrence, however, and have embraced the notion of common security: confidence-building measures, arms control, and détente rather than the threat of force. To the Social Democratic Party of Germany (SPD), the new collective security structure of Europe should be a strengthened, institutionalized Conference on Security and Cooperation in Europe (CSCE). An SPD government would remove all nuclear weapons from German soil and would foster pan-European cooperation in lieu of deterrence. The SPD has talked about a European Security Agency that would comprise both Eastern and Western Europe and make NATO — and, to a great extent, a European defense community — anachronistic in the new Europe.

If this view prevails, the ability of Europe to develop an effective deterrence arrangement would be dealt a fatal blow. Yet this is unlikely, because an SPD government would be subject to pressures from its European partners to remain within a multilateral military framework and because many Social Democrats would be concerned that an alliance-free Germany might tempt the right to push for an independent nuclear force. Thus some link either to a Europeanized NATO or to a more purely European defense force will be seen as necessary.

Central Europeans will continue to be more concerned about their security than Western Europeans. Soviet forces will remain only a matter of hours away from their borders, and the consequences of instability bred by nationalist conflicts are more direct, even existential. As the Warsaw Pact is seen as an instrument of suppression rather than of protection, Soviet attempts to revive it as a political alliance have no real prospect of success. Only Poland has a strong enough fear of a united Germany to sustain any sort of security relationship with the Soviet Union.

What are the alternatives? Central Europeans can hope to enmesh themselves in a larger pan-European system, push for NATO membership, or pursue bilateral treaties with their neighbors or powerful outside states. The NATO option, raised by the former Hungarian Foreign Minister Gyula Horn and others, is not a serious one and is intended more for election campaigns than for statecraft. The most popular alternative among the new leaders of this region seems to be the CSCE combined with membership in the EEC and the eventual development of the European Community (EC) into a political and defense community. The classic strategy of these states in the interwar period was to attempt to create a web of international guarantees for their sovereignty backed up with a series of insurance treaties with Britain and France. The unhappy lesson of that experience as well as that of World War I is that purely national solutions do not work and the balance of power is unreliable. Thus it makes sense for Czechoslovakian President Václav Havel and others to search for larger European frameworks.

The best that these small and vulnerable states can hope for is a tacit security umbrella guaranteed by Western Europe and gradually extended through membership in the EC. Already the security status of central Europe has been transformed in the eyes of most Western Europeans. Because the Eastern bloc no longer exists, these states are no longer considered a Soviet sphere of influence by Europeans and thus no tacit right of intervention is acceptable. A Soviet military action would not be viewed as a repeat of the invasion of Hungary in 1956 or Czechoslovakia in 1968 but would be closer to 1939 in the view of many Europeans. Such a move would be very dangerous and would be more likely to escalate to a pan-European conflict than any crisis since the end of World War II. At the same time, European leaders and publics are sensitive to any provocations or direct challenges to what are considered legitimate Soviet security concerns. Thus, barring a complete implosion of the USSR, the extension of formal military alliances to former Warsaw Pact members is not a serious policy option for at least the next decade. Even if a united Germany becomes a member of NATO, it will not allow NATO forces to be introduced in the former territory of East Germany.

The future security architecture of Europe will consist of a variety of levels. At the pan-European level, an institutionalized CSCE is likely to develop and to receive broad elite and public support. Below that level will be the gradual expansion of the EEC. It is likely to become a monetary and political union as well as develop a defense identity while gradually extending to central Europe associate-member status. As these polities and economies recover, they will eventually integrate within the EEC and gain the security benefits of a European umbrella. Finally, NATO will probably continue to provide the interim framework necessary for the reassurance needed as the Continent Europeanizes its own defense.

Should Europeanization fail because of a resurgence of nationalism in central Europe, especially in Germany, then a security network based on a series of bilateral treaties — i.e., a return to a balance-of-power system — is probable. This system would differ from the interwar system in that it would rely on nuclear deterrence but might also proliferate nuclear weapons in Germany, Poland, and other countries.

Conclusion

European history has returned to the Europeans once again. The era in which the superpowers controlled Europe's destiny is coming to an end. During an interregnum of about half a century, Europe under American protection was able to lay the foundations of a new postnational order through two key institutions, the European Community and NATO. Those once under Soviet domination are faced with the task of repairing the damage done and reintegrating into a common European home. As the forced harmony of Soviet control leaves with Soviet troops, will Europe once again miss opportunities as it did after World War I? Will it return to that time or go even further back, to the prenational heritage of Medieval Europe and of the Holy Roman Empire—to a Europe in which regions mattered more than nations?

The generation of leaders who will guide Europe in the 1990s will have to answer this question. They seem poised to create a Europe beyond the nation-state. Postwar Germans in particular seem to have little inclination to take an independent national route. They are more hesitant than other Germans about unification because they do not want to reawaken nationalism. Their values and attitudes give them a postnational identity that is likely to prefer policies of European integration over a separate German path. Their counterparts throughout Europe share this set of predispositions.[10] The prospects, then, for a Europe quite different from that of pre-1945 seem good. This working model of the EC—combined with forty years of experience in a multinational security organization that has been more than a traditional alliance—means that supranationalism is not utopian.

The question of security may prove to be the most difficult one for this generation, which devalues the political utility of military force and tends to assume that stability in Europe is a given. Its sanguine view of the Soviet Union could be shaken by a more threatening regime in the future. Its distance from the United States, at least in security policy, is liable to undermine transatlantic cooperation in the future. The integration of central Europe may revive a sense that a security problem remains.

Yet if the trends toward the democratization of the Soviet Union continue, the new generation of European leaders in the 1990s has the historic opportunity to create a revived, prosperous, and democratic Europe whose postnational security system could serve as a model for other regions.

NOTES

1. A cross-national survey conducted in January 1990 in seven European countries, including Poland, Hungary, and the USSR, found broad support for membership in the European Economic Community, for social democracy, and for liberalism. "Political, German Reunification Views Polled," *El Pais*, 19 Feb. 1990; reprinted in Foreign Broadcast Information Service (FBIS), *Daily Report: Western Europe*, 30 Mar. 1990, Annex, 1–7.

2. See Timothy Garton Ash, "Eastern Europe: The Year of Truth," *New York Review of Books*, 15 Feb. 1990, 17–22.

3. See, e.g., Alan Riding, "Survey Finds 2 in 3 Poles Opposed to German Unity," *New York Times*, 10 Feb 1990; "Majority in Poll Approves German Reunification," *Le Figaro*, 13 Nov. 1989 and reprinted

in FBIS, *Western Europe: Daily Report*, 22 Dec. 1989, 38; and "Political, German Reunification Views Polled," 2. These surveys, conducted in January 1990, found general approval for German unification in all of Europe except in Poland and the Soviet Union.

4. "Poll Reveals Optimism on Eastern Bloc Future," *Liberation*, 4 Oct. 1989, reprinted in FBIS, *Daily Report: Western Europe*, 30 Nov. 1989, 42–46.

5. A survey of West German opinion taken in February 1990 found that people believed the most important tasks for their government to be environmental protection (mentioned by 60%), combatting unemployment (52%), housing construction (44%), unification (23%), and—least important—military security (3%). "Einheit? Ja, aber Bitte billing!," *Die Zeit* (North American ed.), 16 Mar. 1990, 3.

6. See Stephen F. Szabo, "Public Opinion and the Alliance: European and American Perspectives on NATO and European Security," in *NATO in the 1990s*, ed. Stanley R. Sloan (Washington: Pergammon-Brassey's, 1989), 154–61.

7. "Is NATO Necessary?," *National Journal*, 9 Dec. 1989, 3015.

8. For a fuller discussion of these trends, see Patrick Garrity, ed., *The Future of Nuclear Weapons: Issues in International Security* (New York: Plenum, forthcoming).

9. *Suedeutsche Zeitung*, 9–10 Apr. 1988, 11.

10. For empirical data chronicling the greater Europeanism of postwar Europeans, see Ronald Inglehart, *Culture Shift in Advanced Industrial Societies* (Princeton: Princeton University Press, 1990), 408–21.

Spain's Transition to Democracy: A Model for Eastern Europe?

KENNETH MAXWELL

Spain's foreign and defense policies have been in flux since the 1970s. After a long period of enforced isolation under the Franco regime, the new democracy has moved increasingly into a position of influence in Europe. This process of normalization of international relations was fortified by accession to the North Atlantic Treaty Organization (NATO) in 1982, to the European Community (EC) in 1986, and to the Western European Union (WEU) in 1988. In some ways, the factors compelling this transformation are similar to those facing all Western European governments and reflect the dramatic changes in East–West relations, the long-term impact of the 1989 democratic revolutions in central Europe, and the uncertainties as well as potential dangers of the post–cold war epoch now unfolding.

Spain has also played an increasingly important role on the world stage as a model of the peaceful transition from authoritarianism to democracy. Spain and Eastern Europe, for example, are different in many basic ways; nevertheless, Eastern Europeans have learned from Spain's democratization. More recently, a debate has begun among political scientists as to the relative merits of parliamentary and presidential systems in consolidating democratic polities; again, Spain has been the starting point.[1]

Although the process of democratization in Spain has received a great deal of scholarly attention and a substantial literature now exists on the subject, the interaction of the new regime with the rest of the world has been little studied. That is curious when one considers how central the events in Spain were during the immediate prewar period and how widespread interest in the Spanish Civil War

This essay is based on extensive interviews in Spain and the United States, over the period 1987–90, and a series of meetings with United States and Spanish government officials and military officers at the Institute for Defense Analyses in Washington, D.C., at the Ortega y Gasset Foundation in Toledo, and in Madrid, Spain.

continues among the general public. It may be, in fact, one of the little noted factors that contributed to Spain's negotiated transition that avoided outside interference and the East-West controversy. Certainly, until the end of the cold war, a radical process of regime substitution made it likely that internationalization would follow. Spain's neighbor, Portugal, is the classic case. Because the fall of Portugal's old regime preceded the death of Francisco Franco in 1975, Portugal's turmoil and outsiders' intrusive role in the struggle for democracy provided a salutary lesson of what should be avoided.

The Spanish past, moreover, set important parameters in the international arena. For the United States, in particular, the nature of bilateral relations under Franco provoked much ill will over the United States bases in Spain after democratization. In Spain, however, the diminution of the United States presence was seen as providing an array of options that in no way undermined Spain's basic engagement in a democratic Europe. Ironically, given the internal opposition to Spain's joining NATO and the lack of resonance that talk of the "Soviet threat" had among the Spanish public, Spain's belated entry into the alliance occurred just before shifts in the international system so profound as to bring the very basis of NATO into question, or at least its rationale as an anti-Soviet coalition.

Three dimensions framed the debate about Spain's foreign and defense policies during the 1980s. First, Spain had to surmount the constraints arising from its historical experience. Second, the Iberian or regional context saw a major rapprochement, best summarized as a process of Europeanization. Third, the Atlantic connection, involving bilateral relations with the United States, was subject to substantial modification. In each instance, priorities were reordered, or — perhaps more accurately in the case of Spain — set for the first time.

It should be remembered that, until the mid-1970s, Spain was a dictatorship that the armed forces helped create. In 1981, elements of the army and the paramilitary security forces attempted to overthrow the new constitutional democracy. These attempts, of course, have been only the most dramatic manifestations of a deeper process of change and adjustment. But they exemplify the circumstances limiting Spain's participation in Western Europe and NATO. The military is repositioning itself with respect to civil society, rearticulating and justifying its role within a democratic polity.

For almost fifty years, principally as a result of the Civil War and the nature of the Franco regime, Spain had an insignificant role in international affairs. But in many other respects Spain had been marginal to the European mainstream since the end of the Napoleonic wars and had been severely shaken by the loss of Cuba and the Philippines in the 1890s — events that still condition Spanish reflexes, at least rhetorically, to the United States in particular. Even in the early 1970s, Spain was regarded as a pariah by a large part of the international community and was therefore excluded from many of the organizations established during the post–World War II period, especially in Europe. This exclusion limited what Spain could do internationally and the Spanish elites' exposure to international experience. Thus, for many decades, the country's international relations were severely distorted and self-limiting.

Spain did not share the modern industrialized nations' formative influences and common experiences, such as victory (or defeat) in World War II, postwar reconciliation and economic reconstruction, and the building of European transnational institutions. Indeed, until the early 1950s, Spain was formally excluded from the new international organizations. Throughout the cold war, Spain was firmly anti-Communist, and that, more than anything else, helped it to develop close security relationships, especially with the United States after 1952. But Iberian anticommunism, coming from the interwar decades, was accompanied by a hostility to the postwar Western community's democratic values. In fact, the dissociation of "defense of the West" from "defense of Western values" during most of the post–World War II period has been at the root of Spain's difficulties in integrating foreign and defense policy into a coherent and popularly acceptable doctrine.

After Franco died in 1975, one of the most fundamental tasks of the new democratic regime was to develop a defense and foreign policy more in keeping with a democratic polity and Spain's importance in Europe. Because of the ambiguity of Spain's security relationships before democratization, foreign policy and defense were among the last areas to be normalized in the process of Western Europeanization, and curious holdovers from the old regime continued in new guises. Spain's past also made foreign policy and security arrangements highly susceptible to demagogic posturing, especially in its relations with the United States.

The Transition from Francoism

In Spain, democratization took place by consensus and reconciliation. The new system incorporated the previously clandestine anti-Franco opposition, and the opposition accepted important continuities from the Franco era — especially in the security and military area. Initially, the transition was conducted by a broad but factious centrist coalition, the Unión de Centro Democrático (UCD), led by Adolfo Suárez, a former functionary of Franco's political movement. The UCD achieved remarkable breakthroughs in constitution making and institutional innovation, but it was increasingly unable to contain its centrifugal balances.

Since 1982 Spain has had a majority government (a Socialist majority led by Felipe González Márquez, elected in 1982 and reelected with a smaller majority in 1986 and a disputed one-seat majority in 1989). In 1986 Spain joined the EC. In the mind of the civilian political leadership, the European engagement was essential to ensure the successful consolidation of a European-style democracy, an especially important concern after the failed coup of 1981. Four recent developments, however, help explain some of the special features of Spain's democratization.

First, King Juan Carlos I was instrumental in consolidating democracy. The king, as Franco's designated successor, provided continuity. Moreover, he backed the construction of the broad centrist coalition that was critical to the transitional period through the UCD and worked closely with Suárez.

Second, the strong, moderate, and majoritarian Spanish Socialist Workers' Party (PSOE) emerged as a major competitor for power during the transition. Neither of these phenomena was inevitable. Before 1975 few believed in a monarchical solution to Spain's historical dilemmas, given the strong tradition of Spanish republicanism. In the PSOE, leaders like Felipe González Márquez and Alfonso Guerra González were critical in facing down maximalist demands from the grass roots of the party in 1979 and making the PSOE a moderate party on the Western European social democratic model. This allowed the PSOE to drop much of the Marxist baggage and place electoral over mass politics. The move made the party popular and propelled it into the government in 1982.

Third, Spaniards were aware of the failures of the republican regime of the 1930s and built mechanisms into the Constitution of 1978 to impede the fall of the government. The parliament delegated the writing of the Constitution to a broadly based but small group of experts who worked in total privacy and placed compromise high on their agendas. As a consequence, the Spanish Constitution, with the important exception of the Basques, is universally accepted and does not stand in the way of programmatic decisions by the government.

Fourth, two symbols of past polarizations, the church and the Communist party, moved toward the center. Santiago Carrillo, the Spanish Communist leader during the period of transition in the mid-1970s and a leading exponent of Eurocommunism, had broken with the Soviet Union and embraced a parliamentary path. The church, for its part, had embraced democracy and, more important, provided no legitimacy for the enemies of democracy, as it had often done historically.

During the dramatic years from the death of Franco in 1975 until the aborted coup of 1981, the Spanish army stood moodily on the sidelines. There were rumblings of discontent within the armed forces over the legalization of the Communist party in 1977, the explicit recognition in the 1978 Constitution of the multinational and multilingual character of Spanish society, and the murder by Basque Nation and Liberty (ETA) of the commanding officer of the Spanish army's most important division, as well as other officers and policemen. But when a group of civil guards and army officers took over the Parliament and held the government hostage for several hours in February 1981, the armed forces rallied to the constitutional order. Don Juan Carlos I provided a clear focus for authority and became central to protecting democracy under challenge. By guaranteeing continuity in the midst of transition, the king was able to carry the forces of order with him while embracing the forces of change.

Finally, it is important to stress again the external factor: Spain almost totally avoided international intervention in the 1970s. Here again the king was reassuring, going out of his way to assure the Americans, most notably in a speech before both houses of the United States Congress in 1977, that a democratic Spain was not a threat but a realization of their democratic aspirations.

The Foreign Policy of the New Democracy

In the 1982 general elections the PSOE took 40 percent of the popular vote and 202 of the 350 seats in Parliament, allowing it to form a single party government for the first time in its one-hundred-year history. The socialists acted pragmatically and were reelected for a second term in 1986 and a third term in 1989. The PSOE's connection with French Socialists was strong, and from 1975 on the supportive role of West Germany was important, especially via the Friedrich Ebert Foundation and the trade unions. This conduit provided advice, money, and organizational expertise. Until 1976 the United States had no official relationship with the Spanish Socialists, but the PSOE had informal contacts with individual Americans. These contacts tended to be part of the old republican network; they were influential in transatlantic left and intellectual circles, but they were decidedly not official. The PSOE's views of America therefore tended to reflect the position of opponents to United States administrations and, more generally, the counterculture of the 1960s and early 1970s.

Wells Stabler, who was ambassador in Madrid during the most critical years of the transition, decried the lack of preparation in Washington for the inevitable demise of Franco. Without precise instructions as to what would happen, he was surprised when President Gerald R. Ford's visit to Madrid was announced. Since Franco was then eighty-two years old and could not survive much longer and since the Franco regime did not need shoring up, Stabler saw no reason for the presidential visit. Many Spaniards asked him: "Why did you have to do this? What do you gain from it?" The fact was, according to Stabler, that the "visit achieved absolutely nothing at all except, again from Franco's point of view, indicating that the big friend was rallying around."[2]

Though generally benign, the United States's indifference did not go unnoticed in Spain, and many — especially Socialists — interpreted it as hostility to democratic aspirations. At the time of the attempted putsch of 23 February 1981, Alexander Haig, then United States secretary of state, was reported to have described the assault by Lt. Col. Antonio Tejero and his colleagues on the Parliament as being "an internal matter" and further damaged bilateral relations, especially with the already suspicious left. In 1985, on the eve of his visit to Madrid, President Ronald Reagan spoke of the Abraham Lincoln Brigade, which fought in defense of the republic against Franco: "I would say that the individuals that went over there were, in the opinion of most Americans, fighting on the wrong side." This comment raised a particularly unfortunate memory of United States hostility to the Republican cause in the 1930s, a cause in which General Francisco Franco's supporters had included Hitler and Mussolini. Spanish ministers, among them Prime Minister Felipe González Marquéz, have gone out of their way since then to emphasize to American audiences that they saw the history of the 1930s in a different light. The participation of Americans in the International Brigades, González told a meeting at the Woodrow Wilson Center in Washington, D.C., in November 1986, mitigated America's embrace of Franco's dictatorship.

The sensitivity of Spanish Socialists to foreign-policy issues — particularly American faux pas — is acute because these issues can mobilize the grass roots of the party in a way that embarrasses the leadership. Prime Minister González, in his speech at the Woodrow Wilson Center, expressed a view that is common among his colleagues and that influences their attitude toward the United States. Given the past experience of Spain, he said, no democratic Spaniard assumes support from the Western democracies for a nonauthoritarian Spain; for Spaniards, defense of the West was not synonymous with the defense of democratic values; and the United States's cozy relationship with Franco, including deals to permit bases in Spain, are regarded as Franco's abnegations of Spanish sovereignty and the United States's condoning Franco's dictatorship. It is less important that these views may be unfair, inaccurate, and out of date than that they exist and are powerfully represented in Spanish public opinion and the Socialist government.

Spain under Franco had been excluded from NATO, and its decision to join the alliance in 1982 was controversial. In a break with the consensus policies followed throughout the transition period, Spain—under the centrist government led by Leopoldo Calvo Sotelo—joined NATO precipitously. The decision was motivated at least as much by political objectives as by security needs. The Spanish people did not feel threatened by the Soviet Union and tended to worry more about the potential for conflict in the Mediterranean and with Morocco over the Spanish enclaves of Ceuta and Melilla. Some saw participation in NATO as a means of keeping the army out of domestic politics. The Socialists fought their victorious election campaign in 1982 with an anti-NATO plank; yet, faced with a fait accompli, they promised a referendum on the issue. Under considerable international pressure and with the NATO issue increasingly linked to Spain's application for EC membership, the Socialists, once in government, shifted positions and then had to convince the public, which (according to public opinion polls) was opposed to participation in the alliance, to change its mind also.

Public opinion was no less opposed to the United States presence. Asked on the eve of President Reagan's visit if "the US and its president are loyal and sincere friends of Spain," only 13 percent agreed; 74 percent disagreed.[3] In a 1984 poll on NATO, a question asked about the United States bases received a 70 percent negative result; among PSOE voters, the negative result was 76 percent.[4] The Socialists won the NATO referendum in 1986 but at the cost of an anti-American clause calling for the reduction of American military personnel in Spain.

The NATO issue also complicated Spain's relationship with Portugal, which feared that its own role in NATO would be overwhelmed by Spain's involvement. Portugal categorically rejected serving in any capacity under a Spanish-based unified Iberian command. Spain was also reluctant to integrate its forces into NATO command structures. In addition, British control of Gibraltar—which Spain regarded as a colony on European soil—complicated the NATO issue for Spain. Thus the prospect for disagreements with new and old partners was greater than most officials recognized, especially in Washington; and this failure led to much confusion, recrimination, and considerable difficulties in bilateral relations with the United States, especially over the issue of United States bases in Spain.

The ambiguous and conflictive nature of Spain's reapproximation with the international system on the strategic front stood in marked contrast to the public and political response to Europe, especially the European Community, which was seen as representing the new Spain's ideal of economic prosperity and democratic politics. Europe was both model and aspiration, and, with Franco gone, full membership in the EC was the goal of all Spanish governments following the installation of a parliamentary constitutional monarchy. The path into Europe was not easy, of course, but no major sector of opinion in Spain doubted that the future lay in that direction. Once membership in the EC was achieved, Spain moved rapidly to play a full part in its deliberations.

Civil-Military Relations since Democratization

Despite the coup attempt of 1981 and perhaps in some ways because of it, the process of establishing civilian control of the armed forces has been surprisingly rapid and successful. The Ministry of Defense was established in 1977 and reflected the desire of reformist officers for internal modernization of the armed forces, as well as the need by civilian politicians to establish the primacy of civil over military power in decision making. When the Socialist government began implementing the reform of the armed forces, therefore, it found some effective collaborators among high-ranking reform-minded officers in all three services. Previously, the UCD had excluded the military from the constitution-making process and the relationship between the services and Adolfo Suárez were often tense. Military leaders complained that they heard of measures affecting them from the mass media, not from the government itself. The Socialist government has continued to embark on its reforms in an incremental manner and with broad consultation.

Spain was fortunate in that it faced no serious external threat during the course of democratization. It had avoided the risk of a foreign military involvement during the mid-1970s by rapidly withdrawing from the potentially explosive situation in what was the Spanish Sahara. But Spain faces a major internal threat from terrorism. Paradoxically, this threat has had a positive effect on the integration of the security and intelligence services of the old regime into the new democratic structures.

Several general points can be made about civilian-military relations in Spain. The existence of the terrorist threat helped legitimize the security services and paramilitary forces and preserve an important continuity in these institutions. Since terrorism did not diminish with the end of the Franco regime, these forces, which otherwise would have been subject to scrutiny and perhaps dismantlement, soon became essential to the defense of the democratic state. There were, of course, ambiguities; these institutions had been bastions of the dictatorship and still harbored individuals with decidedly undemocratic values. The nature of the Spanish transition also served to incorporate a large sector of the Francoist bureaucratic apparatus into the new system. Yet it is important to note that the task of defending democracy from assaults was approved by public opinion and helps explain the lack of retribution in Spain against the security services that had long sustained Franco's rule. That is almost unique in the course of change from an authoritarian to a democratic regime.

The corollary of this phenomenon of continuity is that Spain has retained a strong central state government, despite the parallel and key phenomenon of the creation of autonomous regional governments throughout the territory. The state's strength has hindered certain aspects of economic modernization and helped the PSOE to form a quasi-hegemonic control over poor regions dependent on the central government's largess, but it has had the positive effect of limiting the area in which any alternative political vision could be articulated—either on the far right or on the far left. Since the public wanted moderation and Europeanization above all, those who wanted to return to the past, particularly disgruntled military officers, had little influence.

The same phenomenon limited the role of Communists in Spain, especially in the military, where attempts to find converts were quickly repressed. Moreover, the Portuguese revolutionary experience of 1974–75 was a salutary one for the military in Spain. It served to strengthen the military reformers who saw a civilian, constitutional regime as a way to achieve major changes within the military that they wished for and indeed largely articulated before the death of Franco. These reformers, aware of the king's close relationship with the military, welcomed change. They were entirely unsympathetic to what they unflatteringly referred to as "the bunker" (the old-line Francoists). The Communist reading of the developments in the civil society was also inaccurate. The party played a key role in negotiating the transition but reaped few benefits from the process. In fact, the party fragmented and was largely marginalized in the subsequent political process.

The failed coup of 1981 had the beneficial effect of forcing the undemocratic elements within the armed forces into the open. Previously, civilian politicians and the press had been highly circumspect, even fearful, of talking openly of plotting within the military. Afterward, this became a major item of discussion and press exposure. In other words, mysterious forces that had been frightening were identified and no longer seemed threatening. The result was greatly to diffuse the threat from the unreconstructed right.

After the electoral victory in 1982, the Socialists moved skillfully to implement military reforms—a major political objective. Significantly, they placed in the Ministry of Defense a Catalan politician and former mayor of Barcelona, Narcís Serra Serra, who had developed a good relationship with the military before the Socialist victory. Serra has established civilian control, reoriented budget and deployment provisions, and embarked on a major effort to modernize the Spanish military, removing the army's functional role that had been more keyed to internal repression than to national defense.

The Socialists had three major objectives: first, to bring Spanish defense structures more into line with those of Western Europe; second, to professionalize and streamline the armed forces; and, third, to make Spain more independent of foreign arms supplies by the encouragement of domestic suppliers. To modernize these structures is a more radical process than might appear at first sight. In the mid-

1970s the Spanish military, especially the army, more resembled a Latin American force than a NATO army with an elderly and bloated officer corps and 62 percent of its budget spent on personnel (compared with 43 percent in West Germany and 40 percent in Great Britain). In early 1984 the defense law was modified to give greater authority to the prime minister over command and coordination of the armed forces. In this he was to be advised by the National Defense Board and a reformed Joint Chiefs of Staff. The joint chiefs now became a consultative, not a command, body. The 1984 amendment also increased the powers of the minister of defense who became responsible for overall military policy making. In 1985, promotion and appointive power was concentrated in the hands of the chiefs of each service and the minister, and a new position of chief of the general staff was created with responsibility for joint action of the services. These and subsequent reforms placed real decision-making power in the hands of the Ministry of Defense, which then used this power thoroughly to overhaul defense planning and to set priorities for force size and the acquisition of materiél. The heaviest burden of change was suffered by the army. A phased 16 percent reduction in the number of army officers was initiated and reductions of 8 percent imposed on the navy and air force. For the 1990s the number of officers in the armed forces as a whole is intended to reach a level of 58,000, with a total force level of 300,000.

At the same time as these major organizational changes were being implemented, equally important shifts occurred in the system of military justice, limiting the extensive powers exercised by military tribunals during the Franco era. In 1984 the Socialist government adopted a "joint strategic plan" that defined the overall objectives of the armed forces in the new democracy. These consisted of defense of the constitutional order, guarantor of the territorial integrity of Spain, protection of the population from aggression or natural disaster, commitment to the defense and security of the Western world, and the establishment of effective control over the Straits of Gibraltar and its approaches. The practical consequences of these preoccupations — especially those concerning the Magreb — are a strengthening of the southern military region, the strengthening of the Naval Combat Group based at Rota, and the deployment of F-18As. Of course, the lack of specificity about the Soviet threat in Spanish military planning in the 1980s allows the Spaniards to claim with some justification that they were prescient in their view of East-West relations. As of 1990, Spanish defense spending stood at roughly $7 billion, or 2.4 percent of gross national product.

Despite these positive elements in the process by which the Spanish armed forces — in the words of a former chief of the defense staff, Admiral Angel Liberal Lucini — are becoming "like those in any other Western country," the roots of Spanish particularism run deep. The power of this particularist sentiment, which has strong elements of isolationism, also feeds on a resilient anti-Americanism in Spain and complicates thinking about Western defense issues. Many Spaniards seek an alternative to the traditional preoccupation of NATO: a role for Spain within a Spanish-speaking commonwealth espousing a largely anti-American position on politics in Latin America or on such issues as debt and Third World security; a European defense and foreign-policy forum, such as the WEU; or a French-German-Spanish axis on defense issues.

It was against this background that negotiations on United States base rights became so acrimonious and led to the forced withdrawal of the U.S. Air Force tactical fighter-bomber wing from Torrejón, outside Madrid. Again, ironically, despite the bitterness that had accumulated on both sides and Spain's opposition to the use of its facilities for "out of area" contingencies, in 1990 Spain became a major staging area for the United States buildup in the Persian Gulf and, against considerable internal opposition, even deployed naval forces of its own to the Middle East.

Some of these contradictions arose because ideology tended to be more prominent in foreign policy, especially during the first Socialist term, when Fernando Morran was foreign minister (1982–85), than in other areas of Spanish policy, especially those concerning the domestic economy. Complications also arose from the fact that the engagement with Europe, exemplified by the long negotiations over EC admission, became indirectly involved in the NATO issue largely because it provided some leverage to each side at different times during the negotiations; but these tactical moves prevented serious consideration of the consequences and costs of these significant new arrangements. It is striking that the domestic policy of the Socialists has been extremely pragmatic — even conservative in the sense of being antistatist, oriented toward free-enterprise, open to innovations in reindustrialization, and opposed to archaic labor regulation. In foreign policy, the Socialists have on occasion been extremely rhetorical. While this posture may have found favor in some sectors of domestic public opinion — and was considerably moderated by Francisco Fernández Ordóñez, an experienced politician who has held important posts in the UCD governments when he succeeded Morran as foreign minister in 1985 — it has not been without consequences.

Spain, for example, has two vulnerable territorial enclaves in North Africa — Ceuta and Melilla. Morocco claims them in much the same manner that Spain claims Gibraltar. The Socialist government committed itself to Spanish sovereignty in these two cases, mainly as a sop to the military conservatives. Yet, by this high-profile commitment, it created hostages to the future. Both Ceuta and Melilla are ultimately indefensible in a purely military sense, and Spain's intransigence there has undermined the power of its own position with respect to Gibraltar.

This long-term Spanish worry about the consequences of instability in the Mediterranean and the Magreb has most recently been manifested in the Spanish government's enthusiasm for the idea of a permanent Conference on Security and Cooperation in the Mediterranean (CSCM) on the model of the Conference on Security and Cooperation in Europe. Italy supports the idea, but France and the United States are skeptical.

Spain is also committed to a policy of denuclearization. But France, in many respects a model for Spain's NATO relationship, is a nuclear power. France, like the United States and the Atlanticist elements in NATO, wants defense arrangements with Spain because it would serve as a territorial redoubt in the event of a European war. French doctrine would, in any case, have called for a nuclearization of the conflict long before any Soviet or Warsaw Pact troops reached the Pyrenees. But much of this debate, which many in Spain regarded as fanciful at the time, has now become largely irrelevant with the collapse of the Warsaw Pact. Coordination of forces had long existed between NATO and Spain, especially with the navy, and Soviet military planners since the 1950s have taken account of what is, after all, Europe's fourth largest naval force.

Continuing Problems

At the beginning of the Socialists' third term as the governing party, a series of new problems surfaced, all of which are likely to worsen in the 1990s. Perhaps the PSOE's very success made it inevitable that criticism would arise concerning its hegemonic role within the state. Moreover, unresolved problems in the organization of the state have complicated the PSOE's dual role as an administrator and as a political party within a democratically representative polity. First, as administrator, it has been criticized for high-handedness and corruption — both of power and in a more material sense — focusing on Deputy Prime Minister Alfonso Guerra González and his family. Second, as a political party, the PSOE faces the consequences of running the central government, which must deal with unassimilated nationalities (such as the Basques) and autonomous regional governments (such as Catalonia and Galicia) run by regional parties that can aspire to no more than minority-party status on a nationwide basis but are key building blocks to any conservative opposition to the Socialists. These issues complicate center-periphery relations.

While economic prosperity continued and the PSOE enjoyed a clear majority in the Cortes, the difficulties of governance and central-regional government relations remained muted and were almost never mentioned in discussions of the Spanish model. The opposition of large segments of the Basque population to the constitutional settlement of 1978, the continuation of Basque terrorism, and the failure to settle this issue remain major concerns for the future. Basque autonomy may be an unresolvable issue, and one thinks inevitably of nationality problems within the Soviet Union, Northern Ireland, and, worst of all, Lebanon. Spain's failure to solve the Basque problem, despite its overall success in democratization, could be a troublesome indicator for the democratizing countries of Eastern and central Europe, many of which have nationality problems and few of which enjoy the economic and social advantages Spain had during its transition from dictatorship to democracy.

What is important here, perhaps, is the reemergence of the question of constitutional engineering on a Europewide basis, which is implicit in these nationality problems. Germany, according to Christoph Bertram of *Die Zeit*, has traditionally consisted of a multitude of states within one nation, whereas Jordi Sole Tura defined Spain as a nation of nations. Clearly, even if in a less optimistic mode than the discussion to date, Spain provides important lessons for the emerging problems of post–cold war central Europe, the post-Communist regimes in Eastern Europe, and perhaps the Soviet Union itself.

A further troubling issue in Spain — one that is fundamental to any healthy democracy — is the absence of a conservative alternative. The question remains of how a viable democratic alternative to PSOE will arise. Have the Socialists preempted the conservatives' policies so successfully as to undermine the possibility of an alternative government from the democratic right? Even if their forces were to unite to win an election, would they hold together in government, particularly if the conservative coalition was based on disparate interests or a negotiated electoral pact incorporating regionally based parties, within and between which centrifugal pressures could reemerge like the tensions that destroyed the UCD? This vacuum in opposition obviously encourages and aggravates the hegemonic tendencies within PSOE and complaints about its control of the state apparatus, as well as the potential for corruption and the subversion of democratic values.

In addition, 1992 — the quincentennial of the discovery of America — is a symbolic year for Spain with some paradoxical implications. Spain will see the Seville Universal Exposition, the Olympic Games in Barcelona, and Madrid as the "cultural capital" of Europe, as well as the European unified market set against changes in Eastern Europe, Germany, and the Soviet Union. These events are likely to affect Spanish foreign policy, especially on North-South questions, Spain's opening to Latin America, the Middle East, and Africa, and its still-hesitant steps toward full integration into the Western alliance. Important changes of attitude have already taken place, to be sure, particularly Spain's participation in United Nations peacekeeping forces in Namibia and Central America, making a qualitative shift from mere rhetorical engagement to active participation. Spain has also involved itself directly in the Persian Gulf crisis by dispatching naval forces.

Spain, however, limited by its desire to distance itself from United States policy in Latin America, found itself surprised by the electoral victory of President Violeta Chamorro in Nicaragua and has run into problems with its long-time partner, President Fidel Castro of Cuba. And the whole equation on which Spain based its somewhat ambiguous position in the East-West conflict has also changed. The notion of a "common European home" espoused by Mikhail S. Gorbachev and the establishment of new democratic governments in Eastern Europe pose major challenges to the status quo. Central Europe is a potential competitor because it has cheaper labor and could become a source of major migration flows to the West. Spain is already facing a drop in tourism, and remittances from Spanish workers in Western Europe remain an important contribution to Spain's balance of payments. And there remains the great question of the future of the Soviet Union itself. In Gorbachev's vision there is the disturbing image of Europe as a white man's club — not only as a protectionist zone of prosperity that the Soviet Union, like Spain before it, aspires to imitate but also as a defensive economic and social bloc opposed to the Third World in general and Asia in particular. Jerry Hough, for example, in his analysis of Soviet motivations in *Foreign Affairs*, makes much of threats that the Soviets perceive in Asia and the challenge of competitive pressures from the newly industrializing countries (NICs).[5] In a purely economic sense, these fears are reasonable so far as the Soviet Union (or Spain) is concerned. The implications for the Third World are quite serious—especially for Latin America, where Spain has major investments, most notably in privatized telephone companies in Chile and Argentina. Yet, Spanish-American immigrants are facing immense hostility in the Iberian peninsula, where unemployment remains high and much Colombian cocaine trafficking has been redirected to Spain. These foreign-policy issues are only now being addressed but are bound to increase in relevance as 1992 approaches.

Is Spain a Model?

The performance of the Spanish Socialist government, its efforts at privatization, its commitment to a market economy, and its strategy of growth over redistribution have had an impact on the democratic-socialist and social-democratic parties of Europe. The PSOE government and its electoral successes clearly provide social democrats with an alternative to the conservative wave of the 1980s, exemplified by Prime Minister Margaret Thatcher of Britain and Chancellor Helmut Kohl of West Germany. But the key question remains: What is most significant in these phenomena? If all the parties are moving to the right—as the PSOE in government has certainly done on both domestic and foreign-policy questions—what happens to space on the left? Will terrorism or a reactive nationalism take up the slack? Already the Communist party has reemerged in Spain through a united left and is more attractive to the left wing of the Socialist party than at any time since the mid-1970s. Forty-four percent of young Basques continue to believe that violence is an acceptable means of defining Basque national interests.[6] Large-scale unemployment, migration problems, slackening tourism, inflation, and potential industrial competition from central and eastern Europe are all on the horizon in Spain and have implications for the so-far highly successful model of the Socialist government.

Spain's transition to democracy could be a model for Eastern Europe. There is certainly a lot of interest—particularly in Hungary and Poland—in the Spanish example. On a recent visit to Columbia University, Bronislaw Geremek, Solidarity's Parliamentary spokesman, said that while the union was underground during martial law its model was Finland—a model implying escape from direct Soviet domination. Once martial law was lifted, the model was Austria—a model for neutrality between East and West. But once Solidarity achieved its parliamentary landslide in the June 1989 elections, the model became Spain—a model of political and economic reform. Yet, though some elements in Eastern Europe parallel those that affected Spain, other conditions of the Spanish transition are not repeated in Eastern Europe. Clearly, the example provided by the EC, to which Spain had long sought admission, also provides a model for Eastern Europe. However, it is important to note the social and economic change that preceded political change in Spain, especially the economic liberalization policy, carried out by the authoritarian regime, and Spain's participation in the economic boom of the 1960s. One consequence of the economic growth was the emergence of a middle class in the 1960s and 1970s. Tourism and emigrant remittances provided key economic inputs, cushioning the process of political engineering and allowing economic decisions to be postponed until the new institutional structure was in place. Another key element in Spain was the explicit effort of the Spanish leadership during the transition to avoid mistakes of the past, especially the uncompromising stances of the 1930s and the risk of another civil war. The role of King Juan Carlos I was unique to Spain. He used the quasi-authoritarian powers granted to him as Franco's designated successor to implement reform initiatives, divested himself of his powers, and assumed the largely ceremonial role of constitutional monarch in a parliamentary democracy. The American presence in Spain was not popular, but the United States was not there as an occupation force, nor had it been involved in actions to repress freedom. The United States presence, though resisted, was in no way comparable to the Soviet army in Eastern Europe, and the democratization of Spain did not lead to the collapse of the rationale for Spain's integration with the rest of Western democracy but marked the removal of an obstacle to its full and active participation in Western multinational organizations. Pact making was critical to Spanish success by involving the unions, the church, business, and political parties from the left and the right, thus creating an atmosphere conducive to constitutional negotiations and restructuring the economy.

An important point about Spain's democracy has almost always been overlooked, although negotiation and compromise were preeminent characteristics of the transition from authoritarianism, the outcome of its institutional engineering was quite radical and marked a clear break with the immediate past. The constitutional monarchy established in 1978 is a system entirely different from that set up by Franco. The social and economic transformation of Spain, on the other hand, had been incremental and had occurred in the two decades before Franco's death. Raymond Carr, the great British historian of modern Spain, has long argued that in the past Spain sought to impose advanced institutions of representative government on an archaic social structure, almost always with disastrous and often bloody results. By the 1970s, however, Spanish society had changed, becoming modernized, consumer oriented, capitalistic, moderate, and middle class; yet this vibrant new Spain was overseen by superannuated institutions. The transition to democracy reconciled the long-standing differences between institutions and society, but the social changes and the political skill that made democratization possible may be unique to Spain. Eastern Europe may be less fortunate.

NOTES

1. See, in particular, Juan J. Linz, "The Perils of Presidentialism," *Journal of Democracy* 1 (Winter 1990): 51–69.
2. Wells Stabler, comments made at the Foreign Policy Center Conference on Democratization,

Foreign Service Institute, U.S. Department of State, 1986, an edited version of which was published in *Authoritarian Regimes in Transition*, ed. Hans Binnendijk (Center for the study of Foreign Affairs, Foreign Service Institute, U.S. Department of State, 1987).

3. *El Pais*, 6 May 1985.
4. Ibid., 12 Oct. 1984.
5. Jerry F. Hough, "Gorbachev's Politics," *Foreign Affairs* 68 (Winter 1989–90): 26–41.
6. Francisco Oriza, *Juventud Española 1984* (Madrid: Ediciones S.M., 1985): 406.

France, Germany, and the Future of the Atlantic Alliance

ROBBIN LAIRD

The main effort of the French-German interaction on security affairs in the 1980s was to maintain the North Atlantic Treaty Organization (NATO). France sought to anchor West Germany to the alliance. The key event of the decade was the intermediate-range nuclear forces (INF) crisis, and France was afraid that the Soviet Union would be able to pressure West Germany in the direction of neutrality. From the French point of view, if the Soviets had convinced West German officials to reject INF deployments, that would have been an important step toward eliminating West Germany as a Western ally.

West Germany sought to encourage France's fuller participation in the Atlantic alliance. The West German leaders especially wanted to enhance the French commitment (as they understood it) to the defense of West German territory. This concern was expressed in terms of both conventional and nuclear forces. As for conventional forces, West Germany sought to guarantee France's commitment to fight on West German soil from the very outset of hostilities. With regard to nuclear forces, West Germany wanted to see the establishment of much clearer mechanisms to plan for the use of French nuclear weapons, especially on West German soil.

The subordinate theme of the French-German interaction through late 1989 was on NATO's transformation. France encouraged an alteration in how the West German public and elites saw the alliance — trying to de-Americanize it and preparing for the time when the American role would inevitably decline. France sought to maintain a transatlantic alliance by nudging West Germany toward a Europeanization course.

In the aftermath of the INF agreement, West German conservatives became concerned with the fate of the nuclear relationship between the United States and West Germany. France increasingly looked like an important ally in the transformation of the allied nuclear relationship. For a relatively brief period, the relationship between Defense Minister André Giraud and Defense Minister Manfred

Woerner involved a serious discussion of deepening the bilateral military relationship by including France's explicit extended nuclear guarantee to West Germany. Nonetheless, it was transformation within a divided Europe. The Atlantic alliance existed to counter the Soviet Union and the Warsaw Pact. The question was how to restructure the alliance to enhance the European role, to keep the United States committed to Europe, and to continue to counter the Warsaw Pact. A French-German dyad would be developed to reshape NATO with greater European focus and control over a superpower-dominated European security order. The choice was to build either a European pillar or an effective European caucus that would better represent European interests within the alliance.

The French-German Interaction

The elites in both France and West Germany have sought to expand the interaction between them, especially since the mid-1970s. Both France and West Germany have wanted to expand the scope of European cooperation to incorporate security policy. France has favored expanding the European capability to make independent decisions commensurate with the French concept of security independence. West Germany has viewed enhanced Europeanization as a desirable way to get out of the constraints of the superpower-dominated East-West system.

The French-German dialogue has broadened throughout the three basic phases of East-West relations. The first phase was the period of détente in the mid-to-late 1970s. At the time, the confrontation deepened between the United States and the Soviet Union, while European leaders sought to continue a détente relationship. The second phase of East-West relations was the renewed confrontation associated with the INF struggle. The third phase has been the reaction of the West to the Gorbachev revolution.

In the 1970s, the effort to expand bilateral relations was led by President Valéry Giscard d'Estaing and Chancellor Helmut Schmidt. For Giscard d'Estaing, the interaction with West Germany was a useful tool to "normalize" French security policy and to lead France out of the self-imposed isolation of Gaullism. Early in his administration, Giscard d'Estaing and his key advisers articulated the desire to expand the French security commitment in visible ways toward West Germany. They spoke of an "enlarged sanctuary," but heavy criticism from the right and the left caused the president to retreat from too visible a shift in French policy.

Nonetheless, such a shift in policy was pursued covertly. Giscard d'Estaing pursued greater ties between the French military and the NATO integrated command. Also, the French dialogue with West Germany was expanded beyond narrow economic issues to incorporate broader political discussions. Notably, the issues of East-West détente were at the core of the discussions. Chancellor Schmidt, for a variety of reasons, did not wish to enter into a direct confrontation with the United States over East-West policy. Rather, he relied — in part — on the special relationship with Giscard d'Estaing to expand the East-West dialogue, particularly with the Soviets. For its own purposes, France wished to lead the dialogue with the

Soviets "for Europe," especially with regard to French and German long-term interests.

France sought to contain West German aspirations in East-West relations within the terms of the French dialogue with the Soviets. French officials underscored their belief that West Germany would be the channel linking Eastern Europe to Western Europe. France tried to have a close relationship with West Germany in order to ensure that the West German–Eastern European channel would not be used to promote only West German interests. French officials hoped that this channel could be broadened to serve European interests as defined, in part, by France.

The détente phase was followed in the early 1980s by a period of renewed East-West confrontation, centering on the debate over the INF treaty. Leaders in both France and West Germany were replaced during this period of East-West confrontation. A socialist president was elected in France in 1981, and the socialist chancellor in West Germany was replaced in 1982. The focus of the French–West German interaction in this period became the reinforcement of the solidarity between the governments to resist Soviet blandishments and to limit the benefits that the United States could draw from this confrontation to reassert its leadership over the alliance.

President François Mitterrand's agenda in his first term was considerably different from Giscard d'Estaing's. Mitterrand was a pronounced anti-Communist who approached the relationship with the Soviet Union under Leonid I. Brezhnev from an ideological standpoint. In contrast, Giscard d'Estaing — in the classic Gaullist tradition — had approached the Soviet leaders as Russians dominated by visions of state interest rather than ideological or territorial expansion.

For Mitterrand, the goal was to anchor West Germany firmly in the alliance system by developing more European links. It was important to France not to allow the United States to use the conflict over the INF to serve narrow American interests of dominance in the alliance. Rather, France sought to use the INF struggle to strengthen the European component of the alliance.

For Chancellor Helmut Kohl and West German conservatives, the INF struggle was a profound domestic conflict. The left directly confronted the conservatives over the validity of INF deployment. Kohl sought support from Mitterrand's socialists against the West German socialists. Mitterrand's speech in the Bundestag endorsing INF deployment in January 1983 was viewed with great hostility by the West German left and very favorably by Kohl and the conservatives.

For West Germany in the 1980s, the relationship with France was part of the domestic conflict over the approach of West Germany toward security policy. The conservatives saw France as a means to reinforce the solidarity of the traditional alliance against various superpower threats to NATO. From the Soviet Union came the INF challenge and from the United States the Strategic Defense Initiative (SDI) challenge. France has been a good ally, thus underscoring the necessity of preserving what West Germany has accomplished in traditional alliance policy.

France sought to go even further with the West German conservatives. Not interested solely in reinforcing the traditional alliance, the French government sought to expand exchanges with the West German government in order to Europeanize the alliance. In part, the French objective was to build a European pillar. From this standpoint, there has been reciprocal interest on the part of some West German conservative policymakers, notably former Minister of Defense Manfred Woerner.

The reciprocal interest of the French government and West German conservatives to build a European pillar was enhanced from 1986 to 1988, the cohabitation period. During this period, French conservatives sought to expand the French–West German relationship in order to Europeanize the alliance. But the objectives were less the European pillar than using the French-German dyad to transform the alliance into an organization less beholden to the superpower competition. At the core of this effort was the idea of changing the French doctrine and force structure. France would adapt a de facto extended deterrent through the expansion of what it began to call prestrategic weapons. By expanding the prestrategic arsenal, France would make available to West Germany the means for extended deterrence.

The West German conservatives—especially the so-called Gaullist wing—and officials associated with the Ministry of Defense (MOD) were interested in this possible development. They saw it as an opportunity to transform the United States–West German relationship as well, making West Germany less of a hostage to American policy.

Throughout the period up to Mitterrand's reelection in 1988, the French government sought to encourage West Germany to transform the alliance in a more European direction. But, increasingly, the West German government became less interested in Europeanization in this sense and more interested either in maintaining the traditional alliance or in transforming the East-West system to a more cooperative and less militaristic one. The task of Mikhail S. Gorbachev—to build a more political and less military confrontational security system—became more interesting to West German policymakers than the transformation of the alliance via European military integration. Thus French and West German objectives increasingly diverged. A comparison of the divergent public statements of the two foreign ministers is striking. The French foreign minister articulated a policy of vigilance; the West German foreign minister underscored the necessity for a policy of engagement. Their assessments of the Gorbachev regime were also quite different.

Within West German domestic policies, Hans-Dietrich Genscher and the Free Democratic Party (FDP) sought to use the relationship to expand the West German space for maneuver vis-à-vis the United States without making commitments to a new security system dominated by the French definitions of that system. According to Genscher, West Germany operated in a multilateral Western framework and needed the support of its allies to validate national positions. West Germany could not end up in opposition to both France and the United States. But because these two countries maintained only a loose relationship, West Germany had significant room to maneuver.

For example, in the controversy with the United States in 1989 over the question of deploying the follow-on to Lance (FOTL), Genscher sought to co-opt France.

West German leaders spoke of the opposition of the Anglo-Saxons to the West German position of delaying the deployment decision. Even when Mitterrand finally came out against this characterization, West Germany sensed that France could be an ally in altering the alliance doctrine and force structure on nuclear weapons.

For the Social Democratic Party of Germany (SPD), France has posed an ambiguous good in its approach to the alliance. The French pronuclear approach has been unenthusiastically received by the SPD, especially during the INF struggle. Increasingly, however, SPD leaders have embraced the French doctrine as a possible alternative to flexible response. The notion that tactical weapons would be deployed only to the extent necessary to trigger a strategic exchange has been increasingly supported by the SPD leadership. Notably, Egon Bahr has supported the French decision to deploy the Hades from this point of view.

For the SPD, France might be an ally in building a nonsuperpower-dominated European alliance. France's interests are limited to a specific version of such an alliance: the formation of a European caucus to transform the alliance into a political structure guiding the reconstruction of the European security system — promoting reconstruction of structures, not maintaining the current ones.

In the new phase of East-West relations associated with the Gorbachev rethinking and the lifting of Soviet domination of Eastern Europe, the French-German relationship has been placed in a new situation. Now the question is how goals of transforming East-West relations can be linked to French and German alliance policy.

For the West German government, an old commitment — German unification — became a visible, high priority of the government. A latent objective became an active one. In pursuing this policy, the government sought to adjust other elements of policy to this priority.

The West German government clearly sought allies in this effort. The United States remained a preeminent ally for West Germany in shaping the framework within which unification would occur, notably in countering Soviet efforts to retard the process. But unification decisively affects the European political, economic, and military structures within which the Federal Republic of Germany was born. For adjustments, France is the most significant European partner.

France is seeking to adjust to West German aspirations. Notably, the French president has introduced the objective of European confederation. This new structure would emerge in a postsuperpower European security structure and would be the result of the transformation of the East-West security system in a postmilitary phase of development. Thus the evolution of the French-German dyad can be related to the general evolution of East-West relations. The structure of this interaction is summarized in table 1.

The Impact of the Revolution of 1989

The revolution of 1989 suggested that the East-West divide shaping Europe since the end of World War II could be overcome. In the past the hope of overcoming

TABLE 1

The French-German Dyad and East-West Relations

Phase of East-West Relations	French Focus	West German Focus
Détente	Giscard d'Estaing's special role	Schmidt and managing the Americans
INF	Atlantic solidarity	Domestic struggle
Gorbachev	Caution	Activism
Reconstruction	EEC; confederation	Unification; Westernization of Eastern Europe

the East-West divide was a powerful influence on the aspirations of Europeans, but it was primarily a long-range goal. Now what seemed a utopian goal has become an immediate or midrange one.

The Gorbachev revolution in the Soviet Union was an important precondition for the revolution of 1989. Throughout his term as general secretary of the Communist Party of the Soviet Union, Gorbachev has nurtured "new thinking" in Soviet foreign policy. Most fundamentally, the theme of the Gorbachev administration has been the goal of overcoming the East-West divide. His book on perestroika, which sold millions of copies in the West, was simplistic and awkwardly written. But it had a powerful, overriding theme—the Soviet Union was in a process of change that would lead to the end of the East-West confrontation in Europe. The Soviets were no longer the enemies of the West, and the West should be partners in the reconstruction of the Soviet Union.

The reform process in the Soviet Union is complicated and difficult. It has been widely perceived in Western Europe as eliminating the Soviets as an immediate threat to the West. Even before Gorbachev, Western European publics perceived the Soviet Union to be a much less immediate threat than did the American public. After Gorbachev, this gap deepened—and a new element was added. Increasingly, Western European publics began to see the Soviet Union as a declining threat in the middle and long terms as well. Reform has been perceived to be part of a long-term trend in Soviet policy, transforming the Soviet Union from an enemy into a benign or an incompetent source of competition to Western Europe.

These shifts in opinion occurred before the major change in 1989—the crumbling of the Communist regimes in Eastern Europe. The Soviet leaders had debated among themselves from the beginning of the Gorbachev period how to handle the future of Eastern Europe. This debate led to wide swings in Soviet approaches to Eastern Europe in the Gorbachev period. Nonetheless, by 1989, the Soviet leaders had reached the following conclusions:

• Eastern Europe under Communist rule was more a liability than an asset in the reform process of the Soviet Union.

• Reformist Communist parties would be useful, however, to energize change in the Soviet Union.

• The failure of reform communism would not block the process of letting Eastern Europe engage in reform.

- Non-Communist regimes would be acceptable to the Soviets as long as basic Soviet security interests were protected.
- Soviet security interests in the region would be determined through an interaction with Western European regimes.
- The Americans would be important interlocutors in the process of protecting Soviet interests.

As the Soviet Union began the process of letting Eastern Europe reform, it shifted other elements of its policy as well. The Soviets embraced the concept of conventional parity, began unilateral conventional reductions, and promoted a concept of minimal nuclear deterrence. But, above all, Gorbachev argued for the necessity of the Soviet Union's becoming a key player in building the new Europe.

These changes in the Soviet Union and in Soviet policy toward Eastern Europe interacted with and reinforced a number of changes going on in Western Europe in the 1980s. Above all, the notion of accelerating the European construction process had become increasingly important in political debates and in cultural perceptions. The building of Europe associated with 1992 underscored the importance of placing Europe at the center of historical development. The Kantian notion that Europe should be the subject of history rather than its object was in the ascendancy in the mid-to-late 1980s.

The idea of building Europe led Europeans to become increasingly restive with being subordinated in the security sphere to the United States and the superpower competition. The INF crisis exacerbated the restiveness. Although most European publics and elites backed the United States and NATO in the INF crisis, the long-term effect on the European-American relationship was negative. The European governments resented having to be placed in the position of being subordinated to the superpower competition.

As the revolution of 1989 unfolded, the opportunity to move away from the superpower competition was quickly seized upon. European politicians have grasped the importance of using the drift of the Soviet Union from empire to redraft the nature of the transatlantic bargain underlying the Atlantic alliance. Throughout the 1980s, even mainstream European politicians emphasized the importance of rebuilding the alliance. The theme was Europeanizing the alliance. By this, some European politicians meant building a European pillar; the role of Europe would be enhanced within the alliance. For others, the task was to transform the alliance so that the European countries would become significantly more responsible for their defense and the United States would play a subordinate role. For some on the left, Europeanization meant building a European security system that marginalized the superpowers.

The reactivation of the Western European Union, the resuscitation of the Elysée Treaty clause on security consultation in the French-German Treaty of 1963, the Anglo-French security dialogue at the MOD level, and the construction of a Mediterranean security triangle among France, Italy, and Spain (to name the most prominent examples) were key elements in the Europeanization effort. The European governments were seeking to expand their security dialogue through concrete steps at the multilateral and bilateral levels. There was no simple path to changing the transatlantic alliance, but the Europeans were seeking ways to Europeanize the alliance.

These efforts were relatively unnoticed by most Americans, who focused on the traditional alliance framework. The revolution of 1989 accentuated the elements of dialogue among European officials about the future of European security arrangements. The Conference on Security and Cooperation in Europe (CSCE) process — a process that the United States never considered central — quickly became a focal point for the intra-European consultation process. The building of Europe across the European divide now became a key element of the intra-European process. Moreover, the question of how to deal with the emergence of a new Germany became critical to intra-European consultation.

Also ascendant in the 1980s were European discussions on arms-control issues.[1] Before the INF debate, European governments had a limited capability to deal with arms-control issues, which were seen as largely the domain of the superpowers. With INF, heads of state required governments to become more significant players in the arms-control process. Since 1978, the key governments built new departments, added staff, and elevated the priorities attached to disarmament.

By the time of the Conventional Forces in Europe (CFE) and the emergence of the Soviet Union as a serious architect for change in the conventional balance and arms-control process, the European states were ready to assert a much more aggressive stance defining the Western position on arms control. The revolution of 1989 significantly accelerated this process. Now the Western European governments actively sought to influence Eastern European opinion concerning future arms-control agendas. CFE II will see a significantly expanded intra-European component shaping the arms-control process.

The revolution of 1989 had an impact on the various strands of alliance development. Whereas the European effort before the revolution alternated between maintenance and transformation, the revolution placed transformation at the core of the alliance dynamic. Now transformation has become the major theme, with disintegration and elimination dynamics becoming more serious. Maintenance has clearly become a subordinate theme.

The revolution of 1989 posed not only the possibility of overcoming the East-West divide but also the necessity to do so. Notably, the question of German unification came back dramatically on the agenda. But at the same time the end of Soviet domination of Eastern Europe and the prospects for its democratization offered new opportunities. The building of a broader democratic Europe — Eastern and Western — seemed imminent.

Suddenly, the alliance became more of a means to the transition to a new European security architecture than an end in itself. In a divided Europe, the alliance became a focal point for defending Western values against the Communist East, dominated by a militaristic Soviet Union. As the division of Europe began to end, the goals of building a new Europe — democratic, free, capitalist, and social democratic — seemed viable. If the alliance got in the way of this effort, many seemed ready to jettison it. Those who still valued the alliance did so either as an insurance package to protect Western Europe in the period of transition or as an instrument to defend in times of crisis, even when a new political structure had been put into place. The shift from end to means posed a new crisis for transition in the structures and purposes of the alliance (see table 2).

TABLE 2
Alliance Futures

1. Maintenance in short- to-mid term for the purpose of long-term elimination
2. Transformation to Europeanize
   (a) Western European territorial defense with West German participation
   (b) Broad concept of Western European defense with West German participation
   (c) Broad Concept of Western European defense without West German participation
3. Disintegration
   Nationalistic focus
   Narrowly conceived bilateralism
4. Elimination
   National defensive defense focus
   Construction of politically oriented European security structures

Transformation could lead to several variants of Europeanization. All would lead to a serious restructuring of the alliance in which the new Europe played a dominant role. West Germany would either play or not. It would be essential for a viable Europeanization alternative to include West Germany (or the new Germany) as a key architect of the transformation process. Including West Germany would lead either toward a revitalized notion of territorial (but allied) defense or toward the construction of a broader European peacekeeping force. Without Germany, the emphasis of the alliance would shift from an East-West to a North-South security focus.

Disintegration would emerge from an inability to construct a new European security order to replace the Atlantic alliance. National rivalries spawned by the reemergence of the German Question as well as differing approaches to Eastern Europe and the Soviet Union would undercut the ability of Europe to build a new multilateral security order. Also critical would be the attitude of the United States and of Western Europe toward the American role in European and global security.

Elimination would emerge from the construction of a new European security order by vigorously using the alliance as an instrument of transition. Rather than transforming the alliance so that it would remain a viable institution of Western security policy, the emphasis would be on using the alliance as an instrument of transition from the old alliance order to an alliance-free new European security order. In other words, the revolution of 1989 accelerated a number of processes already under way. By opening up the German Question, it unleashed tensions between nationalism and multilateralism in the Europeanization of NATO. Multilateralism has been underscored by Europe 1992, the emergence of intra-European consultation in the West to deal with the East, and the aspirations of a number of Eastern European states on how to deal with the future of Eastern European security.

At the same time, nationalism in Eastern Europe and among the subordinate nationalities in the Soviet Union is the vehicle for seeking freedom. Nationalism has been fueled by the German aspiration for unity and by the reactions of other Western European governments and publics to the emergence of the new Germany. This tension between nationalism and multilateralism is at the core of the building of the new Europe and the recrafting of the Atlantic alliance.

NOTE

1. See Robbin Laird, ed., *West European Arms Control Policy* (Durham, N.C.: Duke University Press, 1990).

Scandinavia and the "Finlandization" of Soviet Security

PHILLIP A. PETERSEN

The existence of a common culture and the development of Nordic cooperation have promoted the image of an informal though genuine alliance among Norway, Denmark, Sweden, and Finland. Since even a united Nordic bloc does not have the resources to form an independent military factor in Europe, however, their respective security policies have long been vulnerable to great-power demands. Ever since the rise of modern Germany, security in the Nordic region has been dominated by the struggle between Germany and Russia. Thus the Finnish decision in 1990 to no longer consider as applicable the military restrictions of the 1947 Treaty of Paris may reflect a resurrection of the old struggle for influence in northern Europe between Germany and Russia. The deviation of the Nordic states from neutrality during World War II, however, was as much a reflection of public opinion in the Nordic countries as it was the reality of their geostrategic circumstances. Therefore, to the axiom that in a democracy the public gets the government it deserves may be added that the public also frequently gets the security for which it is willing to pay. The fate of the Nordic states during World War II may have been predictable from the percentages of state expenditures devoted to defense: Finland, 25 percent; Sweden, 17.5 percent; Norway, 11.5 percent; and Denmark, 10 percent.[1]

Finland concluded that an attack could come only from the east and adopted a Northern Line policy in the hope that Sweden would help guarantee its security. This policy did not fail completely, as reflected in the fact that Sweden allowed arms from its own stocks to be delivered to Finland after 1939, including the anti-tank and antiaircraft equipment in which Finland was almost entirely lacking.[2] Furthermore, when the Soviet Union attacked Finland, a Swedish Volunteer Corps was deployed in Finnish Lapland so that Finnish forces with battle experience could redeploy to the Karelian Isthmus, the only Finnish strategic troop movement during the Winter War of 1939–40.[3] At the end of the war, there were about 8,000 Swedish volunteers in Finland. Military assistance from Britain and France, however, was insignificant. Despite the renewal of faith in the Finnish solider, the Winter War with the Soviet Union demonstrated that without material support from the outside Finland's resources were insufficient for a struggle of any length.

The War of Independence to remove Russian troops from the country and the Winter War with the Soviet Union left the Finns with a national feeling that there was a direct correlation between their determination to fight and independence. By contrast, past wars with Germany had left the Danes convinced they had to avoid war with Germany to preserve their community as a social entity. Since 1864, Denmark had therefore based its security policy on avoiding war with Germany through compromise while fostering a fictional neutrality to improve the Danish position in postwar peace settlements. This so-called negotiation policy led the Danish government to take few precautionary measures in response to the numerous warnings of early 1940, since it did not believe military action could increase the nation's security. With the German occupation of Denmark on 9 April 1940, Wehrmacht assertions that this action was undertaken to protect Danish neutrality allowed the Danish government to continue to assert its sovereignty and neutrality. Although Denmark conceded to German demands, its policy of negotiation is to be distinguished from collaboration because it never linked Danish interests to a German victory. Because Denmark never attempted to accommodate German desires in exchange for favors from Germany, its policy of negotiation resembled Swedish foreign policy during these years.

Although the Norwegian government, unlike the Danish government, chose to respond to heightened tensions in Europe during the "Phony War" of 1939-40 by increasing its defense preparedness, the government did not mobilize to the degree proposed by the military authorities in early April. Its attempt to defend its neutrality, therefore, might have had results similar to Denmark's if the German naval task force directed against Oslo had not been delayed by the combat actions at Oscarsborg fort. With the escape of the king and his government, and the authorization for King Haakon VII to carry on the war outside Norway, Norwegian cooperation with Germany in the manner of Denmark was made impossible.

Swedish neutrality was clearly compromised because of German demands for transit rights through Sweden even before the capitulation of Norwegian military forces in northern Norway on 10 June. Although no amount of intensification of Swedish defense efforts could have prevented a German conquest of Sweden during the spring of 1940, the circumstances led to a Swedish political consensus on rearmament. In the face of efforts by Sweden and Finland to cooperate in resisting demands from either Germany or the Soviet Union, their great-power neighbors strongly opposed either a defensive alliance or a political union. The net effect was that Sweden adopted a growing pro-German orientation as German-Soviet relations deteriorated. Consistent with this shift, Sweden financed a significant portion of the extensive Finnish fortifications along the new eastern frontier.

Although Finland under no circumstances intended to initiate hostilities or allow Germany to do so from Finnish territory, the government assumed that Soviet aggression against Finland would occur in the event of a Russo-German conflict.[4]

Once the Soviets attacked Finland, the Helsinki government conducted the conflict as a separate continuation of the Winter War, signing no treaty of alliance with Germany. From the beginning of the Continuation War, however, Finland's cobelligerency with Nazi Germany undermined external support for Finland's struggle to reacquire territory it lost to the Soviet aggression of 1939–40. No more than one thousand volunteers for the Finnish army were recruited in Sweden, and the Swedish government elected not to equip them with clothing and arms as was done during the Winter War.

As the tide of the German invasion of Russia began to turn, Swedish neutrality was increasingly subject to Anglo-American demands. Although Sweden continued to remain vulnerable to German pressure, as early as the spring of 1943 the German General staff realized that it could no longer take decisive military action against Sweden.[5] The rescue of Denmark's Jews in October and November of 1943 turned out to be a crucial step in establishing the clandestine flow of refugees to and armaments from Sweden. By December 1943, the Swedish government gave its permission to establish and train a national police corps in Sweden for both Norway and Denmark. Despite this official action, however, most Swedish military assistance to Denmark and Norway apparently still took place without the approval of higher authorities.

Even after Germany's staggering defeat at Stalingrad and withdrawal into the Ukraine, it remained the major power in the Baltic and northern Europe. Yet, in January 1943, the United States, with Sweden's support, approached the Soviet Union about mediating a separate Finnish-Soviet peace. All the legally constituted parties participated in the Finnish government, but a "Peace Opposition" demanding a separate peace as soon as possible began to acquire strength in all but the Patriotic People's Movement. By September, leading Finnish politicians began to alter their assessments of the strategic situation, and negotiations with the Soviets were finally initiated through Stockholm at the end of 1943. Unfortunately, the severity of the armistice terms that Stalin offered Finland in the spring of 1944 undermined the Peace Opposition. Only after the Soviet offensive in June was the Finnish nation prepared to pass from war to peace as an unbroken political entity. With the conclusion of a Soviet-Finnish armistice agreement in September, the Finnish government was compelled to wage war in Lapland to expel German forces from its territory. This war was unavoidable and, in fact, helped Finland to establish sound relations with the Soviet Union. Moreover, this relationship led to the development of a "Nordic pattern" of interdependence employed to reinforce Nordic stability politically.

In a House Divided

The strategic reality confronting the Nordic states at the conclusion of World War II was that Europe would be divided, with the United States the dominant Western power on the European continent. Confronted with Soviet dominance of the Baltic region, the Swedish government "repatriated" to the Soviet-occupied Baltic states those Estonians, Latvians, and Lithuanians who had fought in the German armed forces and had fled to Sweden during the final stages of the war. Despite intensive public opposition to forced repatriation, the Swedish government was swayed by the fact that the Soviet Union was indisputably the dominant power in the Baltic region. Sweden strove to reassure the Soviets, confident that the Western powers would support it out of self-interest. On this point, hopes for a Nordic alliance foundered, since "the Norwegians refused to accept a strategy based on expecting the assistance of the Western powers without at the same time declaring political and military solidarity with them."[6] Thus, as Sweden stood by the neutrality it had successfully maintained for 135 years, Norway, Denmark, and Iceland became founding members of the North Atlantic Treaty Organization (NATO) in 1949. Finland, for its part, had already begun the long struggle to reestablish its status as a neutral state with the signing of the treaty of Friendship, Cooperation and Mutual Assistance (FCMA) in 1948.

The Winter and Continuation wars resulted in Joseph Stalin's securing both Leningrad/St. Petersburg and Murmansk through the acquisition of Finnish territory. With the transfer of the Headquarters of the Baltic Fleet from Kronstadt west to Kaliningrad-Baltisk (formerly Konigsberg-Pillau), however, the Gulf of Finland became less critical and return of the Porkkala naval base west of Helsinki was possible during the 1955–56 period. This act confirmed the basic underlying assumption of Finnish security policy since the armistice of September 1944 that "Russia's main interest in Finland is military."[7] Yet the 1948 friendship with the Soviet Union is perceived by Finland to be distinct "from a military alliance treaty, above all in the sense that military cooperation is confined to the territory of Finland and does not take effect automatically."[8] Moreover, the Soviet Union, recognizing that Finland has the primary responsibility for the defense of its territory, has not interpreted the 1947 Paris Peace Treaty limitations on manpower and equipment as a ban against Helsinki's training and arming a large military reserve. In fact, it was the British assumptions about the ultimate fate of Finland's independence, and not Stalin's policy, that led to treaty limitations on Finland's defense forces.[9]

Like most Western analysts, Finns agree that it is unlikely that northern Europe would become embroiled in a war separate from a war in central Europe. Understanding completely that the decisive factors of Finnish security are the strategic value of its territory and the Soviet inclination or reluctance to occupy it, Finland has taken actions consistent with Soviet views concerning the strategic geography of northern Europe. From the contingency planning perspective of the Soviet General Staff, northern Europe was said to contain four strategic regions: (1) northern Norway, Sweden, and Finland; (2) southern Norway, Sweden, and Finland; (3) the Baltic Straits; and (4) the Greenland–Iceland–United Kingdom–Norway Gap (see figure 1). Thus, "from Finland's point of view, there are factors of military geography of a permanent nature which influence our defense policy. The areas which are strategically important to Finland are Lapland and Southern Finland, and the entire airspace of the nation."[10]

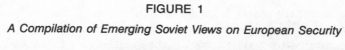

FIGURE 1

A Compilation of Emerging Soviet Views on European Security

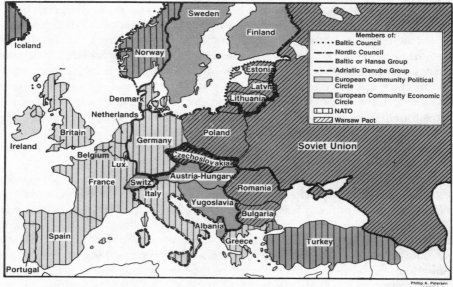

In defining its security policy in terms of confidence in its defensive capacity, Finland has sought to demonstrate its resolve through a predictable and adequate defense capability "founded on long-term planning and well-considered assessments of the tasks of the defense forces and performance requirements."[11] In defining its foreign-policy objective as "good neighborly relations," Finland has sought to protect its people, preserve its institutions, and pursue recognition as a full-fledged neutral member of the international community through cautious consideration of the legitimate security interests of the Soviet Union. However selfishly Finland may have pursued its own interests, it has significantly contributed to Nordic stability. As the president of Finland has argued: "Were she to deviate from her policy of neutrality and harmonious relations and thus upset the prevailing stable situation in Northern Europe, it would not be in the interests of her neighbors in either East or West."[12]

In the view of the Soviet General Staff. victory in a European war was to be obtained by conducting breakthroughs against the weakest ground forces in central Europe to encircle and destroy the strongest of the enemy's forces. Encirclement and destruction of NATO's forward-deployed corps in Germany, an immediate assault-landing operation against Zeeland, and a successful effort to coerce Denmark, the Netherlands, and Belgium out of the Western coalition were perceived to offer the greatest hope of ending a war before it escalated to nuclear weapons or became so protracted as to create unmanageable strains in the Warsaw Pact coalition.[13] Soviet coalitional strategy in central Europe therefore focused on Denmark, since it was the only small front-line state.[14]

All parties recognized that Northern Europe was not where general war between the two main military blocs would be decided. Each side may have hoped, nonetheless, that its actions would cause the opposing coalition to divert sufficient resources to Northern Europe to decrease its chances for victory in central Europe. If NATO could be persuaded that its scarce reserves should be deployed in north-central Norway, they would not be available for the battle for Denmark. Thus, Soviet planners probably thought that they could precipitate a favorable change in the correlation of forces in central Europe by tying down a disproportionately larger number of the enemy's reserves in Northern Europe. To be successful, such a strategy required that the Soviet Union itself not draw too many of its own resources away from central Europe to Northern Europe.

In a Common European Home

Soviet operational planning in the 1970s and early 1980s, largely associated with Marshal Nikolay Ogarkov, attempted to provide security through the preparation of preemptive conventional strategic offensives in the event of war. This ambitious policy exhausted resources, contributing to economic atrophy. It also provoked counterproductive Western political and military responses that actually decreased Soviet security. The combined results led one senior Soviet civilian theoretician to warn in 1990 that when "looking to the future, without radical cuts in the military, we will hardly be able to avoid further lagging behind in the economy. And that would mean that soon we would not even be able to have a modern army at all."[15] It was this growing tension between military policy and security outcome that had resulted in the 1984 removal of Marshal Ogarkov from his position as chief of the General Staff.

The reassignment of Ogarkov was the first of many military policy shifts that would result from a revolutionary transformation in Soviet politics. A non–zero-sum model of security emphasizing threat-reduction, unilateral restraint, and a cooperative stance toward traditional Soviet adversaries emerged as the reform-minded party intellectuals and progressive politicians who were protected over the years by Yuri V. Andropov and his sponsor, Otto Kuusinen, began reconstructing Soviet communism. The Communist system that Stalin imposed on central Europe as a means of ensuring Soviet security had come to be perceived by progressives in the Communist Party of the Soviet Union (CPSU) as counterproductive. As Vyacheslav Dashichev explained to the author in March 1990, "the division of Europe, which was the heritage of Stalinism, brought the Soviet Union into confrontation with all of the Western powers and our economy cannot withstand it." In his view, resolution of the Soviet economic crisis demanded an end to the division of Europe.

While not yet general secretary of the CPSU, Andropov revealed in a 1978 speech the essence of what would emerge as a new security model for Europe: "Europe must become a continent of peace and good-neighborly cooperation. Here, in Karelia, we have to emphasize the significance of the Soviet Union's good-neighborly . . . cooperation with Finland. Soviet-Finnish relations today . . . represent the very kind of *detente* which makes for a more lasting peace. . . ."¹⁶ Although Andropov later became general secretary and was too ill for much of his fifteenth-month tenure to be effective, he did succeed in moving enough of his supporters into key positions to ensure survival of the changes that he set in motion. By the time Mikhail S. Gorbachev was elected general secretary in March 1985, it was understood in the CPSU Central Committee that old methods to speed up scientific and technical development were insufficient to reconstruct the economy. With time, it had become clear that the grave implications of Soviet scientific-technical and economic stagnation required the restructuring of Soviet society. One element of this "fundamental restructuring" involved what Gorbachev called "new thinking," which included the attempt to influence the international environment through a carefully managed public reformulation of national-security objectives and policies. Thus in 1987, after nearly two years of discussion, the Soviet Defense Council adopted a military doctrine consistent with the assessment that security would increasingly be a political task.

Although the "new thinkers" in Soviet security policy probably never had a specific plan for an alternative security structure, what might be properly called a Soviet vision for the future structure of European security was evolving. Using Northern Europe as the model, these defense intellectuals initially thought that a two-tier neutral zone composed of "West-leaning" states (e.g., Sweden) and independent states prepared to defend their territorial integrity (e.g., Finland) might be established through central Europe. Such a zone might provide the Soviets with greater confidence in the determination of Poles, Czechoslovaks, and Hungarians to defend their respective states. Essentially, the new thinkers among Soviet security theorists hoped that they would be able to "Finlandize" states they could no longer control at an acceptable cost. By 1989, the transformation in the character of relations between the USSR and the socialist countries of central Europe was said to be under way, the Soviet Union accepting their market economies and pluralistic systems so long as Soviet foreign-policy interests were not challenged.¹⁷

The non–zero-sum model of security, which may be traced back to Andropov and his appreciation for the superiority of Soviet-Finnish relations over the relationship between the Soviet Union and its non-Soviet Warsaw Pact (NSWP) allies, has since evolved into a vision of European security based on overcoming the division of Europe. While the Soviets talk of the maintenance of both NATO and the Warsaw Treaty Organization, the latter has ceased to exist as an integrated operational command. Authorization for the employment of Polish, Czech and Slovak, and Hungarian armed forces outside their national territories now requires approval of the respective NSWP governments, effectively negating Soviet control over these national forces through the Warsaw Pact operational command structure. Furthermore, Hungary has explicitly stated that it intends to withdraw from the Warsaw Pact by the end of 1991. According to the Hungarian chief of staff, Hungary was already redeploying some troops away from the Western border in early 1990 so as to be prepared to defend itself from any direction, since it no longer has an image of the enemy formulated on an ideological basis.[18]

As for the Soviet attitude, Fyodor Burlatskiy, chairman of the human rights panel of the Supreme Soviet committee on foreign relations, has argued that "if Austria can be neutral, then why not Hungary."[19] Lest anyone misread Soviet commitment to "the principle of noninterference," senior CPSU officials like Central Committee adviser Nikolai Shishlin have noted that the Soviet Union would respect the decisions of its allies even with regard to withdrawal from the Warsaw Pact. As the president of the newly renamed Hungarian Socialist Party summarized the environment, "certainly, in Eastern Europe one cannot conduct policy that is openly anti-Soviet," but "the Soviet Union has ceased to be an ideological power; it no longer regards itself as the avant-garde of world revolution."[20]

Soviet Deputy Foreign Minister Ivan Aboimov summed up the new basis of any continuation of the Warsaw Pact as one in which "alliance relations with the USSR will not be a brake on . . . independent development . . . but a . . . means to preserve stability in Europe until new structures of security are built guarding the common European home."[21] Indeed, the new democracies of Eastern Europe do desire that a pan-European security system be constructed, if only to ensure that the Soviet Union or whatever successor state replaces it is locked into the European political system. The governments of Poland, Czechoslovakia, and Hungary, however, are not seeking the dissolution of NATO. As explained by the deputy head of the Hungarian delegation to the Conference on Security and Cooperation in Europe (CSCE), the new democracies of Eastern Europe understand that a cooperative security system like CSCE is no substitute for a collective security system, such as NATO. Regardless of whether the Warsaw Pact becomes a political organization or ceases to exist, all three governments would prefer to see the long-term survival of NATO.

In Czechoslovakia, strong sentiment favoring withdrawal from the Warsaw Pact has been matched by a countervailing desire to use membership in the organization to influence Soviet behavior. Poland, on the other hand, is no longer interested in prolonging the Warsaw Pact now that it has been reassured about its western border by a united Germany. Thus the Warsaw Pact may have only a short life as a voluntary organization to facilitate transition to a new European security structure. Although the nature of that security structure will probably include NATO, it will certainly not include the Warsaw Pact as it now exists. Some Swiss officials, for example, have suggested the creation of a neutral zone through Europe consisting of Sweden, Finland, Poland, Czechoslovakia, Hungary, Austria, and Switzerland. Since the present neutrals of this group already conduct more or less regular consultations at the highest levels, a more formal grouping could be created either as part of the new European security structure or as a means to ease the transition to a new order.

As a new union is created from the Soviet state, the Warsaw Pact may become chiefly a collective-security arrangement between the Soviet republics that remain in the union and those that choose independence. Lithuania has expressed interest in such an arrangement. Estonian leaders, however, have expressed the desire to make Estonia nuclear-free and ultimately demilitarized. The outcome of the process of moving to a new security arrangement will probably depend most on the negotiation process itself. Any new union will undoubtedly be created through a process whereby the republics grant the central government powers and responsibilities that the republics consider better handled collectively.

The Soviet "Russification" program has created a particularly difficult situation in the Baltic republic of Latvia, where ethnic Latvians constitute no more than half the population. For many years the Soviet government encouraged Russian immigration to Latvia with promises of apartments, and now Latvian families have to wait as long as fifteen years for a flat of their own. Despite the large concentration of ethnic Russians in Lativa, the Latvian Popular Front is as determined to regain political independence as are the Popular Fronts in Estonia and Lithuania. Interestingly enough, since a significant number of the ethnic Russians in Latvia have lived for generations alongside the Latvians, a significant number of them support the restoration of Latvian independence. Ultimately, the Russians will have to make the same individual decisions that citizens of other colonial empires faced. But since the more recent Russian emigrants do not represent a modernizing power in the Baltic states, they will find it more difficult to find a place for themselves in the Baltic states of the new Europe. The repatriation of Russians from the Baltic states will require outside financial assistance if this transfer is to avoid the destabilizing consequence of demands and counterdemands for compensation.

Diplomats from Finland, Sweden, Norway, Denmark, and Iceland have all indicated informally the willingness of the Nordic Council to accept Estonia, Latvia, and Lithuania as members. Such action would undoubtedly be reassuring to the Russians, since it would tend to obstruct the return of German political influence to the Baltic republics. Unfortunately, a critical result of such an expanded Nordic Council, when combined with the "Pentagonal Group" formed in south-central Europe (Czechoslovakia, Hungary, Italy, and Yugoslavia), is the isolation of Poland between its historical enemies. Despite Poland's intensive efforts to draw Sweden closer, the Nordic Council is unlikely to admit Poland. The alternative is seen to be in the development of a Baltic or Hansa Group to reassure Poland and facilitate European integration.

It should also be noted that the independence of the Baltic states would make even more critical the issue of the Kaliningrad oblast. Although Germany, Poland, and Russia probably all regard this as an issue they would prefer to remain buried, it will undoubtedly eventually resurface when it is addressed as a security issue. At the end of World War II, the surviving German population was driven out. The region has remained a closed military area. Having undergone almost no development, if progress toward a common European home leads to the lifting of restrictions, the region's development could well become an international issue. Poland obviously would not welcome any restoration of German economic interests in the region, but Lithuania might find having a common border with the economically most powerful state in Europe a significant boon to its own reconstruction. Finland, however, would not want to see the withdrawal of Soviet military facilities from the region because it would mean a restoration of the security significance of the Gulf of Finland. Keeping the region part of a Russia economically integrated into Europe, therefore, is probably the one solution acceptable to all the states concerned.

The popular support in Norway for joining the European Community (EC) will pull the rest of the Nordic states toward European integration. If Russia is not locked out of Europe, Sweden and Finland will probably apply for EC membership. Swedish foreign and security policy in the post–World War II period reflects a particular set of geostrategic circumstances. If the security environment continues to evolve in the direction anticipated, Sweden and Finland could feel unconstrained from joining the political integration of Europe. Following the general Nordic pattern, Denmark would follow Germany, Iceland would follow Norway, and Finland would follow Sweden. It should be noted, however, that more recently Finland has indicated a willingness to move toward European integration more quickly than Sweden. The key to the pace of this evolution will remain the development of linkages by which Russia can be drawn into the emerging European political and economic system.

The emerging policy consensus among several of the European neutrals and the northern-tier NSWP states and Hungary clearly favors the overarching CSCE security structure composed of the Council of Europe, the EC, NATO, and regional groupings that will facilitate integration and help prevent the exclusion of any state willing to accept a European political culture. As explained by the Estonian legislator Igor Gryazin, "real Baltic independence can exist only if we have a democratic Russia in the neighborhood. An unstable and economically weak Russia would be a threat to our three small republics."[22] Under these circumstances, security will gain a wider definition than it has had since the end of World War II. Nordic cooperation and the Nordic pattern may serve as a model for the development of a common political culture and the security evolution of the NSWP states respectively. "Finlandization" was never a condition but a process, the direction of which was perceived differently by various security theorists. Just as the path of Finnish-Soviet relations since 1944 led to the full restoration of Finnish neutrality by late 1990, the path of the evolution of Nordic security can serve as a useful guide for the transformation of the Soviet Union's relations with its NSWP neighbors and perhaps even with some of its constituent republics.

Notes

1. As cited in Henrik S. Nissen, "The Nordic Societies," in *Scandinavia During the Second World War*, ed. Henrik S. Nissen (Minneapolis: University of Minnesota Press, 1983), 52. The author wishes to express his appreciation to Anita Lindholm for bringing his attention to the existence of this excellent volume.

2. Kari Selen, "The Main Lines of Finnish Security Policy Between the World Wars," in *Aspects of Security: The Case of Independent Finland* (Vaasa: Finnish Commission of Military History, 1985), 35.

3. Anssi Vuorenmaa, "Defense strategy and Basic Operational Decisions in the Finland-Soviet Winter War, 1939-1940," in ibid., 89.

4. Ohto Manninen, "Operation Barbarossa and the Nordic Countries," in *Scandinavia During the Second World War*, 148.

5. Aage Trommer, "Scandinavia and the Turn of the Tide," in *Scandinavia During the Second World War*, 272.

6. Karl Molin, "Winning the Peace," in *Scandinavia During the Second World War*, 361.

7. The phrase was coined by J. K. Paasikivi. As cited in Rene Nyberg, "Security Dilemmas in Scandinavia: Evaporated Nuclear Options and Indigenous Conventional Capabilities," *Cooperation and Conflict* 19 (1984): 67.

8. *Report of the Third Parliamentary Defense Committee* (Helsinki, 1981), 26, as cited in Nyberg, 68.

9. See Nyberg, 70 and n. 64.

10. *Arvio Euroopan Turvallisuus-Polittisesta Tilanteesta Ja Sen Kenitysnakymista Seka Niiden Vaikutuksista Suomen Pulustus-Politiikkaan* [*An Appraisal of the European Security Policy Situation and Prospects for Its Development as well as Their Influence on Finnish Defense Policy*] (Report by the Parliamentary Defense Policy Commission, Helsinki, 28 Feb. 1990), 23.

11. Ibid.

12. Mauno Koivisto, *Landmarks: Finland in the World* (Helsinki: Kirjayhtyma, 1985), 22.

13. See Christopher N. Donnelly and Phillip A. Petersen, "Soviet Strategists Target Denmark," *International Defense Review* 19, no. 8 (1986): 1047-51; and Petersen, "Soviet Offensive Operations in Central Europe," *NATO's Sixteen Nations*, August 1987, 26-32.

14. See John J. Yurechko, *Coalition Warfare: The Soviet Approach* (Koln: Bundesinstitut fur ostwissenschaftliche und internationale Studien, 1986).

15. Georgi Arbatov, as quoted in David Remnick, "Gorbachev's Policy: Turning a Weak Hand Into Grand Strategy," *Washington Post*, 18 Feb. 1990.

16. Yuri V. Andropov, *Izbrannie rechi i stat'i* [*Selected Speeches and Articles*] (Moscow, 1979), 287.

17. Andranik Migranyan, "For Discussion: An Epitaph to the Brezhnev Doctrine: The USSR and Other Socialist Countries in the Context of East-West Relations," *Moscow News*, no. 34, 27 Aug.-3 Sept. 1989, 6.

18. Lt. Gen. Laszlo Borsits, as quoted in R. Jeffrey Smith, "Warsaw Pact—Endgame: In Eastern Europe, the Military Alliance Is Dead," *Washington Post*, 4 Feb. 1990.

19. As quoted in Bill Keller, "Gorbachev's Hope for Future: 'A Common European Home,'" *New York Times*, 30 Nov. 1989.

20. Rezso Nyers, "The Party Remains," *International Herald Tribune*, 14-15 Oct. 1989.

21. Ivan Aboimov, *Argumenty i fakty*, Feb. 1990.

22. David Remnick, "Gorbachev Heartens Baltic Chiefs," *Washington Post*, 13 June 1990.

The Role of the United States in Central Europe

MADELEINE ALBRIGHT

Solidarity won a resounding victory in Poland in 1989. The barbed wire of the Iron Curtain was snipped at the Hungarian-Austrian border; East Germans started migrating to West Germany through Hungary and Czechoslovakia; the Berlin Wall came down; the students marched in Prague and elected the playwright Václav Havel president; the Romanians rioted in Timisoara and rid themselves of their megalomaniac dictator, Nicole Ceausescu; and the Bulgarians marched and demanded an end to the regime of Todor Zhikov, who had been in power since 1956 and was the oldest dictator in Eastern Europe. The revolutions of 1989 compelled world attention. The desire of people to escape tyranny was so strong that, in 1990, even Albania joined the chorus; and in the Soviet Union, Mikhail S. Gorbachev, who set off the chain reaction, had trouble keeping up with the pace.

This essay will consider current and long-term United States policy toward central and Eastern Europe. To do that, it is useful to ask why the United States should be interested in the region and to review past policy. What would the United States like to see happen there politically, economically, and strategically? United States policy toward Eastern Europe has not often been a front-burner concern. Twice in this century, issues simmering in the area have boiled over and scorched those near and far, but Americans have not had to expend much time and energy on the region.

Admittedly, the attention of the world was piqued by such events as the Hungarian revolution of 1956, the 1968 Prague Spring, and by regular Polish uprisings during the 1970s. But this interest has usually been short lived. The aid promised to central and Eastern Europe after the 1989 revolutions is about $1.5 billion — far more than the original $125 million requested by President George Bush in the summer of 1989. If promises made to the people of Poland, Hungary, Czechoslovakia, East Germany, Romania, and Bulgaria are to become reality, the United States must ensure that imaginative programs are implemented as soon as possible and new support—not necessarily financial—is available. In short, American policymakers must develop longer attention spans.

At this point it is even unclear what to call the area formerly known as the Soviet bloc. Those living there do not like to hear the region called "Eastern Europe": that geographic designation should refer to the Baltic republics, the Ukraine, Belorussia, and European Russia. "Central Europe" might be more appropriate, but it should be recognized that there is a northern tier (Poland, Czechoslovakia, and Hungary) and the Balkans (Romania, Bulgaria, Yugoslavia, and Albania). People of these countries want to be called simply Europeans.

It is also unclear what United States policy should be toward the individual countries as well as the overall region. The simplest period of the postwar era is over. No one would deny that there was danger at certain key moments, but the situation was simple—a divided Europe was the prize and the potential battleground. The United States provided Western Europe with financial and military support. As for Eastern Europe, America passed declarations, signed agreements, and expressed its sympathy. But for the most part it was understood that the Soviets controlled that area.

Entirely new circumstances demand that the United States rethink its policy toward Europe. The consensus for the previous policy has been shattered. It is especially hard to develop new relationships because many questions are still unanswered: What will happen in the Soviet Union? How will Europe 1992 develop? What role will a united Germany play? Will the newly emerging democracies survive? How does a new international system with less powerful nation states, more virulent ethnic tensions, more nonstate actors, and more weapons affect the United States? How will power and influence be measured? Finally, how does the United States, in serious need of rethinking its priorities because of budget problems, relate to all this?

It is in the United States's national interest to make sure that the area is stable. As President George Bush has indicated, an investment in Eastern Europe is an investment in the security of the United States as well as in the freedom and well-being of the peoples of Eastern Europe.[1] The West would like to see Eastern Europe composed of functioning democracies, content within their borders, improving their standard of living, and contributing to an international economy. The United States wants the area to be stable, without a power vacuum that would invite outside domination and upset the European balance. Therefore, the United States must determine what is most likely to threaten stability and develop policies to prevent destabilization.

History is a strange teacher. It never repeats itself exactly, but you ignore its general lessons at your peril. In the 1910s, Germany was strong and the Soviet Union had a dynamic leader. Again, in the 1990s, there is a strong Germany and a dynamic Soviet leader. Twice, the United States, safe on the other side of the ocean, considered it necessary to go and settle disputes that threatened its national interest. Those disputes began in the area now called central and Eastern Europe. Granted, Germany is quite different and so are the dynamic Soviet leaders. Another war in the area is unlikely unless Germany and the Soviet Union want to start one, and there is no evidence of that at the present. But conflicts begin when there are economic dissatisfaction, social unrest, potential ethnic conflicts, and power vacuums. If the newly emerging democracies fail because they cannot resolve their serious economic and social problems, they will be replaced by authoritarian governments, chaos, or civil wars. Any maladies that develop will surely infect the Soviet Union; with the availability of weapons, even low-intensity conflicts can spread. The great powers will be drawn in, whether or not they want to be. That is what America must face in central and Eastern Europe.

Even a brief review of United States policy toward the area demonstrates that Eastern Europe is of vital importance; however, for its own domestic and foreign-policy reasons, the United States has not built a steady record of support.

The United States Record

It was Woodrow Wilson's vision of the world that helped to redraw the map and create the independent countries of Eastern Europe. Interestingly enough, the United States has had the same two policy goals in central and Eastern Europe since World War I: the promotion of democracy and the maintenance of stability. Its sense of mission, coupled with its domestic ethnic politics, has led it to promote self-determination and human rights. Its position as one of the guarantors of world peace has required it to pursue policies that avoid war. But all too often it has found that its dual goals have been conflicting ones. For seventy years, therefore, United States policy toward this region has been characterized by genuine concern alternating with ambiguous support. The American reaction has been remarkably similar in confrontations with fascists and Communists.

After 1918 the Allies supported national sovereignty, but, to appease Hitler, they sacrificed Czechoslovakia. The United States was horrified by the German attack on Poland, but it did not understand that its vital interests were threatened until Japan attacked Pearl Harbor.

Late in World War II, the United States Army allowed the Soviets to liberate the whole area. The Yalta agreement guaranteeing free elections was never enforced. "Containment" as a policy gained strength after the region was already a part of the Soviet empire. Despite the proclamation of a "rollback," help for Hungary in 1956 did not seem feasible. John F. Kennedy called himself a Berliner, but Lyndon B. Johnson was unresponsive when the Soviets invaded Czechoslovakia.

For years the United States tried to square the circle by "differentiating," an attempt to encourage political change without risking confrontation. So when Tito broke with Stalin in 1948, the United States launched the idea of giving preferential economic treatment to countries seeking to show their independence from the Soviet Union. In the late 1950s and early 1960s, as the policies of each country began to vary slightly, the policy of "bridge building"— treating each country somewhat differently — emerged.

During the heyday of détente and West German *Ostpolitik*, relations with the

Soviet Union and Eastern Europe improved. The Helsinki Final Act of 1975 was symbolic of the United States's desire to combine principle with pragmatism. While the Soviets showed a greater tolerance for change in their satellites, the United States recognized the de facto division of Europe and did not dispute Soviet geopolitical influence. How to encourage national identity without arousing a Soviet reaction was articulated in what has come to be known as the Sonnenfeldt Doctrine. A version of the differentiation policy was encouraged by the Jackson-Vanik amendment of 1974, which granted most favored nation (MFN) status to Communist countries that allowed free emigration.

During the Carter administration there was an attempt to push the differentiation policy further and give life to the Helsinki Final Act. President Jimmy Carter stressed that a country's human-rights policy, not just its foreign-policy stance, should be a determinant for differentiated treatment. While various steps were taken to improve individual relations and bring certain countries into the international economic system, the emphasis was on a nonthreatening gradual change.

President Ronald Reagan espoused differentiation, but he did not ease tensions with the Soviet Union while General Secretary Leonid I. Brezhnev was alive. The originator of the "Brezhnev doctrine" was capable of acting arbitrarily to prevent what he saw as threatening change. The relative inattention toward the Eastern bloc under the leadership of Yuri V. Andropov and then Konstantin V. Chernenko, from November 1982 to March 1985, allowed reformist forces to gain strength.

Gorbachev came to power determined to deal with the Soviet Union's devastating economic problems. The Eastern European countries could help only if they changed their methods of operating. The Soviet leader saw that he would have to deal on the basis of a new equation: the status quo equaled instability; change equaled stability. Troops would not be used to enforce Soviet policy. Gorbachev's approach made it possible for the United States to feel that its dual goals could be compatible. Both nations' leaders had similar interests, avoiding violence by supporting evolutionary economic and political change.

The Emergence of Gorbachev

It was not immediately evident that the accession of Gorbachev would lead to a new domino effect. For forty-five years the Soviets had managed to keep their empire intact against all odds. While forces of nationalism were decimating the British, French, Belgian, and Portuguese empires, and new countries were being born on a regular basis, the Soviets continued to acquire peoples and maintain control of their Eastern European colonies.

Admittedly, there were problems. In 1948, Tito, the only legitimate Communist leader in the area, defected from the Soviet bloc. Because none of the countries had joined the bloc willingly and their Communist regimes were never regarded as legitimate, trouble surfaced periodically. Interestingly enough, it was always associated with a change in the Soviet leadership. The troublemakers, however, were isolated quickly, and everything went back to business as usual. The 1953 post-Stalin riots in Germany and Czechoslovakia were put down. Georgi M. Malenkov's questioning of Stalinist methods reverberated in Poland and Hungary. In 1956 in Poland the Soviet Union approved a leadership change; in Hungary it rolled in the tanks. When Nikita S. Khrushchev spoke of "different roads to socialism," the Czechoslovaks took that to mean that they could develop "socialism with a human face"; in 1968, the Soviet Union aborted the experiment. Although Brezhnev had ordered the invasion of Czechoslovakia, he and his bloc comrades found it useful to sign the Helsinki Final Act in 1975, committing themselves to abiding by certain human rights. The Poles — always pushing the limits of allowable change — decided they would create an independent trade-union movement. A strong Catholic church and Solidarity, with its 10 million members and dynamic leader Lech Walesa, were too much. This time there were no foreign tanks, and the Polish leadership was persuaded to put an end to it by imposing martial law.

At the end of 1981, the Soviet empire had seemingly weathered the storms and was still together. There had been a cost, however, to the lockstep progress. Instead of promoting growth, command economies were turning developed countries into underdeveloped ones. The Soviet Union itself was at a standstill. Promises of overtaking the United States were laughable. After years of geriatric leadership under Brezhnev, curtailed dreams under Andropov, and infirm direction by Chernenko, Gorbachev came to power.

The change associated with the new Soviet leader did not follow previous patterns. Its effects were not confined within one country; on the contrary, there was a ripple effect. The dysfunctions caused by central planning could no longer be ignored. Emphasis on human rights triumphed. The communications revolution spread the news.

It is safe to say that Gorbachev had not planned to preside over the dissolution of his external and internal empires. What he did see was that, absent its vast military might, the Soviet Union was a Third World country. His first goal was to put the Soviet Union on its feet economically. In addition to releasing creative energies in the Soviet Union, with policies now known as perestroika and glasnost, Gorbachev came to realize that he had to energize Eastern Europe so that it would be in a position to help revive the sclerotic Soviet economy. Although some of the early signals to Eastern Europe from the Soviet Union were mixed, Gorbachev wanted to make those countries function more effectively. While in March 1985 there were forces pushing for change in Eastern Europe, Gorbachev saw that his empire was faced with six old men — the leaders of those countries — whose reaction to the new Soviet initiatives ranged from outright opposition to approbation.

Four of the six leaders indicated that glasnost would come to their countries only over their dead bodies. Nicolae Ceausescu, the youngest at sixty-seven but at that time rumored to have cancer, liked the Gorbachev initiatives the least. He made it clear that he would not follow suit and would continue on his path of squeezing his people dry to pay off the foreign debt and build an ever-grander Bucharest in his own honor. Erich Honecker, seventy-three, let Moscow know that he did not need any advice; he had already undertaken reforms, and East Germany could boast of the highest standard of living in the bloc. Furthermore, all his policies were dictated by his unique position as chief of half the German nation. Gustáv Husák, seventy-two, was also uninterested; Czechoslovakia's standard of living was almost as high as East Germany's, and glasnost—which might invite questions about the 1968 Soviet invasion—did not appeal to the man who had come to power on the back of the Soviet tanks. Todor Zhivkov, the oldest ruler at seventy-four, had been the leader of Bulgaria for thirty-three years. He tried to bring about some reform until his approach failed to meet Gorbachev's expectations. Only Janos Kadar, the creator of "goulash communism" in Hungary, and Wojciech Jaruzelski, who was finding new credibility in Poland—thanks to Gorbachev's imprimatur—welcomed the new Soviet initiatives.

Any idea that Gorbachev favored independent action by the former satellites was belied by his early call for a highly integrated, long-term economic plan for the Council for Mutual Economic Assistance (CMEA). His trips through the bloc and the work he had to do at home, however, must have persuaded him that he could not devote much time to micromanaging developments in Eastern Europe. He seemed to be practicing laissez-faire glasnost, allowing each Eastern European leader to take things at his own pace. He turned his attention to the international scene and to developing his foreign-policy program of "new thinking."

By the end of 1988, Gorbachev's comfort level with developments in Eastern Europe, coupled with his need to cut military costs to improve his budget problems and transfer resources to the civilian sector, set the stage for the dramatic United Nations proposal for unilateral conventional arms cuts. Not only was the Soviet military to be decreased by 500,000 personnel, which meant that large numbers of Soviet troops would be leaving Eastern Europe, but it also became increasingly clear that Gorbachev would not invoke the Brezhnev doctrine as a way to maintain order and orthodoxy in the bloc.

A New United States Policy

When President George Bush took office in January 1989, the reform forces in Eastern Europe were gaining strength. In June, Solidarity won in Poland; a non-Communist headed the government. Hungarians showed their independence by the reburial of Imre Nagy, the hero of 1956. As a sign of United States interest, the president, within six months of taking office, visited Poland and Hungary. He was received enthusiastically. The people in those countries believed that Ronald Reagan's tough stands had contributed to the thaw, and they looked forward to continued United States support. The president spoke of his admiration for what was happening, and he promised assistance. On his way home he stopped in Paris at the Economic Summit and encouraged his partners to join in an effort to help. The administration requested $350 million for the two countries over three years. Congress increased the package, with the passage of the Support for East European Democracy (SEED) Act of 1989, to almost $ 1.5 billion for fiscal years 1990, 1991, and 1992. SEED II, which had not emerged from the Senate by 1 August

1990, would provide additional programs and assistance for the other Eastern European countries.

The new legislation is wide-ranging and comprehensive. It is tailored to create what the United States would like to see happen in the relevant countries. The problem is that, although SEED I was passed in November 1989, by the fall of 1990 not much had happened to put its provisions into effect.

In the fall of 1990, the United States was still in the process of elaborating a policy that will help nurture new political institutions in formerly one-party states, support the growth of market economies to undo the irrationality of Soviet-style command economies, and create European security structures to replace armed antagonistic alliances. In developing new policies, the United States must be sensitive to the common Communist legacy with which these emerging democracies are saddled; it must also recognize the specific variations created by their histories, by their political cultures, and by the different patterns of their recent revolutions.

The Communist legacy. The Soviets established their Eastern European empire for three reasons: first, for security, as a buffer zone to prevent future invasions from the West; second, for economic benefits, to use the manufacturing capability of the satellites to support the Soviet Union; and, third, for ideological purposes, to show that Marxism-Leninism was so attractive that it was being adopted by other countries. The combination produced short-term results and long-term problems as quite different countries were forced to mold their political and economic systems to fit the Soviet pattern.

In order to be reliable security buffers, the militaries of the various countries were made adjuncts to Soviet plans by a series of bilateral military arrangements, which were transformed into the Warsaw Pact in 1955. While they were obliged to spend portions of their budgets on defense expenditures, the satellites did not play an active role in pact decision making. Military doctrine was decided in Moscow, though Eastern Europe would clearly be the first line of battle.

In economic terms, the Soviets created an empire in reverse; the mother country provided the raw materials, the "colonies" provided the manufactured products. In fact, immediately after the war, the Soviets moved some factories to the Soviet Union. The satellites were directed to transform their economic systems to replicate the Soviet command economy. Poland's refusal to collectivize its agriculture was an exception to the policy. The process of integrating the subjugated countries' economies with each other and the Soviet Union was institutionalized through the CMEA, established in 1949 as a counter to the Marshall Plan.

Politically, all the decisions were made in Moscow. The Communist parties of the satellites followed directions, which were transmitted either through Soviet political advisers, the Soviet embassies, or the Cominform—an organization established in 1947 to synchronize ideology. All independent groups were abolished. Puppet parties or organizations carried out the work of the central authorities.

Individual differences. For too long the United States has lumped the countries of Eastern Europe together, thus obscuring the fact that these countries had quite different historical experiences and political influences. Policymakers need to know the character and strength of the leadership group, how united each society is and how willing it will be to put up with hardship, and which institutions can help sustain the bold experiments. To mention only a few salient differences: Czechoslovakia, a functioning democracy in the interwar period, had a legitimate Communist party. Poland has been partitioned, obliterated from the map, and moved west; its nationhood is completely interwoven with the Catholic church. Hungary was an imperial partner in the Austro-Hungarian empire.

Just as the United States thought of the countries in bloc formation, it is beginning to treat their revolutions of a piece. To understand their current needs, it is important to know that while their revolutions have had the common purpose of ridding themselves of illegitimate Communist regimes, they have gone about it quite differently.

The British journalist, Timothy Garton Ash, who witnessed several of the revolutions, wrote that on 23 November, Day Seven of the Velvet Revolution, he said to Václav Havel: "In Poland it took ten years, in Hungary ten months, in East Germany ten weeks: perhaps in Czechoslovakia it will take ten days."[2] One could add that in Romania it took ten hours.

The revolutions differed from one another, not only in the time they took but also in a variety of other determining factors, such as the size and unity of the opposition movements, the viability of the Communist party as a negotiating partner, the presence or absence of charismatic leaders, the role of the church, and the presence of social and ethnic conflicts. As each revolutionary experience becomes more distant and the difficulties of making the reforms work replace the initial euphoria, some of the characteristics of each country's birth will seem less important; however, they should not be forgotten. American policymakers would do well to keep them in mind: the strength of Solidarity as a trade-union movement, headed by a charismatic leader who now refuses to be ignored; the negotiated character of the Hungarian revolution, which opened the door for a highly sophisticated coalition government that could become the model for either success or procrastination; the magic of the Velvet Revolution, which catapulted a small group of dissidents into control of a government and produced elections in which the Communist party got the second largest number of votes; the Bulgarian need to field a stronger opposition movement so that the Communists would lose the next election; the Romanians' curse of having launched their changes with an execution; and, finally, the experience of Yugoslavia, which in 1948 set the example of how a nation could move away from Soviet orthodoxy and might now be providing the negative example of how virulent nationalism can destroy a country. Given these circumstances, what should be the goals of a long-term policy for the United States in this important area?

Political goals; building viable democracies. For forty-five years of Communist dictatorship, no other institutions or voices were legal. The goal of the United States and its allies is to see the countries of central and Eastern Europe with regularly elected democratic governments, supported by strong and independent institutions. By mid-1990, all the countries had held their first elections. Non-Communists were victorious everywhere, except in Romania and Bulgaria — and even in those countries opposition movements had begun to emerge.

Free elections, however, are only the first step toward pluralism. The task for the next stage is to build viable independent institutions that will support the newly legitimate governments. Although the situation is slightly different in each of the countries and will dictate the pacing, generally the requirements are similar. New freedoms and minority rights must be codified in new constitutions or constitutional amendments. Appropriate roles for the new institutions must be determined: How much power should the president have? How can an independent judiciary be guaranteed? What happens to the secret police structure? How will the new parliaments operate? What role will the press play? The election process has to take root at the regional and municipal level. Ultimately, and perhaps most important, a new generation has to be educated to manage the democratic process.

What can the United States do? In the political arena, it needs to continue to provide funding for technical assistance in democracy by providing models, experts, trainers, and exchanges. Political development and party building through the National Endowment for Democracy and its party institutes should continue. Congressional task forces, such as the one established by Speaker Thomas Foley that is already providing information on legislative practices and research techniques, need to be expanded by a regular parliamentary partnership program.

One of the goals of the newly emerging democracies is to develop civil society, a system in which there are autonomous institutions that are not run by the state or subjected to its whims. In addition to encouraging the growth of political parties, the United States should lend its considerable expertise to developing such independent groups. As consequences of radical political and economic changes begin to take hold, there will be considerable social disruption. These groups are an essential part of promoting the dialogue between the rulers and the ruled, and are especially useful in defusing potential conflicts.

The United States must promote and support educational exchanges at all levels. The Peace Corps should be expanded significantly. American teachers in specialized fields should be encouraged to reach out to their counterparts. To avoid spending too much taxpayer money abroad, the United States could give grants to its universities for central and Eastern European students. American students would benefit from such contacts.

The United States must do more to coordinate help. Its embassies are severely understaffed, and volunteer agencies are unclear about where help is needed. More than twenty agencies in the United States government are said to be involved in overseeing and implementing United States policy under SEED I. Confusion is bound to result. The president's proposed $300,000 for a government clearinghouse, known as the Citizens Democracy Corps, might have the worst of all possible effects: damning with few dollars while giving the sense that the issue has been resolved.

Economic goals; healthy market economies. The Eastern Europeans are victims of slavish copying of the Soviet economic command system. According to a May

1990 report by the Central Intelligence Agency to the Joint Economic Committee, the new countries are faced with slow or stagnant growth, declining productivity, energy-intensive and obsolete heavy industries, mounting foreign debts, poor-quality goods and noncompetitive exports, massive environmental problems, and deteriorating infrastructures. As a result, the gap in economic performance between Eastern Europe and the West widened further; per-capita gross national product (GNP) fell to 27 percent of that of the United States.[3]

Additional economic problems have been created by the reforms: unemployment, angry farmers, hyperinflation, nondeliveries of Soviet oil, and a shortage of hard currency—to mention the most visible. Given all the hurdles, any hope for these countries to become productive market economies and participants in the international economic system seems far away. Nevertheless, the success of the whole experiment depends on economic progress. The issue is stated most succinctly in a recent article by Bronislaw Geremek, the leader of Solidarity in the parliament: "We know very well that democracy is the first condition of economic reform. On the other hand, to be frank, the dire economic situation in Poland is now the main danger to democracy in our country."[4] Geremek's statement does not apply only to Poland.

The experience of the immediate postrevolutionary period shows that it is easier to have free elections than to change a command economy into a market one. There are models for a transition from dictatorship to democracy but no guidelines for moving from communism to capitalism.

The task is huge. It is necessary to turn over the ownership of state-owned enterprises to private entities on some equitable basis. Obsolete, energy-wasteful, environmentally destructive plants must be replaced. Currencies have to become convertible. Transportation and communication infrastructures must be put into place. Entrepreneurial and managerial skills must be learned rapidly. Products capable of attracting hard currency must be manufactured. Legislation, capital, training, and patience are needed to make it work. In each of the countries, hundreds of laws need to be passed in order to transform the economy. After he was elected, President Havel said that over 300 laws had to be drafted and passed so as to redefine some 6,000 rules and regulations.[5] New institutions, such as a stock market and independent banks, need to be created. Ways have to be devised to make projects attractive to domestic and foreign investors. Generally, the workers of central and Eastern Europe are skilled, but they need to be trained in state-of-the-art machinery.

The drafters of the SEED acts should be applauded for providing financial and technical help, such as structural adjustment designed to aid economic reforms (including currency convertibility, ending subsidies for inefficient industry, and privatization), the World Bank and the International Monetary Fund programs, debt relief, and restructuring food-aid programs; private-sector development, including loans, grants, equity investments, technical assistance, training, and guarantees; the creation of Enterprise Funds—not-for-profit organizations that combine public and private funding from the United States and the host country to invest in promising, profit-making ventures, with a provision for technical training, worker retraining, Peace Corps programs, and International Executive Service Corps; trade and investment programs designed to encourage United States business to expand its role in Eastern Europe, with new authority for the Export-Import Bank, the Overseas Private Investment Corporation, and the Department of Commerce; educational, cultural, and scientific activities to expand publicly and privately funded scholarships; and environmental and health programs.

The G-24, the group in which the United States participates with other nations working with the European Community secretariat, has also played a vital role. Continued American support for the process is vital. The G-24 activities include the funding of a $1 billion Polish exchange stabilization fund; a $1 billion structural adjustment loan for Hungary; establishment of the $12 billion European Bank for Reconstruction and Development; delivery of food aid and the use of locally generated counterpart funds to supply credit for projects with small farmers, water supply, telephones, and rural banking; and joint or cofinanced projects, such as the Budapest Center for the Environment and the European Training Foundation.

It is not easy for United States policymakers to shift totally from a time of sanctions — with exceptions for good behavior in the human-rights area — to positive support for transitional economies in the form of trade credits, favorable tariff rates, loans, grants, and investment insurance. And this change in attitude is coming while the countries themselves are in a fluid economic state, their new economic legislation is being created, and United States business seems to be skittish and is in tough competition with other Western investors. Progress has been made toward liberalizing the restrictions of the Coordinating Committee on Multilateral Export Controls (COCOM), but it is time to abolish all restrictions for countries in the area that have achieved full democracy and have developed adequate third-country safeguards. Perhaps the greatest economic help the United States could give would be to work out a way to forgive or markedly reduce portions of these countries' debilitating foreign debts.

Security goals; all-European security system. In the fall of 1990, the security picture in central and Eastern Europe was totally fluid. The Warsaw Pact was a mirage. Soviet soldiers were going home, the role of the pact was being debated, and national armies were scaling down and defining new doctrines. Without exaggeration, it could be said that there was a security vacuum in the area.

In addition to pressing political and economic problems, the newly independent countries need to consider an appropriate security arrangement. They are unsure what threatens them the most — the Red army is in retreat, and they have been told that the German army has only peaceful intentions; they may feel most endangered by smoldering ethnic rivalries and potential border conflicts among themselves. If there were to be a border conflict between Romania and Hungary — a not unlikely prospect — what would happen? There is no conflict resolution or security system for the area. To ensure their security, should they restructure the Warsaw Pact, join NATO if invited, or develop a new "all-European" security system?

Under the Warsaw Pact arrangements, the satellites were obliged to spend portions of their budgets on defense and to accommodate large Soviet bases and troops. In 1989, the Eastern European countries reflected Gorbachev's December 1988 arms-control initiatives by cutting their own defense budgets. Today they have to rethink everything. The new governments are cutting military forces and decommissioning weapons and matériel, in keeping with more "defensive" military doctrines. They are also trying to deal with the varied problems associated with departing Soviet troops; the Soviets want them to pay for what they view as luxurious facilities left behind, and the host countries are complaining about the hazardous waste that remains. They are dealing with the positive and negative aspects of converting to a civilian economy: resources saved and consumer goods produced versus potential higher costs, lower profits, and unemployment. Then there is the question of how to make up for the hard currency sales of arms to Third World countries. The need to trade with Persian Gulf countries becomes even greater as the Soviets withdraw their low-priced oil deliveries to their former satellites.

Although some have always maintained that the North Atlantic Treaty Organization (NATO) and the Warsaw Pact were mirror images of each other, the end of the cold war has made their differences quite clear. NATO has been a voluntary association of democracies, designed to defend against invasion from the East. The Warsaw Pact was established in 1955, ostensibly as a counterweight to NATO and West Germany's inclusion in it. It has, however, been a tool for Soviet control over its satellites. Consequently, while NATO's participants are actively seeking ways to keep their alliance vigorous by changing its mission, Warsaw Pact members cannot agree what to do next. Poland, at first, wanted the Soviet troops to stay. Hungary has stated that it wishes to withdraw from the pact altogether. Czechoslovakia has suggested the transformation of the pact into a treaty of sovereign states with equal rights, which would stress disarmament. The temporary commission of pact government representatives, which is preparing recommendations on new structures, has run into substantial differences and is currently able to agree only on a small part of a draft to be submitted to a summit in November 1990.[6]

Since united Germany will be included in NATO, should former bloc countries also be invited to join the alliance? That is obviously a possibility, but some of the countries would prefer being part of a new all-European arrangement in which they had a voice from the beginning, rather than being adjuncts to a group of countries originally united against them. Given the new situation, it might be more productive and forward-looking to concentrate on building a new all-European security system that would be based on NATO and the current Conference on Security and Cooperation in Europe (CSCE) than to focus on expanding NATO itself.

The agenda of the 1990 CSCE summit will include a possible security role, in addition to such issues as conventional force agreement, action on German unification, proposals for free elections, and the rule of law. As Senator Dennis DeConcini and Congressman Steny Hoyer noted, it is essential to look at the structures to see if they can be adjusted to deal with the new security issues.[7] Throughout the cold war, the arms-control talks set the agenda of superpower relations. One of the characteristics of the new era has been that the talks cannot keep up with political developments. So the Conventional Forces in Europe (CFE) talks seem to be out of touch with reality. The most recent NATO summit tried to deal with the new situation and promulgated a new nuclear doctrine, but the effects on actual numbers of weapons is as yet unclear.

The London summit indicated support for the CSCE process, but work on a new European security arrangement seems to be progressing slowly — though more is perhaps going on behind the scenes than is evident. The United States needs to be engaged more actively in developing a new all-European security structure. At the present it is like building a house in a transitional neighborhood and waiting for a break-in before installing a burglar alarm.

In addition to policies that will encourage democracy, free markets, and stable security arrangements, the United States should promote regional cooperation. The next stage will be difficult. Economic hardships will cause dissent, ethnic conflicts might erupt, and demagogy will flourish. While recognizing national differences, the United States must help the newly emerging democracies leapfrog a dangerous nationalistic phase. Their common market, the CMEA, has in fact collapsed. They are beginning to make their own bilateral arrangements with the European Community; but until they are ready to compete in the international market, they must be encouraged to help one another. As America gropes to design new European architecture, it should support ideas that bring countries together to solve specific problems, such as environmental pollution, developing new energy sources, and river transportation. Such functional groupings might not only help to take the sting out of ethnic conflicts and create incentives for cooperation but could also provide the basis for a new European system. Finally, the United States should encourage the next generation of leaders to learn to work together by providing regional training for young parliamentarians.

Conclusion

It is not easy to develop new policies for a region of the world considered outside America's sphere of influence for almost half a century. It is especially difficult when the situation is fluid and the countries are so needy. It may become harder because American enchantment with the drama of the individual revolutions will wane; even the most charismatic leaders will lose their charm and begin to take actions we do not like; and the problems will seem unsolvable. Other areas will demand the United States's attention. The temptation to let the Europeans worry about their own problems will be great. It is even tempting to stress that the United States can help best in coordination with others in the G-24. While cooperation is essential, it would be a mistake to reject a leadership role.

From whatever angle one chooses to view the map of the world, it is undeniable that the region of central and Eastern Europe is strategically important to the Eurasian landmass. The countries in the region have natural ties to the United States that they want to strengthen. They do not want to depend on Germany or Russia for their security, and they provide an important foothold for the United States in an area stretching from the Baltic to the Mediterranean, between Russia and Germany.

If the promises of 1989 are to become reality, and if stability is to be achieved through change, American policymakers must not only develop a longer attention span but must also be more imaginative. Rhetoric must be transformed into real help in real time.

After four decades and billions of dollars spent on building up and defending Western Europe, it is difficult for American political leaders to persuade taxpayers that they must spend their dwindling resources on yet another effort to rescue central and Eastern Europe. It is especially hard when one cannot put a name or a symbol on the enemy. It is even harder when new problems in the Middle East threaten the United States's vital interests. But as George Marshall said when he launched another great effort: "An essential part of any successful action on the part of the United States is an understanding on the part of the people of America of the character of the problem and the remedies to be applied. Political passion and prejudice should have no part. With foresight, and a willingness on the part of our people to face up to the vast responsibility which history has clearly placed upon our country, the difficulties I have outlined can and will be overcome."[8] It is the responsibility of American leaders to explain what the stakes are. Otherwise, as the United States prepares for the twenty-first century, it may discover that it has not done enough to ensure that it be a peaceful one.

NOTES

1. *National Security Strategy of the United States*, The White House, March 1990, 11.

2. Timothy Garton Ash, *The Magic Lantern* (New York: Random House, 1990), 78.

3. "Eastern Europe: Long Road Ahead to Economic Well-Being" (Paper by the Central Intelligence Agency, presented to the Subcommittee on Technology and National Security of the Joint Economic Committee, 16 May 1990), ii–iii, 1–3.

4. Bronislaw Geremek, "Postcommunism and Democracy in Poland," *Washington Quarterly* (Summer 1990), 128.

5. *Inside Eastern Europe*, 9 July 1990, 5.

6. *RFE/RL Daily Report*, no. 136, 19 July 1990, 3.

7. Sen. Dennis DeConcini and Rep. Steny Hoyer, "New Organization for Europe," *CSCE Digest*, June 1990, 2.

8. George Marshall (Commencement speech, Harvard University, Cambridge, Mass., 5 June 1946), as quoted in *New York Times*, 6 June 1946.

The Revival of Politics in Romania

VLADIMIR TISMANEANU

From 1965 to 1987, Romania under Nicolae Ceausescu was a fascinating example of a neo-Stalinist personal dictatorship. The Romanian Communist Party (RCP), created in 1921, was ostensibly the ruling force in that country, but in fact Ceausescu and his clan annihilated the party as a decision-making body. Ceausescu's predecessor, Gheorghe Gheorghiu-Dej, had succeeded in shunning de-Stalinization and in keeping Romania a fortress of Communist orthodoxy. Dej ruled as the chief officer of an oligarchy and ingratiated himself with the party bureaucracy, but power under Ceausescu was exerted by a tiny coterie using the mechanisms of populist authoritarianism, symbolic manipulation, and naked terror. The party apparatus was slowly disenfranchised and eventually emasculated. All forms of opposition and dissent were treated as criminal offenses. The counterpart to domestic repression was Ceausescu's autonomist course in foreign policy that ensured the regime a certain authority in international affairs. Unlike other Soviet-bloc leaders, Ceausescu was not perceived as the Kremlin's puppet, and his initiatives were often praised for their farsightedness.

Until the early 1980s and especially until the beginning of perestroika in the USSR, Ceausescu was able to use this "exceptionalism" as an argument in favor of his political options. Political decay in the late 1980s and the intensification of international pressures on Romania contributed to the weakening of Ceausescu's power. The Byzantine rites could no longer conceal the bankruptcy of the Stalinist system. Romanians were disgusted with a regime whose underpinnings were corruption, repression, and poverty. In December 1989 they launched an anti-Communist rebellion and smashed the whole institutional edifice of state socialism. For several hours on 22 December, there was a vacuum of power in Romania, and it appeared that the country's leap into democracy would proceed smoothly. But then a counterstrike followed and violence became rampant. The anti-Ceausescu bureaucracy, long frustrated by the president's vagaries, came to the fore and pretended to lead the people's struggle against the dictator's supporters. They claimed to be revolutionaries, and many Romanians were taken in by this pretense. A new myth was thus manufactured by the National Salvation Front

(NSF or the Front), the umbrella movement dominated by neo-Leninist zealots whose real agenda is to rationalize rather than to replace the Communist system. They took over in the shadow of the bloody confrontations between the revolutionaries and the secret police (Securitate). Well versed in conspiracies, these apparatchiks orchestrated a colossal hoax and masqueraded as democrats. The NSF was a pseudoform of revolutionary breakthrough, an attempt on the part of the besieged bureaucracy to invent a new principle of legitimacy by renouncing the most compromised features of the system. A spontaneous plebeian revolution was thus abducted by a group of Communist reformers whose main credentials consisted of their more or less outspoken opposition to Ceausescu's eccentric policies. When the revolutionaries realized that they had been duped and their most cherished ideals betrayed, Romania entered a new stage of turmoil. The country's future hinges on the resolution of this conflict between the democratic forces and the counterrevolutionary neo-Communist junta.[1]

The End of Ceausescu's Dynastic Communism

At the end of Ceausescu's reign he was universally regarded as an embodiment of neofeudal despotism, but at the beginning he had been intent on reforming the system and appeared to many Romanians and foreign observers as a maverick Communist.[2] His anti-Soviet foreign policy as well as the liberal policies adopted between 1965 and 1971 ensured him a certain level of domestic and international prestige. The first stage of Ceausescu's rule was thus characterized by increased political and economic links with the West, ideological relaxation, and the endeavor to create a Romanian model of socialism different from the rigid, monolithic pattern advocated by Leonid I. Brezhnev and his supporters in the other Warsaw Pact countries. After 1971, following a trip to China and North Korea, Ceausescu resolutely abandoned all reformist efforts and decided to restore the Communist party's absolute control over the culture and society. He was fascinated by Maoism and Kim Il-sung's oriental despotism, but a more important reason for this shift was his constant belief that history had endowed the Communist party with a special mission and that intellectual diversity could result in disbanding the existing system. True, in August 1968, he condemned the Soviet invasion of Czechoslovakia, but he did so primarily for reasons of self-defense. He never wholeheartedly approved of the Czechoslovak experiment with "socialism with a human face." The Romanian leader's opposition to Brezhnev was rooted in his ambition to act as an independent actor in the international arena and to exert total control over his subjects. Like Gheorghiu-Dej, Enver Hoxha, Kim Il-sung, and Mao Zedong, Ceausescu resented the Kremlin's patronizing behavior. He despised the other Warsaw Pact leaders for their subservience toward Moscow and took great pride in being truly sovereign.

To convince his citizens that he was a genuine patriot, Ceausescu played down traditional Marxist internationalist themes and adopted nationalist symbols and values. Especially after 1971, the official media lionized him as the predestined leader of the Romanian nation, and an unparalleled personality cult was engineered to legitimize his power. The more personalist and authoritarian his leadership methods, the less inclined Ceausescu was to accept any form of collective leadership. During the 1970s, he completely dislodged the political faction that had helped him to establish himself as the absolute leader of the party. Representatives of the party apparatus were replaced by loyal members of Ceausescu's immediate and extended family. Clientelism and nepotism reached their climax in the 1980s when Elena Ceausescu, the president's wife, became the second-in-command. She was appointed a first-deputy premier, a Politburo member, and chairperson of the party's Central Commission for Cadres. All significant personnel appointments were decided by Elena Ceausescu and her most obedient servant, Central Committee Secretary Emil Bobu.[3] In the meantime, the couple's youngest son, Nicu, became a candidate member of the politburo and party boss in Sibiu County in Transylvania. Although renowned for his egregious life-style, Nicu was apparently groomed to succeed his father. Terrified by the ubiquitous Securitate, Romanians were powerlessly contemplating the accomplishment of this dynastic scenario. All the country's institutions functioned in accordance with the preparation of the president's designs to keep power within the family. As dissident poet Mircea Dinescu put it in an interview with the French newspaper *Liberation* in March 1989, it seemed that "God had forgotten Romania."

Ceausescu adamantly opposed the marketization of the Romanian economy. Even during his most liberal period, he was a staunch advocate of central planning and opposed proposals that would have allowed the development of small ownership in such areas as services and tourism. His understanding of Marxism being extremely dogmatic and primitive, he looked askance at all reformist initiatives in other Soviet bloc countries. For Ceausescu, the economic optimum amounted to total autarky. He imposed a number of irrational investments whose unique function was to satisfy his megalomaniac drive. Enraptured with the mythological concoctions fabricated by his sycophants, a prisoner of paranoid delusions, the president was increasingly alienated from his party. He thought of himself in messianic terms and expected Romanians to treat him accordingly.

The Communist party was no longer an autonomous body and existed only to implement Ceausescu's most extravagant plans. Party leaders were humiliated, and the apparatus was increasingly upset with this catastrophic course. Disenchanted and offended, the bureaucrats came to hate the man they had long adored. But Ceausescu, a hostage of the propagandistic mirage he himself had created, ignored this danger. As the party became paralyzed, there was no support for the general secretary other than his faithful Securitate. Headed by General Iulian Vlad, a professional policeman with no ideological convictions, this institution carried out Ceausescu's draconian orders. At the same time, it appears now, the chiefs of the secret police were profoundly aware of the prospects for a popular explosion. Plans were made for such an eventuality.

In 1989 Ceausescu realized that unless he intensified his repressive policy, the whole edifice of what he called the "multilaterally developed socialist society" would immediately and ingloriously crumble. The reform movement in the USSR and its impact on the other bloc countries made the Romanian dictator and his clique increasingly nervous. On various occasions Ceausescu proffered undisguised criticism of perestroika, which he called "a right-wing deviation" within world communism. As a reformist trend was taking shape in Eastern Europe, Ceausescu allied himself with stalwarts of Brezhnevism like Erich Honecker, Todor Zhivkov, and Milos Jakes. An unholy antireformist alliance was formed between these die-hard Stalinists who understood that the winds of change that Gorbachev had unleashed would force them out of power. When events accelerated, Ceausescu was legitimately concerned about his fate and the chances for his regime to remain unaffected by reform.

Emboldened by Gorbachev's policy of glasnost, some Romanians took the risk to criticize Ceausescu publicly. In March 1989 six party veterans addressed Ceausescu in an open letter, denouncing his excesses, his erratic economic policies, and the general deterioration of Romania's international image. The authors were not partisans of Western-style pluralism. Two of them (Gheorghe Apostol and Constantin Parvulescu) had served as general secretaries of the Romanian Communist Party, and their political record did not indicate any heretical propensities. Another signatory, Sylviu Brucan, was a seasoned party propagandist who had also served as the regime's ambassador to the United States and the United Nations in the late 1950s and early 1960s. None of these figures enjoyed popular support, but they were well known within the party bureaucracy, and that was what mattered. Ceausescu reacted furiously to the letter and placed the authors under house arrest. Their refusal to recant showed the limits of Ceausescu's power.[4] Also in 1989, prominent intellectuals began openly to criticize the regime's obscurantist cultural policy. In November, dissident writer Dan Petrescu released a public appeal against Ceausescu's reelection as general secretary at the Fourteenth RCP Congress.

Altogether, Ceausescu's power — impregnable at first glance — was falling apart. Detested by the population, isolated internationally, living in his own world of delusions and fantasies, the aging leader could not understand what was happening to communism. He considered Gorbachev the archtraitor to socialist ideals and tried to mobilize an international neo-Stalinist coalition. In August 1989, he was so irritated with the formation of a Solidarity-run government in Poland that he proposed a Warsaw Pact intervention in that country. Every day the Romanian media lambasted the dangers of reformism and "deideologization." In November 1989, the Fourteenth Congress of the Romanian Communist Party took place, and Ceausescu was enthusiastically reelected general secretary. His major address was a reiteration of his favorite clichés: the rejection of pluralism and the exaltation of the Romanian concept of a "revolutionary-workers' democracy"; the sacrosanct leading role of the Communist party (which for him, of course, amounted to his autocratic power); and the intensification of the class struggle on the international stage. He solemnly pledged to remain faithful to the pristine Marxist-Leninist faith and excoriated all those who had renounced their Communist, i.e., Stalinist, beliefs. With its ritualistic pageants and well-staged hosannahs, the congress was for all practical purposes a political nonevent. It only showed how much Ceausescu and his clique had lost touch with reality. They could not grasp the magnitude of the social crisis in Romania and failed to realize the effect on the Romanians of the revolutionary events in the other Eastern European countries.[5]

But the writing was on the wall for Nicolae Ceausescu and his regime. On 16 December 1989 a demonstration took place in Timisoara, where the police tried to evict Laszlo Toekes, a Hungarian Protestant pastor, from his parish house. When the protesters refused to disperse, the police and the army opened fire. The next day thousands took to the streets with antidictatorial slogans, and a carnage followed. Western radio stations were informed about the massacre in Timisoara, and all Romanians realized that Ceausescu was ready to engage in total warfare against nonviolent and unarmed demonstrators. At that moment there was no return for Ceausescu: to accept the demands of the Timisoara protesters would have only shown how fragile his power was. Instead, he preferred to do what other Soviet-bloc leaders had avoided: he used force in an attempt to quell the unrest. Even at this late hour, he still believed that he could exert total control over the population. He may have even been convinced that the majority of the Romanians would follow his injunctions as they always had in the past. But this time Ceausescu's personality cult backfired: the leader could not fathom the intensity of the popular frustration and thought that only some "hooligans on the payroll of foreign services" could engage in open attacks on the government. The very idea of a legitimate opposition was alien to his mind. Unprepared to meet such defiance, Ceausescu underestimated the danger and left the country on 18 December for a state visit to Iran. On 20 December, when he returned, he delivered an extremely provocative televised speech, and the next day he ordered a mass rally to endorse his intransigent opposition to reforms. On that occasion, however, Romanians refused to follow their leader's behest. Tens of thousands booed Ceausescu in the Palace Square in front of the Central Committee building. For once, they abandoned their fear and interrupted the dictator's oratorical performance. Although Ceausescu tried to accommodate the crowd, it was too late. Television had revealed his stupefaction and confusion, and people saw that he was losing control. That same night, protesting students were massacred in the University Square, and the next morning a huge gathering took place in the Palace Square. The crowd stormed the Central Committee building, and Ceausescu and his wife fled from its roof by helicopter. The man who had garnered more power than any other leader in Romania's history, the once acclaimed "Danube of thought" and "architect of national destiny," found himself betrayed by everyone who had worshipped him only one night before.

The story of Ceausescu's flight and his subsequent capture, trial, and execution on Christmas day remains to be clarified. There are enough puzzling elements in it to make the official explanations provided by Ceausescu's successors more than suspicious. One thing is now clear: immediately after the beginning of the popular uprising in Bucharest, a coup was organized against Ceausescu by some of his closest associates. The most prominent among them was General Victor Atanasie Stanculescu, a deputy minister of defense and the man whom Ceausescu had entrusted with the defense of the Central Committee building and his personal protection. Stanculescu was the last one to talk to Ceausescu before the dictator's flight, and he alone supervised the proceedings at the trial that presumably took place on 25 December. In other words, the end of the Ceausescu regime was ensured by a plebeian revolution, but Ceausescu's personal end was carried out by his own Praetorian Guard.

The Resurgence of Politics

After the revolutionary upheaval that swept away the Ceausescu dictatorship in December 1989, Romanians rapidly discovered the flavor of politics. For the first time in forty-five years the people could speak openly about their worries, criticize the new leaders, and organize independent associations and parties.

Immediately after the revolution the National Salvation Front was formed. The Front's first statement announced its commitment to democratic principles, including the multiparty system and the need to organize free elections as soon as possible. The Front claimed to represent a decisive break with the abhorred Communist regime. The Romanian Communist Party disappeared without a trace from the country's political life. It should be emphasized once again that the RCP had long since lost its autonomy. It had became the appendage of the Ceausescu clique, a huge machine whose unique duty was to extol the president and his wife. Most of the 3.8 million party members lacked any emotional or ideological identification with the leadership. The NSF's announcement of the transition to a pluralist system was therefore welcomed.

Three days later, following a strange trial conducted by a military tribunal, Nicolae and Elena Ceausescu were executed. Since basic legal procedures were ignored, many observers saw the trial as a judicial murder committed to protect the system by demonizing its two most abhorred exponents.[6] The Ceausescus challenged their judges and accused Romania's new leaders of treason and putsch. The NSF Council justified the summary execution by invoking reasons of revolutionary expediency. But many Romanians doubted this explanation and suspected that the purpose of this frame-up, with the defense lawyers being more vituperative of their clients than the prosecutor, was to eliminate the dictator and his wife as potentially embarrassing witnesses in an inevitable trial of the RCP. Since such an occurrence would have involved an indictment of the very system that made possible the Ceausescu phenomenon, the organizers of the secret trial preferred to transfer all the guilt to the two defendants and to silence them as soon as possible. In this sense, Romania's new leaders chose the worst of all alternatives: tyrannicide pretending to be law. By attempting to keep the revolution pure, they sullied it.

As for the composition of the new leadership, informed analysts were immediately struck by the emergence of Communist veterans and apparatchiks to prominent positions.[7] The NSF president himself, sixty-year-old Ion Iliescu, had served under Ceausescu in the late 1960s as first secretary of the Communist Youth Union (UTC) and minister of youth. Between 1970 and 1971 he was the RCP Central Committee secretary in charge of ideology and an alternate Political Executive Committee member. In 1971 Iliescu dared to oppose Ceausescu's "minicultural revolution" and was criticized for "intellectualism and petty-bourgeois liberalism." Following this incident, Ceausescu humiliated Iliescu for his unorthodox stances by assigning him to menial party and state jobs. In 1984 Iliescu lost his Central Committee seat and was appointed director of a minor publishing house in Bucharest. Until the revolution he kept a low profile and did not engage in any daring form of anti-Ceausescu activity. Although he was not among the signatories of the "Letter of the Six," Romanians knew about his political divergences with Ceausescu. In the years that preceded the December explosion, he was widely perceived as a Gorbachevite whose arrival to power would permit Romania to embark on long-delayed reforms. But the violence of the revolution, the exponential rise in political expectations, and Iliescu's refusal to abjure his Communist creed made him unsuited for the task of a radical tribune. It was difficult to see Iliescu as the symbol of the antitotalitarian revolutionary fervor of the youth. Somebody else had to be handpicked to play this role. Born in 1946, the new prime minister, Petre Roman, had no revolutionary credentials except that together with thousands of other Romanians he had participated in the 22 December 1989 seizure of the Central Committee building. On the other hand, he was the son of the late Valter Roman, a former Spanish Civil War fighter who until his death in 1983 was a member of the RCP Central Committee and the director of the party's publishing house. The young Roman could not invoke a single moment of his past when he had raised his voice in solidarity with the harassed dissidents. Fluent in French and Spanish, holding a doctoral degree from the Polytechnical School in Toulouse, Roman was supposed to provide the new leadership with a badly needed European veneer. Unlike Iliescu and Roman, seasoned propagandist Sylviu Brucan (who was born in 1916) could take advantage of his dissident past. After all, he had been one of the authors of the "Letter of the Six," and even before that courageous gesture he had warned Ceausescu against the use of force to suppress working-class unrest in the industrial city of Braşov in November 1987. For his unrepentant opposition to the dictatorship, Brucan had suffered many police harassments. The fourth most visible member of the NSF leadership was Dumitru Mazilu, a former international-law professor who had criticized the abysmal human-rights record of Ceausescu's government in a special report prepared for the United Nations Human Rights Commission.

Initially, it seemed that Brucan was the dominant force within the ruling quartet. To placate charges of a Communist plot to seize the still evanescent power, the NSF leaders decided to include in the larger Council a number of well-known oppositional figures: human-rights activist Doina Cornea; poets Anna Blandiana, Dan Desliu, and Mircea Dinescu; and writer Aurel Dragoch Munteanu. On 12 January 1990, a demonstration took place in Bucharest, where Iliescu, Roman, and Mazilu were accused of trying to preserve the Communist system. Under the pressure of the crowd, the three announced the decision to ban the RCP. Mazilu engaged in a dialogue with the demonstrators that seemed to be an attempt to undermine Iliescu's authority. One day later, *Romania Libera*, the country's most outspoken daily newspaper, published unknown data about Mazilu's past, including his previous job as director of the State Security School in the late 1960s. Upset by these revelations, Mazilu resigned and the NSF leadership remained in the hands of the Iliescu-Roman-Brucan troika.

Several other elements contributed to the political radicalization of the Romanians. One was the rapid constitution of political parties. During the first days after Ceausescu's overthrow, the National Peasant and the National Liberal parties were formed. On 5 January 1990, Radu Campeanu, a Liberal politician who had spent nine years in Communist prisons, returned from Paris after fourteen years of exile. The National Peasants merged with a recently created Christian Democratic formation and became the Christian Democratic National Peasant Party, headed by Corneliu Coposu, a survivor of Romania's Stalinist jails. The Social Democratic Party, the third of the traditional democratic parties in Romania, reemerged under the leadership of engineer Sergiu Cunescu and the honorary chairmanship of Anton Dumitriu, one of the party's historical leaders. It seemed that in several weeks, Romania had experienced an extraordinary leap from the political numbness of Ceausescu's years to the frenzy of a vivid and dramatic public life.

No less important an element has been the rise of Romanian civil society. For those who had been accustomed to seeing Romania as a country without any opposition, this may have come as a surprise. But the truth of the matter was that even under the utterly unfavorable circumstances of the Ceausescu regime, some germs of the civil society managed to survive. One of these, for instance, was the cultural circle surrounding Constantin Noica, a philosopher with Hegelian-existentialist propensities and a Socratic spirit whose disciples came into direct conflict with the official Marxist tenets. Among them, philosopher Gabriel Liiceanu and art historian Andrei Plesu were the closest to Noica. Other members of this "metaphysical opposition" included art historian Andrei Cornea, logician Sorin Vieru, and philologist Thomas Kleininger (who translated Martin Heidegger's works into Romanian). Another center of dissent was the "Iasi group" surrounding Dan Petrescu. Here it is interesting to note the existence of a group of young writers, sociologists, and philosophers in Bucharest who engaged in oppositional activities after 1988: Calin Anastasiu, Dan Oprescu, Stelian Tanase, and Alin Teodorescu. By the end of December 1989, these informal nuclei coalesced to form the "Group for Social Dialogue," an independent association dedicated to monitoring the government's observance of the democratic process and developing civil society in Romania. During the first months after the revolution, the "Group"—as it is usually referred to—became the center of a hectic search for alternatives to the official slide into a Romanian version of "neo-Bolshevism." Its weekly publication, *22*, printed fascinating reports on the Group's meetings with prominent members of the NSF, including Sylviu Brucan. On that occasion, Brucan was overwhelmed by questions regarding the legitimacy of the government and the NSF's controversial tactics.

The major sources of instability in postrevolutionary Romania has been the NSF's hegemonic ambitions. Initially, the Front maintained that it represented a provisional form of government and that its sole mission was to ensure the smooth transition to pluralism in Romania. But on 29 January the NSF organized a massive workers' demonstration against the opposition parties. Populist slogans were launched by the Front's supporters, who charged the opposition with the intention of destabilizing the country's political life. In February, the NSF renounced its suprapartisan pretense, became a political party, and announced its decision to field candidates in the forthcoming elections. From then on, it lost credibility among the youth and intellectuals. One of the country's most influential columnists, Octavian Paler, wrote in *Romania Libera* that the NSF's ambition was to take advantage of its revolutionary image in order to neutralize the opposition and to ensure its victory in the forthcoming election. According to Paler, by turning into a political party, the NSF had relinquished its aura as an emanation of the revolutionary spontaneity of the masses. And Paler's diagnosis turned out to be correct: following this decision, the country experienced a growing polarization of political forces. On the one hand, there was the Front, whose political options were often described as "neo-Communist." On the other hand, there were the opposition parties, dominated by the three above-mentioned "new old parties." In the meantime, the NSF created a large number of satellite parties, ready to endorse its platform and hope for a share in power. During the May 1990 elections, more than eighty political parties presented candidates. Out of them, NSF critics argued, about forty were sympathetic to the Front. The opposition could hardly organize, and its political discourse was not accessible to the population because of the obstacles created by the Front-run government. But the NSF itself was far from being a real political party: its often decried neo-Bolshevism was a survivalist strategy on the part of the beleaguered nomenklatura of the four decades of Communist rule. More an umbrella movement than an ideological party, the Front played on and encouraged fears of instability and chaos. The NSF had to admit its own weaknesses in February when it invited the other parties to join a peculiar miniparliament called the Provisional Council of National Unity. By co-opting representatives of the opposition into this fragile body, the ruling troika aimed to put an end to public unrest.

But discontent in Romania had deep social roots and could not be easily mitigated. The Front's indulgence in half-truths and aggressive warnings could but further irritate the revolutionary forces. It was perhaps Iliescu's major illusion that a Romanian version of perestroika would satisfy the population. To his dismay, the NSF leader had to learn that, instead of decreasing, the radical ferment was continuing to gather momentum. The students and the intelligentsia spearheaded this struggle for the fulfilment of the revolution. For many Romanians, the NSF has outrageously abused their confidence, usurped political power, and tried to institute an "enlightened" version of the Communist regime.

The widespread sentiment that the NSF's hidden agenda consisted of the restoration of the old regime without the grotesque outgrowths of Ceausescu's tyranny was not groundless. After all, Romanians knew that the dreaded Securitate had not been dismantled. A few of Ceausescu's henchmen were brought to trial only for their participation in the 16–22 December slaughter, not for the role they played in the functioning of Europe's most vicious despotism since Stalin's death. Instead of purging the administrative apparatus of the servants of the old regime, the NSF had appointed them to key positions. This situation was well known to the Romanians, and it accounted for the growing tensions that were soon to reach an explosive point. The wounds in that country were too deep and too recent for the NSF to admit openly its Communist heredity. True, the Front created its own social base among frightened apparatchiks and their families, and among some sectors of the industrial working class and of the peasantry. During the electoral campaign, Iliescu and Roman went out of their way to brandish the specter of unemployment and the threat of the country's "occupation" by Western multinational companies.

Conceived by unreconstructed Leninists, the NSF strategy failed to excite the youth and the intelligentsia — because it neglected the dynamism of society's self-organization, the force of the collective passions for freedom and democracy, and the contagious effect of the democratic movements in the other Eastern European countries. The Front was living with the illusion that Romanians would accept a simple revamping of the Communist system. On 11 March 1990, the "Proclamation of Timisoara" precisely articulated the political expectations and values of those who had started the revolution. In effect the real charter of the Romanian revolution, the document emphasized the unequivocally anti-Communist nature of the uprising in December 1989. Article 7 of the "Proclamation" questioned the revolutionary bona fides of those who had emerged as the beneficiaries of the upheaval: "Timisoara started the revolution against the entire Communist regime and its entire nomenklatura, and certainly not in order to give an opportunity to a group of anti-Ceausescu dissidents within the RCP to take over the reins of political power. Their presence at the head of the country makes the death of our heroes senseless." This was political dynamite in a country still run by former luminaries of the Communist nomenklatura. To give this view even more poignancy, article 8 of the "Proclamation" proposed a set of guidelines for the elimination of former Communist officials and security police officers from public life for a certain period of time: "We want to propose that the electoral law, for the first three consecutive legislatures ban from every list all former Communist activists and Securitate officers. Their presence in the political life of the country is the major source of the tensions and suspicions that currently torment Romanian society. Until the situation has stabilized and national reconciliation has been achieved it is absolutely necessary that they remain absent from public life."[8] Soon thereafter, the "Proclamation" became the rallying point of all democratic forces in Romania: the statement was endorsed by hundreds of independent groups and associations, including the "Group for Social Dialogue." Even more emphatically, the document opposed the right of those who had served the Communist regime to run as candidates for the presidential office. The "Proclamation" hit its target: the offended nomenklatura reacted with its traditional weapons, including slander, innuendo, and intimidation. The Front-controlled newspapers (*Adevarul, Azi,* and *Dimineata*) and the "free" Romanian Television tried to dismiss the relevance of the "Proclamation," calling it an unrealistic and potentially disruptive document. There were insinuations that it could play into the hands of far-right groups abroad. But for millions of citizens who signed it, the "Proclamation of Timisoara" became the program for Romania's emancipation from communism.

By the end of April 1990, thousands of students, workers, and intellectuals seized the University Square in Bucharest, where they organized a sit-in to protest the government's refusal to consider the public demands formulated in the "Proclamation." The main organizers of this "Commune of Bucharest"—which lasted several weeks—were the "December 21" Association and the Independent Group for Democracy. They were joined by hundreds of other informal initiatives. Although the government sent police troops to disband the demonstrators (who had camped in the Square), the around-the-clock demonstration continued.

Confronted with this unwavering challenge, Iliescu committed a major blunder when he called the protesters *golani* (tramps). This was a very costly mistake, because the term was ominously reminiscent of Ceausescu's outbursts against the "hooligans" in Timisoara during the first days of the revolution. In a matter of hours, thousands of Romanians proudly began to declare themselves *golani* in solidarity with the demonstrators. Although Iliescu apologized for using this word, many Romanians considered it indicative of a mind-set.

Another source of tension in the aftermath of Ceausescu's downfall was the growing ethnic conflict in Transylvania with regard to the grievances of the Hungarian minority. In March 1989 bloody clashes took place in Tîrgu-Mures, and each side blamed the other one for these incidents. Romanian spokesmen deplored the radicalization of the Hungarian political demands, whereas Hungarian activists accused *Vatra Romaneasca*, a Romanian cultural movement with nationalist undertones, of having engineered the bloodshed. The government behaved in an erratic way, first playing neutral and then unqualifiedly embracing the *Vatra* approach. This in turn antagonized the Hungarians who spoke of the continuity of Ceausescu's chauvinistic policy and accused the NSF of using nationalism for electoral purposes.[9] It appeared that the new leaders were ready to relinquish their initial generous promises toward ethnic minorities and resume the time-honored ethnocentric policies of the deposed dictatorship. This could only feed frustrations among the Hungarian minority and complicate relations with the Republic of Hungary.

Civil War or National Reconciliation?

Learning the democratic process is difficult in a country with few democratic traditions. On 21 May 1990 Romanians could vote freely for the first time in more than fifty years. Paradoxically, instead of overwhelmingly defeating the neo-Communist NSF, a large majority of Romanians gave Iliescu and his formation the benefit of their doubts. The opposition parties suffered a crushing defeat, and the Front's presidential candidate triumphed with more than 85 percent of the national vote. The NSF candidates also obtained the majority in the bicameral Parliament. Once again, compared with other former Communist countries, Romania was exceptional. The secret of the NSF's landslide lay in the systematically entertained ambiguities about this party's real attitude toward communism. For instance, the day before the election, the daily *Azi*—the official newspaper published by the NSF—maintained that Iliescu's victory would be the best guarantee against a return to communism. According to statements made by Ion Iliescu, Petre Roman, and Sylviu Brucan, the Front did not have anything in common with the execrated RCP, the party of the former dictator Nicolae Ceausescu. On the contrary, according to this self-serving mythology, the NSF was the embodiment of the purest dreams of the anti-Communist upheaval that swept away Ceausescu and his clan in December 1989. On various occasions, Iliescu recognized the historical failure of the Communist utopia.[10] Any thoroughgoing discussion on the legacy of communism was skillfully avoided as the NSF leaders proclaimed that the RCP had passed away together with Ceausescu. Simultaneously, the Front's propaganda exploited the widespread apprehensions among Romanians regarding the dangers of a sweeping transition to a market economy.

The opposition was fragmented and unprepared for such competition. Clinging to the memory of their bygone splendor, the "historical parties" failed to stir responsive chords among middle-aged Romanians who saw these formations as structurally different from what they had been accustomed to for decades. The Front's rhetoric sounded familiar, and many were ready to trust Iliescu because he appeared the closest to their understanding of politics. Thus, a paternalistic temptation motivated the decisions of the majority to support the NSF. This paternalistic temptation reached disturbing levels in such electoral slogans as "when Iliescu comes, the sun rises." On the other hand, one should mention the government's intimidating actions during the electoral campaign when the opposition's activists were often harassed and slandered. Ironically, for many Romanians, voting for the NSF appeared as the only alternative to a slide into anarchy.

The NSF victory, however, did not mean the end of the democratization process in Romania. Neither did it imply a long-term victory for the Front, which, after all, is a heterogenous formation whose leadership includes former Communist bureaucrats, technocrats, intellectuals, revolutionary romantics, and political adventurers. They will have to meet the demands of an increasingly dissatisfied population in a country with limited economic resources. For the moment, the Front has managed to capitalize on the ordinary Romanian's fear of the opposition's intention to marketize the ailing Stalinist economy and the possible economic fallout—the fear of the unknown. Promising job security and increased food supplies, the NSF could assuage many misgivings about its revolutionary credentials. If these policies fail, the Front will be held responsible for the dismal economic situation and a new wave of unrest will follow.

The dictator's fall signified the end of more than four decades of brutal Stalinism. But it has not led to the end of communism in any form. Neither has it ushered in full-fledged pluralism. The question arises: How can one save a spontaneous revolution from being co-opted by those adept in the Leninist techniques of manipulation? The issue is to explain both the tremendous amplitude of the revolutionary upheaval and also its failure to engender political forms attuned to the rising hopes and expectations of the Romanians.

Romania is different from the other Eastern European countries because it had never undergone de-Stalinization. It had never passed through the process of moving from the absolute and totalitarian rule of one man to the (slightly less absolute) authoritarian rule of a Communist Politburo. The distinction between these two forms of oppression may seem irrelevant to Westerners, but it is striking to people who live under them. A single absolute ruler, in the mold of Ceausescu, means a rule unchecked and unmoderated in its arbitrariness, ignorance, and cruelty. A Politburo, even one made up of self-serving individuals, at least provides a moderating check against the worst depravities of any one member. The degree of hatred that oppressed people feel toward their masters is bound to be different in the two cases. It is in this context that the NSF's present position in Romania and its relative success in the current domestic political scenario may be understood. As one Western commentator recently put it, the NSF's platform bears little resemblance to that adopted by Solidarity in Poland or by Václav Havel in Czechoslovakia. The NSF is akin to those reform-minded Communists who are desperately trying to rescue the sinking ship of communism in Eastern Europe without totally abandoning it and who have, as a result, been given short shrift by the electorate in the other countries. The NSF still clings to the dream of a socialism with a human face, but as Adam Michnik recently pointed out, "there is no socialism with a human face, only totalitarianism with its teeth knocked out."[11] Indeed, the NSF's international image has been seriously tarnished by its persecution of the opposition and its reluctance to admit the need to apply a Polish-style "shock therapy" to the ailing Romanian economy. Iliescu and his associates will not be able to govern without offering a social contract to the increasingly disaffected Romanians. Thus, it is likely that the government will try to broaden its political base and avoid the exclusive exercise of power. As the economic situation becomes increasingly tense, the Front will be confronted with movements of despair and rage. Under these circumstances, the NSF—or any party that would be its successor—will try to establish a populist authoritarian regime. Liberalization will subside and new laws will be enacted to secure the Front's supremacy. Iliescu's encomiastic treatment by the official propaganda suggests that the Front considers charismatic leadership—a self-styled version of "enlightened despotism"—as a possible consensus-building strategy.

New political parties will emerge in the near future. Instead of being past-oriented, these formations will articulate the political and social interests and aspirations of various categories of Romanian citizens. It will be their task to familiarize Romanians with democracy and to make them understand the virtues of freedom. Between the revolution and achievement of political pluralism lies the shadow of a people scared into submission by the long experience of totalitarianism. It is likely that the NSF itself will split between partisans of limited reforms and those who advocate the decisive break with the old institutions and habits. The awakening of the civil society will contribute to the flourishing of grassroots movements and groups whose role will be to exert continuous pressure on the government and permit citizens to experience genuine political participation. For the time being, young Romanians are viscerally suspicious of political parties. Like their peers in Hungary, Poland, and Czechoslovakia, they resent authority and fear the institutional solidification of their activism. The older generations, on the other hand, tend to be innately conservative and suspicious of any "foreign" influences that may deprive them of the little they have gained under the NSF—a trait that the Front propagandists have exploited to the hilt. It is thus likely that umbrella movements will soon be formed to magnetize the political energies of those Romanians who voted for the NSF because of their lack of enthusiasm for the still uninspiring opposition parties. The backbone of this emerging civic culture exists already: the hundreds of informal groups and associations that endorsed the "Proclamation of Timisoara" and formed a national alliance to pursue the goals codified in that document. But the national trauma of the dictatorship and the political fallout of the revolution have left a legacy. The independent social forces will eventually have to coordinate their actions in a broad democratic movement. In other words, the opposition itself is not limited to its current expressions. The existing political spectrum should thus be seen as provisional, the first station on Romania's road to freedom.

Notes

1. For the nature of the post-Ceausescu political power in Romania, see Vladimir Tismaneanu, "New Masks, Old Faces: The Romanian Junta's Familiar Look," *New Republic*, 5 Feb. 1990, 17–21; and idem, "Between Revolutions: Vying for the Spoils of the Christmas Uprising," *New Republic*, 23 Apr. 1990, 23–25.

2. For analyses of Romania's political system under Ceausescu, see Mary Ellen Fischer, *Nicolae Ceausescu: A Study in Political Leadership* (Boulder and London: Lynne Rienner, 1989); Kenneth Jowitt, *Revolutionary Breakthroughs and National Development: The Case of Romania* (Berkeley: University of California Press, 1971); Michael Shafir, *Romania: Politics, Economics and Society* (Boulder: Lynne Rienner, 1985); and Vladimir Tismaneanu, "Personal Power and Political Crisis in Romania," *Government and Opposition* (London) 24 (Spring 1989): 177–98.

3. After the revolution, Bobu was tried and received a life sentence for his "participation in the genocide against the Romanian nation."

4. See Vladimir Tismaneanu, "The Rebellion of the Old Guard" and the full text of the "Letter of the Six" in *East European Reporter* 3 (Spring/Summer 1989): 23–25.

5. See Nicolae Ceausescu's report presented to the Fourteenth RCP Congress, *Scinteia*, 21 Nov. 1989 (English translation in FBIS-Eastern Europe, 22 Nov. 1989, 58–84). For the antireformist direction of the Congress, see Alan Riding, "Romanian Leader Refuses Changes," *New York Times*, 21 Nov. 1989, and "In Romania, Fear Still Outweighs Hope," ibid., 24 Nov. 1989.

6. See Olivier Weber, "La revolution confisquee," *Le Point* (Paris), 30 Apr. 1990, 46–47.

7. See Jean-François Revel, "Roumanie: flagrant delit," *Le Point* (Paris), 12 Mar. 1990, 87.

8. See "Proclamatia de la Timosoara," *Romania Libera*, 20 Mar. 1990 (English translation, FBIS — Eastern Europe, 4 Apr. 1990, 60–63).

9. For an in-depth examination of the nationalities conflict in Transylvania, see Vladimir Socor, "Forces of Old Resurface in Romania: The Ethnic Clashes in Tirgu-Mures," *Report on Eastern Europe*, no. 15, 13 Apr. 1990, 36–43.

10. See "Un entretien avec Ion Iliescu: Le large sourire du 'pere de la nation,'" *Le Monde* (Paris), 17 May 1990.

11. See Steve Crawshaw, "In Search of the Paris of the East," *The Independent*, 19 May 1990.

The Impact of Europe 1992
on the United States

STEPHEN COONEY

It should surprise no one that a transformation of the economic and political landscape is taking place simultaneously in Eastern and Western Europe. As Austrian Chancellor Franz Vranitsky noted in justifying his country's application for membership in the European Community (EC), perestroika and 1992 are two sides of the same European coin. Or, as the general counsel of a major French company once remarked to this author, there is a wind of deregulation blowing in Europe — from Reagan's America, through Thatcher's Britain, and now across the Continent.

While no one can equate the postwar democracies of Western Europe with the authoritarian Communist governments of Eastern Europe in any moral or political sense, there is one essential similarity in the economic sense. By the early 1980s both Western and Eastern Europe were suffering economically from excesses of central-government planning and control, budgetary indiscipline, and the distortions of government subsidization run amok in response to domestic political priorities. The problems were much worse, of course, in Eastern Europe, because these countries lacked the regulator of democratic control over governments whose economic policies were bankrupt. But in Western Europe the phenomenon of "Eurosclerosis" seemed to demand new thinking in response to persistent problems of low growth, unemployment, inflation, and government deficits.

The proposal to complete the development of a single internal European Community market by the end of 1992 (EC-92) represented a creative response to this situation. EC-92 foresaw efficiency and competitiveness gains from the unification of EC markets on the international level. In the late 1970s, the dynamic had moved in the other direction, thanks to EC-constructed or EC-endorsed produc-

The author is director, International Investment and Finance, National Association of Manufacturers, but the views expressed in this essay are his own and do not represent the policy positions of the association.

tion cartels and national quotas aimed at protecting national production and employment bases through a policy of *sauve qui peut*. At the time, the rule of unanimity, based on the "Luxembourg compromise" of 1965, was slowing the development of EC integration policies even in the areas of competence clearly granted to it by members under the Treaty of Rome of 1957. The solution proposed under the EC-92 approach is to improve national economic performance by creating a more integrated EC-wide market, facilitated by constitutional changes in the EC structure itself.[1]

Many cynics say that national competitiveness within Europe will never be buried, and EC-92 will therefore never amount to more than cosmetic fluff. The nature of the program and its relative success to date will be reviewed below, but here it should be made clear that the United States private sector takes EC-92 very seriously. The private sector takes it seriously because EC-92 is driven by a certain inherent economic logic that has tended to overcome or to erode political resistance to change throughout the history of the postwar era in Europe. The struggle for national economic advantage within the EC framework will persist. After all, states, localities, and regions still struggle for economic advantages under the United States constitutional system. But a major, and on the whole positive, change is taking place within Europe.

The Primary United States Interest in 1992 Is Economic

United States foreign-policy attitudes toward Western Europe are heavily influenced by a focus on the North Atlantic Treaty Organization (NATO). The first question that observers ask is, What will be the impact on NATO and the United States leadership role? This concern with the "structure of the alliance" is, for example, at the center of a recent analysis of EC-92 in a *Foreign Affairs* article by Robert Hormats, formerly assistant secretary of state and a respected American observer of United States–European relations.[2]

What tends to be forgotten is that NATO itself is an instrument, not a policy goal. The goal that NATO addresses is the military containment of the Soviet Union. Even as an instrument of military containment, however, NATO has always been seen as only half the solution — the other half being the economic prosperity and political stability of the individual European nations. Because the postwar Soviet military threat was seen as working on two levels — overt military pressure and domestic subversion — United States policymakers instituted responses to both those levels: NATO and the Marshall Plan.

Since EC-92 is primarily an instrument of economic policy, perhaps the first reaction should not be to determine the impact on United States political and military leadership of the Western alliance but to consider how it affects the other side of the policy equation — the economic well-being of Western Europe. Removing internal market barriers to create a more dynamic EC market is good economic policy, and the United States should not discourage it. EC-92, it is reasonably clear, has been a major part of the successful response of Western Europe to the economic crisis of the 1970s and early 1980s.

In Eastern Europe, by contrast, the Communist economic system was effectively destroyed, bringing the political system down with it. Within a few months, it appears that a peaceful "rollback" of communism has been achieved to a degree that an old "cold warrior" like former United States Secretary of State John Foster Dulles would have hardly dreamed possible. EC-92, by displaying the vigor, creativity, and high level of voluntary international cooperation with which Western democracies can deal with economic crises, played no small role in discrediting the regimes of Eastern Europe and the Soviet Union.

United States economic policies have also served as a free-market beacon, showing other countries how a decentralized economy led by the private sector generates jobs and growth. Since 1970, furthermore, the goal of economic performance has been elevated to greater prominence than in the early cold-war years. Industrialized, socialist, and Third World countries have all searched for successful economic models that can deliver the goods, whatever political changes are necessary to accommodate economic goals. But the twin trade and federal-budget deficits have undermined the United States position in the world economy and today threaten its political leadership. United States enjoyment of what appears to be the ultimate demonstration of the success of free-market economics — the triumph of liberal democracy and the failure of communism — is dampened by the persistence of its own major economic problems.

In short, the United States must eliminate its trade and current-account deficits, which exceed $100 billion every year. And it must do this without an austerity policy and a major shrinkage of demand, which would not only lower the United States standard of living but also threaten the recovery of growth and trade that has occurred worldwide since the late 1980s. Domestically, a big part of the answer is to eliminate the United States federal budget deficit that depresses productive investment and overstimulates American consumption of imports. But this is not the only answer. The United States must also continue the rapid growth of exports that has already occurred since the fall of the dollar and the recovery of growth in most world markets.

In this context, the EC market may be the key one. It is already the largest United States regional market, and a reasonably well-integrated one, unlike the "Pacific Rim" market. The United States needs EC-92 to be successful not only because of its long-term military and strategic goals in Europe. It also needs the business of a successful, dynamic, and open EC market. The remainder of this essay will therefore explore both the concept and the prospects of EC-92 and what a successful and dynamic EC-92 program has meant and will mean for the economic future of the United States.

EC-92: An Expanding Concept

The very failure to complete the common market as originally envisioned led to the development of EC-92. For this reason the key EC-92 document, the white paper of 1985, is entitled "*Completion* of the Internal Market" (emphasis added).[3]

Both the political momentum of the program and the impulse of the dramatic events in Eastern Europe, however, have altered the character of 1992 into something requiring an altogether broader vision. Hence the formal adoption of the Social Charter and the European Monetary Union (EMU) projects at the Strasbourg summit of EC heads of government in December 1989.

How realistic was the United States concern, prominent in 1988 and early 1989, that the EC was really creating a "Fortress Europe"? At no point, it seems, was the major thrust of the program the creation of a protectionist "Fortress Europe." On the other hand, there has always been the consciousness that non-EC countries could end up gaining greater advantages from some aspects of EC-92 than members of the EC itself. Therefore, the program has contained discriminatory features to ensure that this would not happen, at least not without reciprocal benefits for the EC. Some of these problems that have also affected United States policy will be considered in the last section of this essay.

The initial driving force behind EC-92 was the awareness that market integration under the Treaty of Rome had lost momentum by the late 1970s. De facto trade barriers that continued to prevent the realization of a truly integrated market created substantial costs for EC producers and consumers. According to the European Commission's official study, summarized in the report *The European Challenge—1992* by Paolo Cecchini, the result of eliminating such barriers (or the "cost of non-Europe") may equal 3 to 6 percent of Europe's gross domestic product, or a total of $250 billion annually.[4]

These costs were tolerable in the 1950s and 1960s as the European economies boomed. But the impact of Eurosclerosis created rising concern, not only with the burden of inefficiencies within Europe but also with the implications for the declining world competitiveness of EC industry. The initial set of proposals to establish a fully open internal market by 1992 focused on these de facto obstructions to free trade within Europe.

In 1985 the recently appointed European commissioner for the internal market, Lord Cockfield of the United Kingdom, produced the internal market white paper that has revitalized the European Community. Backed by recent decisions of the European Court of Justice, the Cockfield proposal contained a target list of about 300 directives and other policy actions, aimed at eliminating effective barriers to the internal market. Taken together, these directives would eliminate all remaining physical barriers to the movement of persons and goods within the European Community, eliminate differences in national technical standards as barriers to the free movement of goods, eliminate national differences in indirect tax rates as a trade barrier, and eliminate barriers to the free flow of capital within the EC. Moreover, Lord Cockfield insisted that the entire package had to be achieved by a specific date—1992—or the whole process would be blocked by member countries picking the benefits they wanted and dragging their feet on the rest. Cockfield's program was both encouraged and fully backed by the European Commission president, Jacques Delors.

One major constitutional change in the Treaty of Rome was required to make the process work. The rule of unanimity on all items deemed to be of essential "national interest" had to be scrapped, at least so far as the basic internal market reforms were concerned. This change was adopted by the Single European Act (SEA), formally ratified by all members in mid-1987. This series of amendments established that most internal-market directives would be adopted by qualified majorities. No one member government could block directives by withholding its consent.[5]

Most of the major technical directives aimed at enhancing the internal market have been proposed, debated, and approved with a rapidity that is surprising to veteran observers of the European Community. These include most of the directives that will affect United States business interests. The rate of implementation of directives in member state laws has been less satisfactory. And some of the other major elements of the original program, particularly the harmonization of value-added tax rates among members and the free movement of individuals across national frontiers, have created more serious political difficulties. There is not yet a basic agreement among members on the essential outlines of harmonized policies to be implemented by 1992. Significantly, under the SEA, proposals in these areas are still subject to unanimous approval by members rather than to qualified majority votes.

In January 1989, President Delors became the first head of the commission appointed by member governments for a second term since the very first president, Walter Hallstein. The commissioner of the internal market program since the beginning of 1989 has been Martin Bangemann, formerly economics minister of Germany. Bangemann replaced Lord Cockfield, who was not reappointed by the British government. Prime Minister Margaret Thatcher strongly disagreed with some of Cockfield's policy stands and the fast pace of the 1992 program that he supported. "Arthur," she is reported to have said, "has gone native." But the continuation of a strong team under Delors's leadership, including another former British Conservative cabinet member, Sir Leon Brittan, as commissioner for competition policy, has contributed to an intensification of the EC-92 process.

Prime Minister Thatcher's well-publicized disagreements with the direction of EC-92 do not involve the original program so much as the expanded vision that has been encouraged, largely by EC President Delors and President François Mitterrand of France. Thatcher has repeatedly cited commission reports, which indicate that Britain actually has the best record to date of implementing EC directives into law. Her concern is with what she perceives as a wrong direction taken in expanding 1992 to include a "social dimension" of the harmonization of worker rights and a full-fledged monetary union, including a single currency and a central bank.

Neither of these initiatives directly threatens the international economic interests of the United States. The agreement to free capital movements and to eliminate national capital controls, already set for 1 July 1990, addresses the major practical concern of United States companies operating in the EC. The battle over the "second and third stages" of the Delors report on economic and monetary union is primarily a political issue, in that free capital movements and the continuation of the European Monetary System of tightly regulated currency parities already place strong constraints on the freedom of national monetary policies.

Similarly, EC social policy does not yet contain any elements that discriminate against United States economic interests. The "social dimension" does contain some concepts that could lead to a premature effort to harmonize working conditions in Europe and thus discourage new investment and the creation of new jobs — an equal concern both to American companies that operate in Europe and to EC-based companies. To date, what has been agreed — with the prominent dissent of the British government — is the Social Charter, a document of uncertain legal status serving only as "a reference point for taking fuller account in the future of the social dimension of the Community,"[6] according to the official Strasbourg communiqué.

The greater significance of these two issues is that they add a new European political dimension to the EC-92 process. Since 1988 this departure of the EC-92 program from narrower economic concerns already in the EC's sphere of competence, along with the establishment of a lead role for the EC itself in formulating aid policies for Poland and Hungary (as agreed at the Paris G-7 economic summit), has been encouraged by the changes in Eastern Europe. Not only the internal market but also the future constitution of Europe may be at issue. In the long run, it will be important for United States interests whether the EC maintains a "Europe of States" (a phrase coined by Charles de Gaulle and a policy adopted by Thatcher) or intensifies political integration to provide a common EC front for dealing with the new situation to the East.[7] But it appears that this decision will be made by Europeans themselves, without decisive influence or input from the United States.

The Impact of EC-92 on United States International Economic Interests

The EC has become the only major regional trading partner with which the United States has restored a trade surplus since the early 1980s. The rapid improvement of the United States trade position with the EC and the prospect of further export gains flowing from the dynamic growth effects of EC-92 perhaps constitute the most significant aspect of EC-92 for American foreign policy.

It has become a cliché to say that unsatisfactory economic performance is undermining the United States global leadership position. The budget deficit, the trade deficit, and the need to finance these deficits with a large inflow of foreign capital into the United States have seriously weakened the American claim to global economic leadership — and possibly to political leadership as well.

The major initiative in the 1980s to stem the rise of the United States trade deficit and then to reverse it was the 1985 policy decision to seek a reduction in the exchange rate of the American dollar. Coordinated actions by the United States government with the governments of other major industrial countries led to a fall of about 50 percent in the dollar against the Japanese yen and the major European currencies by the beginning of 1988. Since then, the dollar's trend has been mixed with periods of sharp rises and subsequent falls, aided by continued governmental exchange market policies.

The overall decline in the dollar's value since 1985, combined with the resumption or strengthening of growth in major United States export markets served to reduce the American merchandise trade deficit from $152 billion at its highest level in 1987 to an estimated $110 billion in 1989. Since 1987, the United States has reversed the trends of the earlier 1980s and entered into a period of export-led growth. From 1981 through 1987, a worsening United States trade balance acted as a drag on growth in real gross national product (GNP). But from 1988 through the first three quarters of 1989, improving trade performance contributed to GNP growth. Real United States annual growth averaged 3.6 percent, compared with only 2.8 percent without the direct impact of trade deficit change. However, because of the leveling out of dollar exchange-rate performance and an expected moderation in growth abroad, both the United States Treasury and the International Monetary Fund (IMF) expect a possible worsening of the United States trade deficit again in 1990–91.[8] Hence the critical importance of foreign markets for the United States in the early 1990s.

The EC has been the key market in the improvement of the United States trade deficit from 1987 through 1989. As table 1 shows, the net improvement in the United States trade balance with the EC of $23 billion since 1987 has accounted for more than half of the overall net improvement of $42 billion. From a United States deficit of over $20 billion annually with the EC in both 1986 and 1987, the trade balance improved dramatically, achieving a small surplus in 1989. This dramatic turnaround is to be explained by a number of factors. One is the resumption of dynamic growth in the EC, which has explicitly been linked to the forward dynamic effects of the 1992 process.[9] Furthermore, unlike Japan, where there has

TABLE 1

United States Trade Balances, 1985–89[a]

Trading Partner or Region	United States Trade Balance ($ billions)		
	1985	1987	1989
World	−126	−152	−110
European Community	−19	−21	2
Canada	−16	−11	−9
Japan	−46	−59	−50
East Asia newly industrializing countries (NICs)[b]	−22	−34	−25
Latin America[c]	−16	−12	−11
Organization of Petroleum Exporting Countries (OPEC)	−9	−13	−9

Source: U.S. Department of Commerce, United States Trade Performance in 1988 (Washington D.C., September 1989); Highlights of U.S. Export and Import Trade (FT-990), December 1986; and "U.S. Merchandise Trade," (FT-900), October 1989.

[a] January–October 1989 at annual rate.
[b] Taiwan, Korea, Singapore, and Hong Kong.
[c] Both Latin America and OPEC totals include Venezuela and Ecuador.

been similar currency appreciation against the dollar and strong domestic growth combined with a large and continuing United States bilateral deficit, the EC market is relatively open to American goods so that any change in the exchange rate affects relative demand.

The EC may remain the key foreign growth market for many American companies, especially if EC-92 creates a more dynamic and open EC market. Europe is the most important United States regional market and will probably remain so indefinitely. In 1989, 24 percent of United States exports were shipped to the EC, which has overtaken Canada (22 percent) as the largest regional or national market. Japan's share of 1989 exports was 12 percent, half the EC level, and the four East Asian newly industrializing countries (NICs) listed in table 1 accounted for another 10 percent. These are also important and rapidly growing markets, but, especially in Japan, there remain market barriers to United States exports and investment that are greater than the barriers in the EC, while regional integration is far less. The same is true of Latin America, which takes 12 percent of United States exports, more than half to Mexico alone. Latin America is further handicapped by its low level of development and by its financial problems, in addition to market fragmentation.

The improvement in the United States balance with the EC has primarily been on the export side. United States export growth there has been near or above double-digit rates since 1985 — 9 percent in 1986, 14 percent in 1987, an amazing 25 percent in 1988, and a further 15 percent on an annual basis in the first three quarters of 1989. By 1990, United States exports to the EC will probably surpass $90 billion; thus they will have doubled in only five years. The scale of such export growth is hard to comprehend. For example, that five-year export increase to the EC for 1985–90 will be about equal to the estimated total United States exports to Japan, the world's second largest national market, in 1989 ($45 billion). The boost American exports have received from the EC has been the equivalent of suddenly finding a new island export market the size of Japan off United States shores.

There remains the problem of protectionist trends in EC-92, which have led to concerns over "Fortress Europe." Surely, it is sometimes argued, the EC will not simply allow United States companies — whether as exporters or investors — to share prominently in the benefits of the EC market. Two factors weigh strongly against such a policy aimed at the United States.

First, the United States market has been open to EC trade and investment. Indeed, the strong growth of EC exports to the United States market in the mid-1980s was largely responsible for "jump-starting" the sluggish EC economies of that period. From 1981 to 1985, the United States trade balance with the EC worsened as rapidly as it did with Japan — from a $14 billion surplus to a deficit of $18 billion, or a turnaround of over $30 billion. During the period 1981–85, 43 percent of all GNP growth in West Germany was due to its growth in exports to the United States; 39 percent, in Italy; and 26 percent, in France.[10] Even though EC export growth to the United States market slowed in 1988–89, the reversal of the United States trade deficit with the EC has been accomplished within a framework of continued EC export growth overall to the American market. The average rate of growth has been 6 percent a year since 1985, and the United States is the EC's largest world export market.

Under these circumstances, the EC is unlikely to be unduly concerned by changes in the bilateral balance with the United States, as long as it maintains its dynamic growth and as long as it is clear that EC products and companies have reasonable access to the trading partner's market. This is clearly not the case with Japan, which is why that country, not the United States, tends to be the primary target of "reciprocity" provisions that are part of many EC-92 proposals. It must also be remembered that the EC is not a monolith. There is often substantial disagreement between EC members' interests on how to deal with such external trade problems. An excellent example is the contrast in the views put forward on the external dimension of EC-92 in 1989 by the major French and West German industry associations.[11]

The other factor militating against protectionist policies is that EC companies need advanced United States capital-goods exports and technologies to maintain and improve competitiveness. People who criticize the quality of American goods in stores often overlook that the United States comparative advantage on world markets is primarily in manufactured capital goods, which account for a third of all United States exports.

These industries have benefited greatly from the EC growth recovery leading up to 1992 because, as the EC's own latest economic forecast points out, EC investment growth — especially in equipment — has been extremely high in the last few years.[12] The author recently surveyed in congressional testimony the comparative performance of ten United States high-technology sectors, primarily capital goods, in trade with Japan and the EC. From 1985 through 1988, United States exports in almost all of these areas showed high double-digit growth and a dramatically improved trade balance. For example, computer exports increased by 67 percent, and the American surplus grew by $2.4 billion, to over $6 billion. Despite heavy EC government subsidies for Airbus, United States aircraft exports nearly doubled, and the surplus increased from $1.3 billion to $3 billion. In power-generating equipment, which includes all types of engines and parts, there was a $1 billion swing, as a substantial United States deficit improved to a small surplus. In comparison, despite similarly favorable exchange-rate changes for United States exporters, the comparable trade balance with Japan on a product-by-product basis worsened or showed little change.[13]

Specific EC-92 Concerns of United States Interests

Despite the favorable outlook for United States economic interests, neither United States policymakers nor the private sector should overlook specific EC-92 policy proposals or other EC policies during the same period that may have discriminatory or adverse consequences for American interests. Some of the concerns of the American industrial community, for example, have focused on the harmonization of standards and certification; public procurement; and rules of origin, local content, and common commercial policies.

Harmonization of standards and certification. With the development of EC-wide product standards and testing procedures on the basis of mutual recognition and equivalence promises in order to create a large market, products will theoretically have to meet only a single standard to be sold in all member countries. While new EC-wide standards are supposed to be developed in accordance with existing international standards, often there are no accepted international standards or such standards may differ from EC-established essential minimum safety requirements.

Many United States producers have expressed concern that they will have no access to the system in order to ensure that their products are not disadvantaged by new standards and testing procedures. The EC and the European private standardization bodies in 1989 responded to these comments by publishing information on standards projects at early stages of development and by agreeing to consider consultation with accredited non-EC bodies on specific problems that may arise.[14] The EC has also said that it will consider mutual recognition agreements with non-EC bodies on testing and certification after developing its own harmonized system. But any such agreement must be based on effective reciprocal access.

Public procurement. Both United States industry and the United States government have expressed support for strengthening existing EC rules on the opening of member-government procurement and extending EC rules to utilities (telecommunications, energy, water, and transportation) excluded from EC or General Agreement on Tariffs and Trade (GATT) discipline. But the utilities directive establishes an EC content provision that requires a member country to favor bids containing at least 50 percent EC content over non-EC bids within a margin of preference and allows member governments to ignore non-EC bids altogether. This provision may be included in the directive only as a bargaining chip for the purpose of ultimately securing a multilateral procurement agreement that includes these sectors and grants EC producers rights of reciprocal access. But American companies are complaining that the public-procurement EC content rule has increased customer pressure in Europe for goods produced within the EC.

Rules of origin, local content, and common commercial policies. Completion of the internal market may result in the replacement of the formal or informal national import quotas that still exist in the EC with EC-wide measures. United States interests are particularly concerned that the EC may replace national quotas on car imports from Japan in some major member countries (France, Italy, Spain, and the United Kingdom) with EC-wide quotas that would also be applied to cars that may be produced by or with Japanese companies in the United States and subsequently exported to Europe. This could be done by requiring that cars sold by Japanese companies or affiliates pass an EC content test to avoid inclusion in the Japanese quota.

Other measures enacted by the EC outside the EC-92 framework have increased concerns that EC policies are being driven by a desire to encourage import-substitution investment in the EC. These include a decision on the rules of origin on semiconductors that would be subject to the high (14 percent) EC tariff and a decision that the Japanese copier company Ricoh circumvented EC antidumping duties by shipping products from its factory in the United States. In response to such concerns, the European Commission, in the statement of 1 November 1989, disclaimed any intention of using rules-of-origin decisions to distort investment or trade and accepted a United States proposal to negotiate a multilateral rules-of-origin agreement.[15]

This is only a partial list of some of the major issues that have created problems for American companies in the context of EC-92. First, what should be noted about these and other contentious proposals is that they are often a double-edged sword — often containing market-opening features as well as provisions that may disadvantage United States economic interests. But whether American companies are the target of these provisions or simply caught in the cross-fire of EC proposals aimed at Japan is irrelevant to those responsible for determining how best to take advantage of the expanding EC market.

Second, in many cases the EC has been responsive to United States complaints about its policies and has modified or offered to discuss provisions that cause concern. This does not mean that most of these problems are yet resolved — part of the problem, as with the Japanese car quotas and the harmonization of testing and certification, is that the EC itself has not resolved its own internal-policy debates. But it does mean that a dialogue has been established and the United States government has revised earlier views that a comprehensive "Fortress Europe" policy is being developed.

One final point addresses a key feature of some of these issues and is also crucial in determining the long-term United States interest in EC-92. Many policies that are in dispute between the United States and the EC are alleged to contain an element of "forced investment"— increasing investment in production facilities to obtain fully equal treatment within the EC. This issue is not only a direct policy concern between the United States government and the EC Commission and member governments, but it also tends to pit American economic interests against one another. It remains to be seen whether the companies that invest in the EC will have advantages over those that seek to service the EC market primarily through exports.

Economic pressures further complicate this issue by encouraging companies to invest locally in order to become major players in a foreign market for the long term. Such United States investment will almost certainly increase in the EC. United States direct investment in manufacturing in the EC by the end of 1988 accounted for about half of total United States direct foreign investment in manufacturing worldwide; it had increased in value by almost one-third since 1986. The interests of United States exporters and investors are not contradictory: about one-third of United States exports to the EC consistently go to the EC affiliates of American direct investors.[16] Almost certainly a large part of this relationship is accounted for by the heavy United States export emphasis on capital goods.

Conclusion

In *The Revolt of the Masses*, first published in 1930, the Spanish political philosopher José Ortega y Gasset suggested that Europe was not becoming Americanized but that the United States was the first country to become modernized. This thought seems particularly relevant to the era of EC-92. The members of the European Community will maintain their individuality, different from one another and from the United States. But this does not preclude the growing convergence of functional similarities in the economic and business sphere; countries on both sides of the Atlantic have much to learn from one another.

It is also probable that the growth of economic interrelationships has now increased to the point where it cannot be forcibly reduced without causing serious economic damage to both parties. In the early 1980s the rapid growth of United States imports from Europe, perhaps encouraged by an unwise and unintentional combination of United States policies, had a beneficial effect in stimulating a revival of economic growth within the EC. With the fall of the dollar and stronger growth in the EC, the trade balance has now shifted dramatically back to the neutral point — but EC companies have also established a large direct investment presence in the United States. The relationship has now matured, so that, as in textbook economics, it may be the major macroeconomic swings that govern the bilateral economic relationship. Thus, the growth dynamics of EC-92 could enable the United States to improve its overall current account and trade balances. But this relationship need not lead to a permanent position of dependence in either direction.

NOTES

1. Michael Calingaert, *The 1992 Challenge from Europe: Development of the European Community's Internal Market* (Washington, D.C.: National Planning Association, 1988), part 1.

2. Robert Hormats, "Redefining Europe and the Atlantic Link," *Foreign Affairs* 68 (Fall 1989): 71–91; Stanley Hoffmann, "The European Community and 1992," ibid, 43–46.

3. Commission of the European Communities, *Completing the Internal Market* (Luxembourg: Office for Official Publications of the European Communities, 1985).

4. Paolo Cecchini, *The European Challenge—1992: The Benefits of a Single Market* (Aldershot, U.K.: Wildwood, 1988), 98.

5. The official summary, *Treaties Establishing the European Communities*, abridged ed. (Luxembourg: Office for Official Publications of the European Communities, 1987), contains the full text of the Single European Act and notes all changes to the original Treaty of Rome. An excellent short survey of the revised process is Sandra J. Thompson, "The Making of an Internal Market Directive," *Business America*, 1 Aug. 1988, 12.

6. EC Office of Press and Public Affairs, *European Community News*, no. 41/89, 11 Dec. 1989, 6.

7. Hoffmann, 33, 41–42.

8. U.S. Department of the Treasury, *Report to the Congress on International Economic and Exchange Rate Policy* (Oct. 1989), 14; International Monetary Fund, *World Economic Outlook*, Oct. 1989, 14–15.

9. Commission of the European Communities, Directorate-General for Economic and Financial Affairs, *Economic Forecasts*, 1989–1990, Sept.-Oct. 1989, 2.

10. *U.S. Trade Balance at a Turning Point* (Washington, D.C.: National Association of Manufacturers, 1986), 13–14.

11. Bundesverband der Deutschen Industrie, *Completion of the Single European Market: Consequences for the European Community's External Economic Relations — German Industries' View* (Cologne: BDI, 1989); Conseil National du Patronat Français, *Volet extérieur du Marche unique européen et Politique commerciale commune* (Paris: CNPF, 1989); English translation available.

12. EC *Economic Forecasts*, 4.

13. See this author's prepared statement, provided at the hearing of the U.S. House of Representatives Committee on Science, Space and Technology, 101st Cong., 1st sess., 17 May 1989, 4–6, and table 1 in this essay.

14. A good overview of United States industry concerns was provided in the hearings on *Europe 1992: Product Standards and Testing*, U.S. House of Representatives, Committee on Foreign Affairs, Subcommittees on International Economic Policy and Trade, and Europe and the Middle East, 101st Cong. 1st sess., 13 Apr. 1989. The author has discussed the United States industry perspective and the EC response in more detail in testimony before the U.S. Government Working Group on European Community Standards, Testing and Certification Issues (U.S. Department of Commerce, 26 July 1989).

15. EC Office of Press and Public Affairs, *European Community News* no. 39/89, "The European Community Will Continue to Apply the Rules of Origin in a Way Which Will Not Affect Trade or Investment," 1 Nov. 1989.

16. U.S. Department of Commerce, Bureau of Economic Analysis, *U.S. Direct Investment Abroad: Operations of U.S. Parent Companies and Their Foreign Affiliates — Preliminary 1987 Estimates*, July 1989, table 16; and Bureau of the Census, *Highlights of U.S. Export and Import Trade* (FT-90), Dec. 1987, U.S. Exports table 5.

Spiritual Resistance in Eastern Europe

JOHN A. COLEMAN, S.J.

The map and rulers of Eastern Europe have shifted so many times since 1792 that it would be foolhardy to generalize about this Balkanized, often obstreperous, and culturally diverse region. In 1975, Gerard Simon asserted: "In most countries of Eastern Europe, the church is no longer a first-rate social force; it is not independent and strong enough to determine current social development."[1] Even then, his generalization did not ring true for Catholicism in Poland and Yugoslavia or Lutheranism in East Germany. Standard social- and political-science accounts of life in Eastern Europe (with the glaring exception of Poland) doggedly continued their analyses as if the churches did not exist or exert any political leverage or cultural sway. Only rare social-science monographs, Keston College's *Religion in Communist Lands*, and occasional papers from Radio Free Europe skillfully explored the role of the churches.

The churches' restricted role under Communist regimes needs to be seen in context. As Bogdan Denitch, discussing the Yugoslavian church in the mid-1970s, noted: "The religious organizations are the *only* organizations outside the formal political system permitted to exist. Insofar as they are subject to governmental and party pressure, they are far less subject to that pressure than any other group making a claim to independent and separate loyalty would be. No other group which does not support the legitimacy and desirability of the existing social order, irrespective of its political pedigree, has been permitted an independent organized existence. Certainly, no group with supra-national organizational ties has been allowed to exist."[2]

To be sure, after the Communist takeover in the late 1940s, a general pattern employed tactics to harass the church, foil internal church autonomy, and restrict religion to the church sanctuary and private sphere and to keep it out of society as such. Show trials of Cardinals Joseph Beran of Prague, József Mindzenty of Budapest, and Aloysius Stepinac of Zagreb horrified the world for their manifest travesty of justice. Yet it is worth recalling that, apart from show trials, almost all the tactics used by Communist regimes against the church have had precise parallels in postrevolutionary France, the Austrian empire under Joseph II, and the czarist regime in Russia. These tactics include state bureaus of religious affairs; attempts to foster autonomous national churches free from Rome or, failing that, autonomous organizations of regime-loyal priests; restricted correspondence or contact with Rome; the abolition of religious orders in Hungary and Czechoslovakia; the abolition of religious schools; the state licensing of priests; the abolition of all church charitable work with the poor, sick, or imprisoned; and the restriction of church meetings for religious instruction.

The Vatican has seemed to take these various antireligious strategies in stride since the early 1960s, perhaps because of past persecution of the church by Bismarck and Garibaldi, by the Directory and the Third Republic in France, and by Mexico. Yet religion has endured.

Indeed, with some exceptions like Lithuania and Czechoslovakia, at least since the mid-1970s religion has arguably been much freer in Eastern Europe than in Zaire, Malawi, Burma, or parts of non-Communist Southeast Asia. As Hans Jakob Stehle has noted of the metaphor of the church of silence in Eastern Europe, the church in Poland "was never, even in times of stress, a silent church but always a militant and usually victorious church."[3] In every crisis in Polish society since the end of the Stalinist period the church emerged stronger, more vital, and with new public concessions and privileges. Similarly, in 1985 the church in Yugoslavia was stronger than it had been in 1945.

Myths about the Church in Eastern Europe

Neither the Communist parties nor the various national units of Catholicism represented monoliths. In Poland, the Znak parliamentary group, the Catholic Intellectual Clubs (KIK), and the editors of the influential Catholic journals *Wiecz* and *Tygodnik Powzechny* represented a progressive Catholicism inspired by the vision of the French Catholic writer and editor of *Esprit*, Emmanuel Mounier. Other Catholic factions continued the conservative nationalism and realpolitik of Roman Dmowski. In Yugoslavia, Catholic factions included a deep-standing rivalry between the diocesan clergy and the more numerous Franciscan order in Bosnia-Hercegovina. Personal rivalries between Zagreb's Cardinal Franjo Kuharic— ecclesiastically moderate but opposed to any species of Christian-Marxist dialogue — and Archbishop Frane Franic of Split, who supports this dialogue, have fostered conflict between those who support dealing with the state and those opposed to such a dialogue. A final internal cleavage in the Yugoslav church contests the independent and progressive theological society, Christianity Today (organized as a self-managed public entity under Yugoslav law), against the clerical hierarchy in Croatia, which seeks to impose its control directly on the theological group.

Czechoslovakia and Hungary under communism included both an "official" church (recognized and, to some extent, co-opted by the regime) and an underground resistance church, both at loggerheads. The point to make, then, is that within each national church could be found servile loyalty to the Communist regime (e.g., the Association Pacem in Terris in Czechoslovakia, the group Pax in

Poland) as well as accommodationist but autonomous Catholics who espoused the ideal of Albrecht Schonherr, the Lutheran bishop of East Germany: "the church not *of* or necessarily *against* but the church *in* socialism."[4] In some churches, underground resisters turned to *samizdat* publications, unlicensed ministry through house churches, and explicit alliances with the democratic opposition. Corresponding factionalism appeared in the various Communist parties, ranging from hard-line atheists to pragmatic accommodators of the religious impulse to "secret" believers within the party.

Religion in Eastern Europe is practiced outside the church, and much "secularization" has occurred even without Communist regimes. Precise statistics for church practice in Eastern Europe can be hard to come by. In Yugoslavia, there are well-trained, Marxist sociologists of religion. In Poland, sociologists at the Catholic University of Lublin compile religious statistics (with the danger of church censorship of unpleasant findings of irregular practice and heterodox belief). But secret devotees of the church and those who worshiped in parishes distant from their home do not show up in most surveys. In general, however, the statistics show an overall decline in practice from 1945 to 1990, with an increase in the late 1970s and 1980s. Given the extraordinary rise in urbanization, industrialization, and social mobility in postwar Eastern Europe, the increased secularization of society might have occurred in any event—even without overt persecution of religion or discrimination against believers. Poland, Slovenia, Slovakia, and Croatia have relatively high levels of religious practice; elsewhere in Eastern Europe the practice approximates the low levels of Western Europe.

A decade-long spiritual revival among the young in Eastern Europe has had many sources. The unevenness of religious policy in various countries encouraged those still suffering religious restrictions to contemplate—or demand—change. Those who experienced new concessions from the regime could hope for further concessions as part of "normalization." For their part, the Communist regimes, seeking greater legitimacy after the mid-1970s, made overtures to the religious communities. A new boldness in religious literature—both *samizdat* and legal publications—inspired confidence. Croatia's *Glas Koncila* and Polish Catholic journals became trusted sources of information and commentary. Religion itself came to serve as a symbol of a form of protest against oppressive regimes.

After 1980, the "Polish syndrome" and the Polish pope evoked great optimism in many countries, although the religious revival predates the election of Pope John Paul II. Moreover, in many of these countries, young people talked about and practiced religion outside the institutional church. Today, despite a greater receptivity than ever in the churches' recent history, it is not a foregone conclusion they will benefit from the new spirituality, especially if they remain sterile bureaucratic apparatuses.

Catholicism remains the dominant religion of Poland, Lithuania, the western Ukraine, Czechoslovakia, Hungary, and western Yugoslavia. As David Martin has noted, "the union of vigorous intellectual and ritual dimensions in Catholicism, plus the range of multiple associations it builds up with culture and with the international community, give it a unique power of resistance and make it a unique focus of totalitarian attention." Martin has also written that "authoritarian systems in opposition tend to curb the authoritarian impulses of the system as a whole."[5] It is unclear whether a strong church in opposition will gain equal strength in the new tasks of social and political reconstruction.

Protestant spiritual resistance is most interesting in Czechoslovakia and East Germany. In Hungary, the Protestants were, if anything, more accommodating to the regime than Catholics. Moreover, the important role of Lutheranism in East Germany can be left aside, since Germany will soon be united. One presumes that there will be a renaissance of German Lutheranism as a result. In any event, the ratio of Catholic to Protestant forces will be different in a new Germany.

Each church in Eastern Europe responded differently to Communist religious policy, which varied from country to country. Their strength in mounting spiritual resistance to totalitarianism depended on four factors:

1. *Internal church autonomy.* Internal autonomy was, undoubtedly, the single most important variable for predicting an independent church-society strategy, one that looked beyond mere survival in the parish sanctuary toward exercising greater spiritual impact on society. Not surprisingly, the countries with the greatest degree of internal church autonomy (e.g., Poland, Yugoslavia) also had the most developed strategy of spiritual resistance. In these countries, the church could publicly criticize the revisions of the nation's constitution in the 1970s, something the Hungarian or Czechoslovakian churches could not do.

"Church autonomy" refers to the ability of the church to nominate and assign its bishops and priests; communicate church policy through bishops' conferences and pastoral letters and sermons; communicate without interference with the Vatican and the world church; and control the recruitment and training of seminarians. Only Poland and Yugoslavia approached this normal church autonomy. Where autonomy did not exist, it was properly the first priority in any church-society strategy, as it was in the Vatican's *Ostpolitik.*

2. *The mobilization of the laity for a wider role in society.* Mobilization of lay members for their citizen role is a prerequisite for a church with political impact; it needs such facilities as the Oasis movement in Poland, clubs of Catholic intellectuals, a lay press, and base communities. Mobilization in Eastern Europe was strongest in Poland and Yugoslavia. Only in those two countries could one speak of a self-consciously Catholic intelligentsia. One would expect that training such a group would be the church's first priority in its new period of rehabilitation as a publicly juridical body in society.

3. *Alliance with other democratic opposition movements.* Spiritual resistance was strongest when it was linked to other resistance movements, especially a democratic opposition movement. As Max Weber noted, religion effects social change in "elective affinity" with other social movements and interests. Where the church maintained links to other democratic opposition groups (e.g., Charter 77 in Czechoslovakia, the alliance in Poland with the Committee for the Defense of Workers), its leverage for spiritual resistance was thereby enhanced and its credibility reinforced.

4. *Internal church renewal.*   Vatican Council II — with its new focus on cultural and political issues as described in "The Church and the Modern World"— for the most part has passed Eastern Europe by. David Martin has suggested that, in general, the church in Eastern Europe "minimizes the impact of the Vatican Council because this would create divisions for the government to exploit." He also noted the truism that "heavy pressure and chosen or enforced isolation make for conservatism."[6] Similarly, Gerard Simon remarked that "the necessity to concentrate on defense and apology did not allow the church to turn its attention to internal reforms."[7] That task now awaits the church in Eastern Europe and may cause it to pursue both institution building and religious renewal more than outward political activity. Only in Yugoslavia have the various reforms instituted by Vatican II — liturgical renewal, ecumenism, a new theology open to worldly reality, a new social teaching, and more democratic forms of communication — been embraced by significant sectors of the church. Elsewhere, theological conservatism remained the order of the day.

Resistance in Hungary

Catholicism in Hungary does not enjoy the national cultural or symbolic power found in Poland or Croatia. Indeed, Hungarian Catholicism must vie for any national role encumbered by a long history under the Hapsburgs of a "Josephinian Church," so called because Emperor Joseph II (1741–90) forged a church to serve government interests, follow government regulations, and act as a branch of the civil service.

The Counter-Reformation in Hungary avoided the violent military confrontations in the religious wars that occurred in neighboring Czechoslovakia, although civil pressures were applied to coerce Protestant reconversion. Catholic forces never removed a Protestant stronghold in more remote Transylvania. There, at the 1550 Diet and later, under Gabriel Bethlen, Calvinists proclaimed religious freedom and Protestant liberties in the name of Hungarian independence. Protestant nationalism emerged again in the nineteenth century to become the "rallying point of all anti-Hapsburg nationalist sentiments."[8] The rallying symbol of the 1848 uprising, Louis Kossuth, was a Protestant.

Meanwhile, the Austrian Hapsburg rulers expected the Catholic church to preach obedience to secular authority and, by and large, it did so. Even after the *Ausgleich* of 1867 (with the enactment of a Hungarian religious bill of disestablishment), the Catholic church remained a "quasi-established" church, since all major appointments of archbishops, bishops, abbots, and canons were subject to government veto. During the nineteenth century, Protestants led the way in the revival of Magyar as an "official" language. At present, Protestants represent about 26 percent of the religious believers in Hungary: 21 percent Calvinist Reformed and 5 percent Lutheran versus 71.5 percent Catholic. During the Communist period, however, little was heard from the Protestant churches about the ancient liberties. If anything, the Reformed church in Hungary was even more accommodating to the regime than Catholicism.

In the interwar period, Hungary represented a class state and the official church was considered on the side of the ruling class. After 1945 (and especially after 1947 when Communists came to power), the church suffered enormous restrictions. In 1945, church property amounted to 34.6 percent of Hungarian land-holdings. These were expropriated over the objections of the bishops. Meanwhile, unlike the Polish bishops, Hungarian Catholicism, under the redoubtable and aristocratic leadership of József Cardinal Mindzenty, followed a catastrophic policy of reactionary resistance without wily compromise.

Between 1948 and 1956, the Hungarian church underwent major curtailment. It lost almost all of its 3,344 educational institutions (in 1945 the church controlled 40 percent of all elementary schools and 27 percent of all secondary schools), as well as its welfare organizations, hospitals, and printing houses, and all lay organizations were suppressed. Mindzenty's successor as head of the bishops, Joseph Grosz, was sentenced to fifteen years of imprisonment in 1951. In 1950, 3,500 religious-order priests and nuns were interned. A renegade movement of proregime peace priests, headed by Monsignor Miklos Beresztocz, began in 1949. In August 1950 — decidedly under the gun — the Hungarian bench of bishops signed an accord with the state, accepting the self-limitation that the church had absolutely nothing to do with secular society. All but six religious orders were disbanded, and the number of members of religious congregations declined from 11,538 in 1948 to 250 in the early 1980s.

For the first years after 1950, in the dioceses where consecrated bishops were still allowed, the de facto bishops were officers of the state ministry for religious affairs (the "bishops with moustaches") who controlled diocesan agendas and appointments. They proceeded to appoint the proregime peace priests to the best parishes and banish zealous priests to rural exile.

Through the 1950s and 1960s, church statistics show a steady decline in baptisms, church weddings, religious funerals, number of priests per 10,000 Catholics, and attendance at religious instruction. No new church construction was allowed. The church lacked trained personnel and access to religious literature. All doctors of theology fled the country. In 1949, when religious instruction was still allowed, voluntarily, in the schools, 80 percent of the Catholic children attended. When the law changed in 1965 to allow only highly restricted religious instruction on church premises (taught only by priests, without heat or the use of any audiovisual aids, and allowed only if the parents publicly signed a request for released time), only 40 percent still attended catechetical class. By 1975 this number plummeted to 7 percent. As Miklos Tomka noted, after 1950 "the powerless majority maintained its contacts with religion; those who possess or sought to acquire power distanced themselves from religion."[9] The church had minimal contact with society. The best to hope for was not a *modus vivendi* but a *modus non moriendi* (a way of not dying).

During the 1960s both the Vatican and the state sought a *modus vivendi*, beginning with a formal agreement in 1964. The Vatican sought to fill vacant episcopal sees with cautious bishops at least minimally loyal to Rome, but these appointments remained subject to government veto. The government wanted "official" dialogue partners to offset a small but influential quasi-underground church where students, professionals, and others pursued private prayer, religious instruction, and worship. It also sought legitimacy for the regime and help in overcoming low morale (Hungary has the highest rate of suicide in Europe and a major problem with alcoholism). Out of this *modus vivendi*, the Hungarian church represented the flagship for the Vatican *Ostpolitik*. Eighty-two bishops were appointed or transferred in a twenty-five year period. In 1976 Lazlo Lekai was allowed to succeed Cardinal Mindzenty as primate. He pursued what came to be known in Hungary as "the politics of small steps" in church-state relations. The bishops made a deal to find the church's place in socialism and to control sectarian excess in the semi-underground base community movement. Ironically, by dealing only with the bishops, "the state strengthened the centralized and clerical disposition of the church."[10] Bishops remained aloof, formalized administrators, pastorally quite distant from the most zealous pastors and believers and suspect of being more loyal to the regime than to the church's own mission.

In the conclave that elected John Paul I, Stefan Cardinal Wyszynski — Poland's primate — chided Cardinal Lekai for his pusillanimity. Upon his election, Pope John Paul II, in rapid succession, addressed three strong letters to the Hungarian bishops, demanding that they show more backbone and initiative. Under this prodding, Bishop Josef Cserhati of Pecs, the spokesman for the Hungarian bench of bishops who had argued that the church must "accept the social targets and structure of the Socialist People's Party," now called for greater freedom for the church.

A law in effect since January 1990 allows full freedom to the church. Hungary enjoys full diplomatic recognition with the Vatican. In a sense, Vatican *Ostpolitik*, for which Hungary and not Czechoslovakia was the success story, backfired. For some time, the Hungarian bench of bishops will be filled with aloof, cautious, and isolated bishops who enjoy little credibility with priests and people. On the eve of the new opening for the church, Tomka could summarize the organizational state of Hungarian Catholicism: "The official church remains weak; not even in its own sphere of influence can it guarantee authority, communication and working discipline. The effectiveness of the church does not depend on organizational factors but on personal qualities. This means that the official church is more a latent principle and juridical form than a real functioning structure. It provides the mere background for the real kernel — islands (a youth pilgrimage, some well-functioning parishes) — all without a common conception, division of labor or systematic interconnections."[11]

In a recent interview, Father Lazlo Lukacs, the newly appointed director of public affairs for the bench of bishops, commented: "If you can understand the instinct of a dog when the dog puts its nose up and it's been slapped, you can understand why, after forty years, the church is reluctant to put its nose up. This makes it very difficult to animate the bishops, the clergy and the laypeople."[12]

The lower clergy is no better off. A graying, shrinking cadre, a dispirited group suffering uncertainty about the function of the priest, the lower clergy allowed itself to be loaded with many honorary titles, red sashes, and decorations from the Communist government. Emmerich Andras commented: "The priest is much less called upon for his services, contact with him is avoided and any approach on his part is met with certain reserve."[13] There is a widening generation gap within the church, and — against Vatican II mandates — no real presbyterial councils have taken place. Few Hungarian priests have read Vatican II decrees or know of new theological currents in the church.

Moreover, the most vital element in Hungarian Catholicism, the semiunderground base community movement, remains in tension with the hierarchy that sought a Vatican condemnation of organizations like the Catholic pacifist group led by Father Gyorgy Bulyanyi. Amazingly, the Hungarian bishops (again explicitly against the Vatican II teaching) sided with the government in declaring that no Catholic could be a conscientious objector. Bulyanyi's quasi-sectarian group continues at loggerheads with the hierarchy and accuses it of cowardice. As one commentator noted of Cardinal Lekai's successor: "The past record of the newly appointed Primate, Archbishop Laslo Paskai, suggests that he will be no less politically obedient to the government than his predecessor. As head of the 'peace priests' organization, *Opus Pacis*, Paskai has identified himself with the policies of the Hungarian government. Last October [1986], the Bishops' Conference, under his chairmanship, issued a circular letter which sanctioned the right of the state to require all citizens to perform whatever service is necessary for national defense. This was widely regarded in Hungary as an attack on the pacifism of [Bulyanyi's group] to demonstrate that the post-Lekai era would produce no change of policy."[14]

No Hungarian Catholic prelate, priest, or active Catholic layperson represented a formidable voice of Hungarian dissidence. No Hungarian Catholic *samizdat* emerged. Even the base community movement remained a purely religious movement, more akin to Amish resistance than to political pacifism. Everything points to a continuation of a Josephinian servile church for some time in the Hungarian political order. Dramatic shifts in direction toward a more self-consciously public or civic role for Catholicism can only be expected from pressure from the Vatican. In interviews given while traveling in the United States in the fall of 1989, Cardinal Paskai gave no indication that the leadership of Hungarian Catholicism had any plans for the transformation of its highly secularized and dispirited society.

Resistance in Czechoslovakia

If Czechoslovak Catholicism's past as a cultural national symbol is darker than Hungary's, its future may be brighter. Early on, Jan Hus (martyred in 1415 by the Roman church in a nefarious betrayal of a safe-conduct promise) stood for the use of the vernacular in the liturgy and national independence. During the Reformation, about 90 percent of the Czech lands turned Protestant. However, the victory of the Hapsburgs in the infamous Battle of White Mountain in 1620 led to forced reconversions from Protestantism. Virtually all citizens of Czechoslovakia are nominally Catholic or unbelievers.

In the Czech lands, the Catholic bishops tended to be German aristocrats. The church remained distant from the Czech national renaissance of the nineteenth century. Already in the early 1900s, a schismatic Czech church movement, the Los von Rome Bewegung, sought an autonomous Catholic national church. As Pedro Ramet put it, in the Czech lands, "the Catholic church and the Hapsburg state were two faces of a single enemy."[15] After independence in 1918, Thomas Masaryk favored the schismatic national Hussite church. Ramet commented, "Czechoslovakia was susceptible to anticlerical programs quite independent of the communist takeover."[16]

Slovakia, before 1918, was ruled by Hungary rather than by direct rule from Austria. More agrarian and peasant based than the Czech lands, Slovakia joined the new nation after World War I but with some reluctance. Statistics show the different valence to Catholicism in the two parts of the country. Some 36 percent in the Czech lands are practicing Catholics, while more than 50 percent in Slovakia adhere to the church. In the interwar period, the church supported a Catholic political party, the Slovak People's Party of Father Andrej Hlinka. During World War II, Hitler allowed a semiautonomous puppet regime in Slovakia, headed by Monsignor Josef Tiso, who was executed after the war for treason. A majority of Catholic priests in Slovakia supported Tiso, while Protestant pastors went into resistance.

Hence, Catholicism entered the postwar period and the early Communist years in great discredit for its acquiescence to Hitler, including Tiso's compliance in the final solution for the Jews. Except for the brief Prague Spring, Czechoslovakia remained the severest regime in Eastern Europe on religious policy. Other countries in Eastern Europe saw an earlier period of Stalinism give way to a *modus vivendi* with the church in the 1960s and beyond — often, as in Hungary, because of a desire to bolster regime legitimacy or counteract societal morale problems like the high rate of suicide by drawing on the church's residual moral capital.

Unlike Cardinal Mindzenty — who never admitted mistakes — at the Second Vatican Council, Josef Cardinal Beran acknowledged serious shortcomings in Catholic pastoral outreach in pluralist societies. The Communists supported Father Josef Ployhar's association of regime-loyal "peace priests" and used state salary subsidies to reward priest lackeys of the regime who gave up religious instruction, avoided contact with the youth, or preached less.

In the early 1950s, 3,000 monks and 10,000 nuns were interred in concentration camps, accused of bacchanalian orgies and plotting counterrevolution. Religious orders were suppressed. Seminaries were subject to severe restrictions in recruiting students and placed under effective state control. Not until the spring of 1968 under Alexander Dubcek did the bishops establish some control over their own seminaries. Even then, the authorities insisted, for example, that the Catholic seminary in Bratislava include propaganda courses on atheism as part of its curriculum. As late as 1987, seminarians protested a training program controlled by the "peace priests."

Throughout the 1970s and 1980s anti-Catholic activity in Czechoslovakia was especially severe (only in Romania and the Soviet Union was religious policy so strict). Priests could function only under a government license, and the most zealous were refused licenses. Priests and laity were jailed for the subversive act of introducing Bibles and religious literature to the country. Except for Prague's courageous Frantisek Cardinal Tomasek, the church lacked clear leadership. In 1985, ten of the thirteen episcopal sees lay vacant. The Vatican was impeded in naming new bishops, and 1,161 of the 4,336 Catholic parishes lacked resident priests. "Official" religious instruction of youth was almost nonexistent. The Catholic weekly newspaper *Katolicke Noviny* was under effective regime control; for example, it censored or revised papal documents. A large proportion of the licensed clergy belonged to the regime-loyal Pacem in Terris priest association. Dissident priests or lay workers were subject to suspicious unexplained disappearances and deaths. A thoughtful article on the church in Czechoslovakia could refer to the status of the church there as a *modus moriendi*.

In contrast, there was a network of "secret church" bishops, priests, and believers — a catacomb church that met in houses, engaged in prohibited religious instruction, and published Catholic *samizdat*. Indeed, the regime feared these catacomb Christians even more than Charter 77, all the more so because of a tacit alliance between the two groups. An unlicensed priest, Václav Maly, was prominent in Charter 77.

Residual religious loyalties, however, remain strong. Statistics for 1984 showed 31.2 percent of believers in the Czech lands and 71.6 percent Slovakian Catholics were baptized; 15.8 percent versus 53 percent in the two lands married in the church; and 50.6 percent versus 80.5 percent were buried with church funerals. One indication of the greater strength of the faith in Slovakia versus the Czech lands was the mass pilgrimage in 1987 to celebrate the millennium of St. Methodius, the first bishop of Moravia. Some 100,000 to 200,000 Slovaks attended, while only a small group from the Czech lands took part, even though the pilgrimage site was in their territory.

The thaw in church-state relations in Czechoslovakia in 1989 has allowed the church to appoint zealous pastors to the vacant episcopal sees. Moreover, the tacit alliance between Catholic groups and Charter 77 has given the church a national credibility for the first time in recent history. Still, the Czech church needs education for the clergy and laity as well as communication and capital aid. In the words of a Raskob Foundation task force on churches in Eastern Europe: "In many areas there are no churches, no trained personnel to teach religion, no clergy for pastoral service and virtually no basic tools for communication . . . . Without such essentials, freedom of religion is without meaning." Archbishop Daniel W. Kucera of Dubuque, after a recent visit with the new Czechoslovak bishops, commented that they "need catechetical and parochial programs; they need to know how to run parish councils . . . . They know that things will happen very fast, and they need coordination and networking."[17] They also need help communicating within the church.

Pope John Paul II made a pastoral visitation to Czechoslovakia during 21–22

April 1990. He has scheduled visits to Hungary and Poland in 1991 and has shown a strong desire to visit Yugoslavia. In his speeches in Czechoslovakia, the pope touched on the division between regime-loyal and underground priests: "In order to continue their assistance to the faithful, quite a few [of the priests] had to accept from those in authority at that time a *modus vivendi* not shared by all. In the Lord's name I exhort you to forget the conditioning of which they were the victims and in a renewed pastoral commitment to build anew the full unity of the priesthood under the leadership of the bishops."[18]

Such reconciliation, without recriminations, between those who suffered imprisonment and those who were co-opted by the regime may be organizationally more difficult than the pope's exhortation suggested, all the more so since the newly named bishops belong to the first group. The Czechoslovak college of bishops represents a unique profile. As John Paul II said to this new group of bishops: "A significant characteristic of your college is the fact that a majority of you, for a certain period, were not able to exercise your priestly ministry publicly and engaged in civil occupations, mostly blue-collar workers, experiencing from within the daily living conditions of people today, the problems of the laity, the difficulties of the workplace."[19]

The bishops may have their own problems, however, asserting their authority and relating to priests and laity who sometimes have not known the authority of a bishop for more than a generation. The bishops have inaugurated an ambitious ten-year program of spiritual renewal of the nation to culminate with the millennial feast of St. Adelbert in the year 2000. Each year emphasizes a different social, moral, or spiritual theme linked to an intensive program of church preaching, pastoral programs, and retreats. A similar decade-long spiritual renewal program in Poland during the 1960s was successful in renewing the church.

The pope, during his visit to Czechoslovakia, stressed the social role of the church: "The church's life does not consist in liturgy and the sacraments alone; it must also reach the fields of culture, education, social action and charitable activity . . . . In a free and democratic society, the church and state should, in mutual respect, foster healthy collaboration for the sake of the integral development of the human person."[20] The papal tone was surprisingly pluralistic, stressing cooperation with other churches, religious freedom, and collaboration "with the other forces of society which are especially sensitive to the problems of the nation's moral health."[21]

Especially under the leadership of a unique cadre of bishops and zealous, formerly underground clergy, Czechoslovak Catholicism seems more prepared than the church in Hungary for the new post-Communist nation building. Future issues will include (1) the relation of Catholicism (which enjoys a longer and more credible link toward Slovak nationalism than to Czech national consciousness) to Slovak desires for national independence and (2) the extent to which the church implicitly sponsors a Christian Democratic Party in Slovakia. The unexpected electoral success of the Civic Forum in Catholic Slovakia in the 1990 elections augurs well for a Catholicism open to exercising its moral influence in a pluralistic society. Naturally enough, the same question can be raised about the future of Catholicism in Poland.

Resistance in Poland

Polish Catholicism represents one of the most successful cases of oppositional nationalism. Unlike other institutions, the church has never betrayed the nation. The role of the church in postwar Poland has been well documented and its organizational strength publicly assessed. Remarks here will therefore be limited to the future of Catholicism and politics in Poland.

At present, there seems little reason to fear a clerically dictated state. The leading Catholic intellectuals, such as Prime Minister Tadeusz Mazowiecki, are likely to resist clerical control of politics or the move toward a Polish Christian Democratic Party. Surprisingly, since it is contrary to most "official" Catholic positions, Polish intellectuals, journalists, and politicians have asserted that religion must remain a private matter. Perhaps those who fear a resurgence of prewar clerical politics will be encouraged to remember that during the post-1921 Polish Republic (with a constitution modeled on France's Third Republic), "the Catholic church was pushed on the fringes of political life."[22] A national synod in the near future will probably signal the terrain that the church will seek to carve out in national life (abortion will be one vexing issue). However, with Catholics pitted on both sides of the growing Walesa-Mazoswieki divide, the church is likely, especially during the current papacy, not to take sides explicitly. The intellectuals are clearly voting for pluralism. As Zbigniew Nosowowski, editor of the Catholic monthly *Wiecz*, put it, "the church has fulfilled its role in confronting communism; now it has to give prophetic witness in another way, within a pluralist society."[23]

With the death of Stefan Cardinal Wyszynski and the translation of Karol Wotijla to Rome, the leadership of the Polish episcopacy has been diminished. The new primate, Józef Cardinal Glemp, has lent his name to a neologism, *Glempic*, which means "to say nothing at length and in soothing terms." For decades, internal opposition among the bishops themselves and between bishops and lower clergy or among the laity has been submerged to present the appearance of a united opposition. Already at the time of the third session of the Vatican Council, important Catholic lay voices (the editors of *Wiecz* and *Tygodnik Powszechny*) sent a memorandum to the papal secretariat of state, criticizing their bishops for being overly doctrinaire. In 1984, parishioners in Ursus engaged in a hunger strike against Cardinal Glemp, protesting his transfer of a popular priest, Mieczylaw Nowak.

The seamless web of Catholic unity is likely to unravel in public just as Solidarity has begun to break into factions. Especially as a new austerity hits the country, the long-standing divergence between priests and people in living standards (Polish priests live well) could become a bone of anticlerical contention.

Polish cultural politics in this century veer between the often anti-Semitic chauvinist nationalism of Roman Dmowski and the more cosmopolitan vision of Józef

Pilsudski and the Constitution of 1791. Both visions are strongly represented in the church, at every layer. The primate probably leans more to the vision of Dmowski. Among the Polish Catholic journalists and politicians, the more cosmopolitan vision prevails, as exemplified in the side they took in the dispute over a Carmelite monastery in Auschwitz. In interviews, this more cosmopolitan group does not see any essential difference between their Christian humanism and the revisionist secular humanism of people like Jacek Kuron and Adam Michnik. Differences between these two visions will continue to plague Poland and the Catholic church in that country. But the anniversary of the 1791 Constitution should favor the more cosmopolitan group.

Catholic social teaching would seem to have little sympathy for "rugged capitalism" or brutal supply-demand market economics. Sooner or later, versions of a more public social Catholicism (with its stress on distributive justice, basic human needs, and economic democracy) seem bound to emerge within Polish Catholicism. In this regard, the view of some government spokespersons — according to whom the church's charitable network should provide the social safety net to make up for the state's abrupt turn to the market — seems very unrealistic, given the limitations of church resources.

Sociological evidence of Polish religion shows it does not represent a monolith of practicing Catholics or orthodox beliefs. Weekly mass attendance in urban Poland is not much higher than it is in Canada or the United States. Again, among the Polish urban population only 49.7 percent think premarital sex is wrong; only 47.3 percent reject divorce; only 34.4 percent accept church teaching on artificial birth control; and only 54.2 percent oppose abortion.

A leading Polish sociologist of religion, Barbara Strassberg, has argued that Polish Catholicism has evolved from one form of selective religion (folk Catholicism of a peasant class) to a new form where "people believe in only some elements of dogma, participate in religious practices in a more and more irregular way and accept the church's authority only in some matters."[24] The genius of Polish religion lies in the fact that it is not dogmatic. Thus, without the need to play a clear role as the oppositional ideology and umbrella organization for dissidents as it did under communism, the church, if it becomes more dogmatic, may not gain automatic acquiescence from its constituency. As a cultural and patriotic forum, however, one can expect the church to continue to act as the guardian of the nation's soul. But different factions within the church are likely to emerge more publicly. In the new climate of Eastern Europe, the church can be expected to be a force to direct current social development.

Prognosis for the Future

The issue of religion and politics in Eastern Europe in the immediate future will cause the church in Czechoslovakia and Hungary to focus on internal institution building (recruiting priests, establishing training centers for lay cadres, and trying to make up for the lost generations who have had minimal religious education), on evangelization efforts to reach out to nominal Catholics, and on healing the rifts between the regime-loyal and underground church of the Communist period. This will leave little time or energy for political activity.

In these two countries and in Poland, two issues close to the church seem likely to become politically significant and may divide Catholics from non-Catholics (and some Catholics from other Catholics). The first is abortion. Abortion rates in these three countries — especially Poland — are high and abortion laws more liberal than in the rest of Western Europe. Despite the recent advice of Zbigniew Brzezinski to church officials in Poland (on the occasion of his receiving an honorary doctorate from Poland's Catholic University in Lublin) that they not expend their energies in issuing orders or setting restrictions but in educating and encouraging the public, it seems likely that the bishops will raise the abortion issue, especially in Poland.

Joachim Koncziela, chairman of the Department of Social Sciences at Lublin, warned that a protracted debate about Poland's liberal abortion laws could result in a "polarization of attitudes" that might hinder economic and social reforms. The other explosive issue regards religious or Roman Catholic instruction in schools, which Koncziela fears would cause a "new ideological isolation of non-believers."[25] In Hungary, Prime Minister Jozsef Antall, a devout Catholic, "has pressed one of the policy proposals most offensive to Free and Young Democrats: that there should be religious instruction — initially it was even implied that this might be compulsory Catholic instruction — in schools."[26] The issues of abortion and religious instruction are almost certainly to be pressed by the bishops, even though many Catholics in these countries will not agree with them.

Finally — and ironically — it may not be the institutional church as such but the autonomous Christian Democratic movement that may be the most potent vehicle of Catholic leverage in the new Eastern Europe. European bishops have a penchant for supporting (at least covertly) Christian Democratic Parties. Such parties have emerged in Hungary and Slovakia and in Catholic Slovenia and Croatia. Cardinal Glemp has proposed such a party as a possibility for Poland.

Eastern European countries have looked to the West, especially to Germany, for political models of their new constitutions and democracies. As Timothy Garton Ash recently noted of these fledgling democracies: "The West German parties, together with their rich and active party foundations, also play an important role. At the moment the CDU [Christian Democratic Union] seems to be the most successful, the SPD [Social Democratic Party] having the problem that all over East Central Europe ex-communists are now calling themselves social Democrats."[27]

It seems, given the price the church has paid for its ties with Christian Democratic parties in Europe, that thoughtful church leaders might think twice about wanting such parties where they do not already exist. To some extent, they usurp the bishops' task of addressing issues of church and culture and tame the prophetic voice of the church. Although nominally ideological parties of Christian inspiration, they almost always become interest parties, as most political parties must be, and serve definite class constituencies, thus compromising the universal, transcendent moral claims of the church. But they support the church position on abortion and religious instruction in schools more than secular parties. Despite its official neutrality, the church usually becomes closely aligned to Christian Democratic parties where they exist. Ironically, then, it may be this more secular outreach vehicle, ideologically akin to the church but organizationally independent, that will serve as the major vehicle for a Catholic impact on the political order in Eastern Europe in the near future. The Christian Democratic parties have the personnel, resources, and money to play a key role in the activation of the new politics of Eastern Europe and an interest in doing so. Rather than the churches, these parties will be the major direct Catholic vehicle for politics in the immediate short term.[28] Indirectly, however, in accord with the general moral stance of international Catholic social teaching since the end of World War II, the churches can be relied on to lend moral support to democracy, the rule of law, and a regime respectful of human rights.

NOTES

1. Gerard Simon, "The Catholic Church and the Communist State in the Soviet Union and Eastern Europe," in *Religion and Atheism in the U.S.S.R. and Eastern Europe,* ed. Bohdan Bociukiw and John W. Strong (New York: Macmillan, 1975), 219. (Emphasis added.)

2. Bogdan Denitch, "Religion and Social Change in Yugoslavia," *Religion and Atheism,* 383.

3. Hans Jakob Stehle, *Eastern Politics of the Vatican 1917–1979* (Athens, Ohio: Ohio University Press, 1981), 47.

4. Albrecht Schonherr, "Opportunities and Problems of Being a Christian in a Socialist Society," in *Churches in Socialist Societies,* ed. Norbert Greinacher and Virgil Elizondo (New York: Seabury, 1982), 47–48. (Emphasis added.)

5. David Martin, *A General Theory of Secularization* (New York: Harper and Row, 1978), 51, 222.

6. Ibid., 218.

7. Simon, 219.

8. Leslie Lazlo, *Church and State in Hungary: 1919–1945* (Ph.D. diss., Columbia University, 1973), 39.

9. Miklos Tomka, "Stages of Religious Change in Hungary," in *World Catholicism in Transition,* ed. Thomas Gannon (New York: Macmillan, 1988), 171.

10. Ibid., 173.

11. Ibid., 182.

12. Cited in Tim McCarthy, "Hungary Asks Why the Euphoria is Fading," *National Catholic Reporter,* 20 Apr. 1990, 10–13.

13. Emerich Andras, "The Situation of the Catholic Clergy in Hungary," in *Churches in Socialist Societies of Eastern Europe,* ed. Norbert Greinacher and Virgil Elizondo (New York: Seabury, 1982), 59.

14. John Eibner, "Controversy in the Hungarian Church: Fr. Bulanyi on Trial," *The Month,* 20 (April 1987): 152.

15. Pedro Ramet, *Cross and Commissar: The Politics of Religion in Eastern Europe and the U.S.S.R.* (Bloomington: Indiana University Press, 1987), 75.

16. Ibid., 76.

17. Jim Castelli, "Bishops Plan Church Aid to Eastern Europe," *National Catholic Reporter,* 1 June 1990, 6.

18. John Paul II, "Czechoslovakia's Task of Renewal," *Origins,* 3 May 1990, 791.

19. Ibid., "The Tasks of the Bishops," 795.

20. Ibid., "Overcoming the Tower of Babel," 798.

21. Ibid., "Czechoslovakia's Task of Renewal," 792–93.

22. Norman Davies, *God's Playground: A History of Poland*, vol. 2 (New York: Columbia University Press, 1982), 404.

23. Cited in Peter Hebblethwaite, "Walesa's Drive toward the Presidency," *National Catholic Reporter*, 1 June 1990, 10.

24. Barbara Strassberg, "Polish Catholicism in Transition," in *World Catholicism in Transition*, 196.

25. Mary Rothschild and Edward Schau, "Report from Poland," *Commonweal*, 13 July 1990, 406.

26. Timothy Garton Ash, "Eastern Europe: *Apres le Deluge, Nous*," *New York Review of Books*, 16 Aug. 1990, 52.

27. Ibid., 53.

28. For studies critical of Christian Democratic Parties and their impact on the church, see *The Church and Christian Democracy*, ed. Gregory Baum and John A. Coleman (Edinburgh: T. and T. Clarke, 1987).

Protecting the Environment: A New Focus for the Atlantic Alliance

ALLEN L. SPRINGER

At the May 1989 summit of the North Atlantic Treaty Organization (NATO), President George Bush called on members of the alliance to place a higher priority on environmental issues. The subsequent summit declaration affirmed the "need to address worldwide problems which have a bearing on our security, particularly environmental degradation." Recognizing the "importance of safeguarding the environment," alliance members pledged themselves to new environmental initiatives.

Critics were quick to see this new interest in the environment as an attempt to turn attention away from the Lance missile modernization debate and the generally eroding sense of direction in the alliance. Yet the emergence of the environment as a significant political issue appears to have a more solid foundation. At the Paris Economic Summit two months later, environmental concerns were again high on the conference agenda. Well-publicized studies about the dangers of acid rain and global warming helped shift the focus of the World Energy Conference, held in Montreal in September 1989, from its earlier emphasis on energy supply and price stability to the long-term ecological implications of increased consumption of fossil fuels.

The environment has become a major foreign-policy issue. This essay discusses some of the reasons why environmental issues are particularly relevant to United States–Europe relations in the 1990s. It also examines the institutional setting in which environmental concerns have been and will continue to be addressed.

The Relevance of the Environment

It may not be readily apparent why environmental degradation, however important a global and continental issue, should deserve serious alliance attention. Few environmental threats either span or are confined to this "regional" grouping whose members are distant geographically. Moreover, there is some irony in suggesting that NATO, long committed to the protection and maintenance of rigid territorial boundaries, focus on problems that are often seen as aggravated by precisely that insistence on "artificial" political barriers. Yet there are at least four reasons why, if only on a political level, the environment should be an important component of United States–Europe relations, not only in NATO but also in the Organization for Economic Cooperation and Development (OECD), in other regional organizations, and in bilateral relations between the United States and the European Community.

First, one need not be a skeptic to suggest that the alliance needs a fresh sense of common purpose. Environmental issues provide an attractive focus for a security organization apparently facing a diminished military threat from the Soviet Union. The nuclear accident at Chernobyl made clear to many the ecological interdependence of the Continent and suggested the possibility that the most serious challenge to Western security might come not from armed attack but from environmental catastrophe. Americans have come to realize that, just as the Atlantic Ocean cannot insulate them from European politics, neither can it protect them from the effects of problems like ozone depletion. Environmental isolationism makes even less sense than its political counterpart. Moreover, the ocean that has been the central unifying concept behind the "Atlantic partnership" is itself threatened by oil pollution and the dumping of toxic chemicals, which cannot be controlled by national legislation alone.

Second, it is clear that Western public opinion takes environmentalism seriously. A poll commissioned by the United States Information Agency just before the Paris Economic Summit revealed that people in Great Britain, West Germany, Canada, and Japan viewed environmental problems as the most important issue to be discussed in Paris. By overwhelming margins, the people of these four countries and of France and Italy considered pollution an "urgent and immediate problem" and favored environmental protection even at the cost of economic growth. This certainly suggests an opportunity for those searching for politically attractive directions to new alliance activity. The growing strength of environmentally active groups like the Green party in countries like West Germany, Belgium, and even Great Britain, as seen in the 1989 elections to the European Parliament, should also serve as a warning to those committed to traditional patterns of alliance behavior. Coming into greater political prominence are people ready to question such former articles of faith as reliance on nuclear weapons to deter Soviet aggression, given the devastating ecological consequences that would almost certainly result from their use. The debate over the Lance missile modernization program was clearly linked to a growing public discomfort with nuclear weapons, a concern also reflected in new worries about the safety of transporting and storing nuclear materials on West German soil.

Third, environmental issues can become the source of discord among alliance members. The infamous "cod war" of the 1960s and early 1970s between Great Britain and Iceland was the result of British opposition to Iceland's attempt to extend its maritime jurisdiction to protect coastal fisheries. The memory of the threat that conflict posed to NATO's continued possession of key military bases in Iceland is probably one reason for the care with which the United States and other countries have attempted to encourage Iceland to restrict its whaling practices. In the economic sphere, inconsistent national antipollution measures can lead to trade dislocations and controversy within the OECD. The lack of a coordinated environmental policy can also serve as an obstacle to European economic integration, which has been a long-sought goal of the alliance as a strong "second pillar."

Fourth, environmentalism offers a potential bridge to Eastern Europe. Air and water pollution and problems of deforestation faced by countries like Czechoslovakia are far more serious than those in the West. The Chernobyl accident brought to countries like West Germany and Poland a sense of shared vulnerability to external environmental threats. A new, growing environmental movement in Eastern Europe, coming at a time of rapid political change, presents new opportunities for cooperation that can help overcome past political divisions.

What is good politically for the alliance and related institutions can also significantly benefit those searching for solutions to pressing environmental problems. While there are few global environmental threats to which the United States and its European allies can effectively respond solely on a regional level, regional cooperation can play an important role in furthering global action. There are several reasons for this.

First, developed countries in the West bear a special responsibility for many of the environmental problems they face. As in the past, they consume a disproportionate share of the world's resources and produce a disproportionate share of its pollution. Fortunately, with this trend comes the capacity to make a significant difference in overall global pollution levels through coordinated regional action. Ozone depletion is a good example. In 1977, OECD countries produced about 80 to 90 percent of the global supply of chlorofluorocarbons (CFCs), widely suspected to be a primary cause of ozone depletion. OECD countries took the lead in responding, first individually and then later in the 1985 Vienna Convention for the Protection of the Ozone Layer and the subsequent Montreal Protocol on Substances that Deplete the Ozone Layer. Although these two agreements were negotiated under the auspices of the United Nations Environment Program and include many non-OECD countries as signatories, the key provisions concerning the formula for bringing about CFC reductions and the use of trade sanctions to secure compliance were essentially hammered out in negotiations between the countries of the European Community (EC), Japan, and the "Toronto group," which included Canada, the United States, Finland, Norway, and Sweden.

Second, existing patterns of Western regional cooperation can be adapted with relative ease to environmental issues, compared with the challenge of building institutions on a global level. Despite some differences among OECD members, generally shared values make possible more decisive action here than in a world setting where pressing problems of hunger and overpopulation may make certain environmental interests, such as the protection of endangered species, a relative rather than an absolute concern to some of the poorest nations. In a 1970 article in *Foreign Affairs*, George Kennan suggested an even more active role for Western regionalism.[1] Kennan proposed that environmentally conscious Western countries create an International Environment Agency, staffed by apolitical scientific experts, to serve as a more effective advocate for global environmental interests than could be established within the framework of the United Nations. Such a regional organization would seem particularly divisive and inappropriate in 1991, but the idea of taking advantage of the relatively clearer consensus on environmental matters that may exist on the regional level does have merit.

Third, Western nations have the economic resources to provide both inducements to encourage desirable environmental practices and punishments for those who fail to protect international environmental interests. By acting in concert they can use this potential to greater effect than by acting individually.

With regard to positive incentives, one area that seems appropriate for coordinated action is the protection of tropical rain forests. The government of Brazil has every reason to expect some form of outside assistance in maintaining the "lungs of the biosphere," especially from those whose extensive use of fossil fuels has made the danger of global warming particularly urgent. Whether that assistance takes the form of direct aid or some form of "debt for nature" exchange, the delicate task of putting together an equitable aid package can be made easier by informal conversations among potential donors outside the glare of publicity that attends broader global negotiations.

Indicative of what can be done in a more punitive vein are efforts to protect African elephants, which declined from a total of nearly 10 million in the 1930s to 1.5 million in 1979 to about 650,000 today. Unilateral bans on ivory imports, by Japan, the United States, and the EC have helped drive down the world price for ivory, which should limit some of the incentive for poaching. These actions also helped precipitate a 1989 decision by the Convention on International Trade in Endangered Species (CITES) to establish a moratorium on international trade in ivory. As with similar efforts by major "port" states to encourage adherence to the standards of the 1973 Convention on the Prevention of Pollution from Ships (MARPOL) by denying port access to ships of nonsignatories, carefully coordinated regional action could convey a stronger message. Against such a strategy, of course, must be balanced the danger of triggering a retaliatory response.

The Institutional Setting

Any discussion of the institutional context of United States–Europe environmental relations must make clear the range of intergovernmental organizations currently at work within the region on environmental issues. International commissions regulating busy waterways like the Rhine and the Danube rivers date back to the nineteenth century. Canada and the United States have successfully employed the International Joint Commission since 1909 to help resolve a number of disputes arising along their 3,000-mile border. Specialized institutions focus on such problems as fisheries management in the North Atlantic (North Atlantic Fisheries Organization) and the pollution of the Baltic Sea (the Helsinki Commission). Among the most interesting recent initiatives is the work being done to protect the Arctic environment by a group of Arctic countries, including Canada, Denmark, Finland, Iceland, Norway, Sweden, the Soviet Union, and the United States. Given the multiple American interests in the Arctic, as well as the possible side benefits of cooperation with this diverse group of countries, continued United States participation in this effort seems ensured.

Three strictly European organizations with broad areas of responsibility also deserve mention: the European Community, the Council of Europe, and the Council for Mutual Economic Assistance (CMEA). All three bodies have taken an interest in environmental matters.

The European Community, now with twelve members, is by far the strongest institution. Despite the failure of the 1957 Treaty of Rome to refer specifically to the environment as an appropriate area for community activity, the EC has undertaken a number of environmental initiatives. In charge is the Directorate General for Environment, Consumer Protection, and Nuclear Safety, created in 1972 as a division of the EC Commission, which serves as the organization's executive arm. The Council of Ministers, to which the commission makes recommendations, has exercised its power to issue binding directives on subjects ranging from the quality of surface drinking water to the disposal of polychlorinated biphenyls (PCBs) and the protection of migratory birds. The council has adopted a series of "Action Programmes," which have formed the basis for a coordinated community environmental policy. Acting on behalf of the EC, the commission has been a party to a number of important environmental conventions, including the Barcelona Convention for the Protection of the Mediterranean Sea against Pollution (1976) and the Berne Convention on the Conservation of European Wildlife and Natural Habitats (1982).

As the EC moves toward increased economic and political integration in 1992 and beyond, the importance of its work in the environmental field will doubtless increase. While this consolidation is generally a positive development, there remains some concern that efforts to achieve a consensus within the community on potentially divisive issues could lead to policies that impose greater costs on outside parties, particularly the United States and other developed countries in the West. The recent EC controversy with the United States over importing beef raised with growth-enhancing additives, though not strictly an "environmental" dispute, suggests the kind of disagreement over standards used to define a "threat to human health" that could become more common. If nothing else, the EC is becoming an increasingly complicated entity with which to negotiate. Understandably, "internal" considerations played a pivotal role in the initial formulation of the EC position on controlling CFC emissions, a position with which the United States and other countries outside the community took issue. The ultimate success in reaching a compromise on the CFC question may indicate a positive role for the commission in unifying what might otherwise be twelve individual positions.

Still, the potential friction between the EC and its developed allies makes a regular process of consultation on environmental matters all the more important, whether within the OECD or in some other arena.

The Council of Europe is a more broadly based organization than the EC, with twenty-one member countries that include all the states of Western Europe and Turkey. Formed in 1949, the council is primarily a forum for the exchange of ideas and information, not a regulatory body. The council's Committee for the Conservation of Nature and Natural Resources was set up in 1962 and has served as the focus of efforts not only to conserve resources but also to find common solutions to problems of air and water pollution. Two council publications, *Newsletter-Nature* and *Naturopa*, play an important role in bringing European countries together on environmental matters and making them aware of national legislative initiatives.

Since 1949, the Council for Mutual Economic Assistance (CMEA) has linked the socialist countries of Eastern Europe by providing an organizational framework for sharing economic information and encouraging technical and scientific collaboration. The CMEA has a long-standing interest in the protection of water resources and has recently begun to cooperate more closely with Western Europe on long-range air pollution. If the CMEA is to survive in the changed political climate of the 1990s, one test may be its ability to address the environmental problems facing its members.

From an American perspective, however, the three most active arenas for direct United States-Europe environmental cooperation have been NATO, the OECD, and the United Nations Economic Commission for Europe (UNECE).

NATO's Committee on Challenges to Modern Society

As is true of all the organizations discussed here, NATO's involvement in environmental issues was not envisioned in its original charter. Primarily a defense organization, NATO is remarkable for taking an interest in environmental matters as early as it did. In 1969, President Richard M. Nixon used the occasion of NATO's twentieth anniversary to propose the creation of the Committee on Challenges to Modern Society (CCMS), which would focus the "experience and resources of the Western nations" on the task of "improving the quality of life of our people." Then, as today, an environmental initiative by an American president was greeted with skepticism by some who saw the effort as an attempt to create a new agenda for a moribund alliance. Nevertheless, the North Atlantic Council accepted the idea and made the CCMS a regular committee of the organization, thus forming what became known as the "third dimension" of this military and political alliance.

Rather than attempting to serve as a standard-setting body, a role quite inappropriate because of the consultative processes on which NATO relies, the CCMS has hoped to stimulate national legislation through the use of an innovative "pilot study" approach. An individual nation, working alone or with others, spearheads a study of a reasonably specific environmental problem, absorbs all related costs, and then takes the initiative to try to get any suggested policy changes adopted by other states. Using this technique, important studies have been conducted on problems ranging from air pollution to the dumping of hazardous waste to the preservation of historic monuments. In some cases, NATO studies and recommendations have led to concrete international action outside the alliance; for instance, NATO's work on oil spills helped bring about the important 1973 MARPOL agreement. National reporting procedures are also used to encourage NATO members to take the results of CCMS studies seriously.

The CCMS has also convened an annual Environmental Roundtable, which has focused on a different issue of concern to member states each spring since 1974. Among the topics addressed in recent meetings have been national risk assessment procedures (1984), the future of biotechnology (1986), and indoor air quality (1987). In 1980, the CCMS sponsored in Brussels a meeting of all alliance environmental ministers to discuss a wide range of common environmental problems.

The CCMS has not been without its critics. Since NATO defends the status quo in Europe, some see the alliance as unable to respond effectively to environmental problems that transcend the political frontiers that it protects. Its limited membership and clear Western orientation make cooperation with countries in Eastern Europe difficult, though not impossible. Others argue that the CCMS should take advantage of NATO's essentially military nature to examine some of the environmental effects of military operations. While there are obvious institutional reasons why such efforts would encounter resistance within NATO, efforts by the CCMS to look more directly at reasonably discreet issues, such as aircraft engine noise (a study undertaken by the United States and West Germany), might help create a more favorable sense of NATO's responsiveness to legitimate environmental concerns within its area of control. Since 1980, the CCMS has sponsored a number of international seminars focusing on such concerns as the protection of animal and plant life in military training areas.

Some have suggested that the CCMS has been too timid or done too little, but others — particularly in the United States government during the Reagan administration — have argued that the CCMS has attempted too much. As other organizations became active in the environmental field, concern arose over undesirable duplication, and the United States limited its involvement in some CCMS studies and plenary meetings.

Despite these objections, NATO should continue its involvement in environmental matters. The pilot study certainly seems to be a cost-effective way to deal with common environmental problems in a reasonably focused way. The flexibility shown by the CCMS in bringing in nations outside the alliance has helped avoid the sense of regional exclusivity that might otherwise exist. Moreover, the alliance's reputation as an "action-oriented" organization and the level of influence it enjoys at the highest levels of government within its member countries gives its environmental initiatives an unusually high profile.

The changing political environment in Europe and the progress in arms control that it has made possible also present a new set of environmental concerns that go well beyond the more focused work of the CCMS. A proposed ban on chemical weapons will require a careful and costly procedure to dispose carefully of existing stockpiles. If the talks on Conventional Forces in Europe (CFE) go forward as expected, huge amounts of military matériel on both sides of the East-West border must be destroyed. Major force redeployments throughout Europe, which are expected with the development of new continental security arrangements, bring with them environmental implications that are difficult to comprehend fully now but which must be addressed in the future.

Organization for Economic Cooperation and Development

The Organization for Economic Cooperation and Development (OECD), formed in 1961 as a successor to the Organization for European Economic Cooperation (which had overseen the Marshall Plan) has a broader geographic base than NATO. It includes not only the countries of Western Europe, the United States, and Canada but also Australia, New Zealand, and Japan as full members. The primary mission of the OECD is to encourage economic growth and international trade both within the group and globally, although it has also been concerned with coordinating economic aid to developing countries by member states. Structurally, the OECD is governed by a council that has the power, generally by unanimity, to make decisions binding on the members and to issue nonbinding recommendations. Given the need for unanimity, the OECD is essentially a consultative body whose strength comes from the status of its members and their common need for coordinated and consistent policies.

In 1970, the OECD council established the Environment Committee with a reasonably broad charge — to investigate the "economic and trade implications" of environmental problems and to encourage "cost effective" means of dealing with them. Since then, the committee has been active in a number of different areas, particularly air pollution and other problems of transfrontier pollution.

In addition to supporting technical research, the OECD has put forth a number of influential statements of legal principles governing the environment. Among the most important are the "polluter pays" principle, mandating that the environmental cost of economic activities be reflected in the price of goods and services, and the "prior notification" principle, which requires that a country considering a project with potential transboundary effect at least notify and consult with other countries potentially affected by its environmental consequences. The OECD has also helped develop the rules of private international law governing transboundary environmental injury by encouraging the right of "equal access" for foreign victims to the courts of a polluter's nation. Following the Chernobyl accident, the OECD's Nuclear Agency, which had previously established a nuclear "incident reporting" system for use by OECD countries, began work on private-law remedies for transboundary nuclear damage. This work has become particularly significant because of the seeming erosion of state responsibility for transboundary damage that attended the failure of European countries to push the Soviet Union more forcefully to compensate the non-Soviet victims of Chernobyl.

The OECD has also been involved in the question of environmental impact assessment, an approach first adopted by the United States in the National Environmental Policy Act of 1969. In 1987, the World Commission on Environment and Development (Brundtland commission) commended the OECD for its 1986 recommendation to member countries that they apply environmental assessment procedures to their bilateral assistance programs.

The unanimity required for OECD action diminishes the organization's legal clout, and its primary mission — to encourage economic growth — may seem to compromise its responsiveness to environmental values. The OECD is also limited both by the geographic diversity of its membership and by its general exclusion of Eastern European countries. Nevertheless, few question the organization's value, either as a regional forum for discussing common environmental issues or as a catalyst for more focused environmental initiatives.

The United Nations Economic Commission for Europe

The United Nations Economic Commission for Europe (UNECE) is one of five regional commissions operating under the general authority of the United Nations Economic and Social Council. Created in 1947, the UNECE adds an important dimension to United States–Europe relations by including countries of Eastern and Western Europe, as well as the United States and Canada, in its deliberations. It also provides a vital link between the European region and other regional and global organizations. Not surprisingly, an organization with such a diverse membership has little regulatory power. The UNECE can engage in research, promote consultation between member governments, and make recommendations to them (but only by unanimous agreement).

The UNECE's interest in the environment dates back to the 1950s, beginning with the problem of water pollution on inland waterways and leading to discussions of human settlements and air pollution. Its increasingly comprehensive approach to regional environmental management made the UNECE an important catalyst for the global Stockholm Conference on the Human Environment, sponsored by the United Nations in 1972. The UNECE's most tangible success to date is the 1979 Convention on Long-Range Transboundary Air Pollution (LRTAP). Led by Norway and Sweden, particularly concerned about the effects of acid rain on Scandinavian lakes and forests, the attending parties pledged to limit their contributions to the long-range air-pollution problem. They also created procedures for consultation, exchange of scientific information, and monitoring sulphur dioxide levels and established the Executive Body to recommend further, more concrete measures. At its first meeting in 1983, the Executive Body called for a 30 percent reduction in sulphur dioxide emissions by 1993, a proposal later embodied in a 1985 protocol. The Executive Body has also encouraged work on the impact of nitrogen oxide and other pollutants.

The LRTAP convention exemplifies both the positive and negative characteristics of the UNECE as a forum for regional environmental diplomacy. The UNECE's broad geographic membership made possible an agreement encompassing both polluters and victims of pollution (not always discrete categories) and focusing on air pollution, which had never before been the subject of multilateral agreement. It was also the first major environmental agreement between Eastern and Western nations. Their cooperation is essential, since air pollution does not respect East-West divisions. The creation of ongoing structures provides an opportunity for continued and expanded cooperation in the environmental field, thus enhancing the prospects for the "bridge to Eastern Europe" discussed above. On the other hand, the convention has been unusually careful to limit the obligations of its signatories. No specific emission limits or enforcement provisions were included. Even the obligation to control pollution was stated in conditional terms. Under article 2, parties are required only to "endeavor to limit, and as far as possible, gradually reduce and prevent air pollution." This suggested to critics that the need to achieve consensus in so diverse a group led to agreement on the "lowest common denominator," although more decisive action was required. Indeed, there was some concern that the parties were, by treaty, approving antipollution obligations less stringent than those already required under customary international law. One can hope that the subsequent success in negotiating the more restrictive 1985 protocol indicates that, whatever the limitations of the 1979 convention, the procedures it set up can help produce a more effective regime to control regional air pollution.

Conclusion

This essay argues that both environmental and alliance interests can be served in the 1990s by increased attention to the environment. To claim that environmental issues deserve a high priority, however, is not to suggest that now is the time for building major new environmental institutions on a regional level. Just as it is largely for political reasons that United States-Europe cooperation on the environment makes sense, there are solid political reasons for working within the existing regional framework. For all their political and organizational limitations, CCMS, the OECD, and the UNECE can achieve environmental goals on the regional level if the governments are willing to rely on these organizations.

Moreover, the danger of moving too decisively on a regional basis must be recognized. Differences between the United States and the European Community on environmental policy can be managed through improved consultation. Despite the publicity recently given to threats to the global ecology, many of the environmental problems faced within the Atlantic area are reasonably localized. Most can and should be solved on the national level. Cooperation within CCMS and the OECD can suggest successful regulatory approaches, and the OECD can help prevent some of the trade distortions and friction caused by potentially inconsistent national legislation. Yet to raise them directly to the international arena would only complicate the regulatory process.

Other threats can be dealt with at the subregional level and are best left there, where distinctive patterns of continental cooperation make more efficient solutions possible. Acid rain is a good example. Whereas the LRTAP convention established some helpful general principles to govern atmospheric pollution, there is no reason for Canada and the United States to await the difficult process of building a regional consensus. Action can be taken now to protect the North American environment using the tools and processes that 200 years of generally happy coexistence have made available.

Perhaps the most important reason to be wary of an overly aggressive United States–Europe environmental initiative is the possible reaction of developing countries. It has taken nearly two decades and much careful, patient work within the United Nations Environment Program (UNEP) and other global organizations to reassure many nations in the Southern Hemisphere that protection of the environment was not an objective dreamed up by Western imperialists in the late 1960s simply to squelch Third World development and to sustain their domination of the global economic order. The new and fragile sense of pragmatism that seems to have settled over discussions of such global challenges as the protection of tropical rain forests should not be jeopardized. Ultimately, global ecological problems require globally negotiated solutions, and regional groupings like NATO should try to facilitate rather than to supplant that effort.

NOTE

1. George F. Kennan, "To Prevent a World Wasteland: A Proposal," *Foreign Affairs* 48 (April 1970): 401–13.

The Politics of German Unification

DAVID GRESS

Karl Marx, one of the most famous and influential of all German philosophers, was right in saying that "men make their own history, but they do not know the history that they make." Rarely has this been more true than in central Europe, the Soviet Union, and Germany in the years since 1987. Soviet President Mikhail S. Gorbachev, for whatever reasons, decided to sacrifice Communist power in East Germany. That power fell swiftly and decisively—not just in East Germany but also in Poland, Czechoslovakia, Hungary, and elsewhere in Eastern Europe. As a result, the region is in turmoil, the like of which it has not experienced since the late 1940s, with the radical difference that today the turmoil is caused by growing freedom, not encroaching despotism. It is unprecedented for Marxist states to relinquish control of their subject societies and for their inhabitants to learn freedom rather than fear. Siegfried, the hero of Wagner's *Ring*, is born without fear: neither dragons, nor gods, nor walls of fire teach him the fear that is necessary if he is to grow up and fulfill his destiny. The central Europeans face the opposite problem: raised and trained in fear, they must learn the freedom that comes from overcoming fear. For decades, central European dissidents called on East Germans, Poles, Czechs, Slovaks, and Hungarians to live "as if they were free." Few were able to follow this exhortation, which had inevitable and often fatal costs. Can the many follow it now, when the bonds of coercion are loosened?

This question can be answered with no more certainty than the question of German unification. The central Europeans of today truly do not and cannot know the history that they are making, nor can we. It is an awkward time to judge the course and outcome of any of these developments, particularly German unity. This essay can only put the background and the beginnings of the process into its broader historical, political, and philosophical context.

Such an enterprise is not undertaken without political, moral, or ideological judgments. What is already abundantly clear about German unification and its international reception is that one's attitude toward it and one's view of its prospects and consequences depend largely on how one interprets German history and on one's view of freedom and economic self-interest as driving forces of human behavior.

This survey of the politics of unification therefore considers the various understandings of contemporary Germany. These understandings flow from basic moral and political beliefs, especially about modern German history and the purposes of German politics, held by those who are involved, either directly or as observers, in the process of unification.

Gorbachev thought that the East German opposition groups that called for reforms in the fall of 1989 could maintain an independent, socialist German Democratic Republic (GDR). He forced General Secretary Erich Honecker out of power, hoping to legitimize East Germany, making it better able to fuel neutralist sentiment in West Germany. Neither Gorbachev nor most observers realized that nationalist feeling had not died in East Germany; forty years of denying that there was a nationalist issue had merely pushed aside the problem of division, not solved it. Observers with a sense of the true character of East German society foresaw the end of the GDR when Hungary opened its borders to Austria on 4 May 1989. Opening the borders, first to Czechoslovakia and then, on 9 November, in Berlin did not result in stability but in a frantic rush westward of people who clearly did not believe there was any reason for staying. In the last two months of 1989, West German leaders returned abruptly to the older view that the division of Germany was a source of instability and insecurity because it was based on the denial of freedom and self-determination, and such denial inevitably produces conflict.

When the desire for democratic liberty and national self-determination concur, the combination can be irresistible and revolutionary. European history is full of examples, from the French Revolution through the revolutions of 1848 and the unifications of Germany and Italy in the 1860s. Since the end of World War II, Western Europeans have, with reason, regarded their self-determination and liberty as secure and have therefore been able to devote their energies to integration, growth, and social and cultural advancement at a higher level — that of the European Community (EC). In central Europe — including East Germany — by contrast, the Communist rulers denied both self-determination and liberty. Moreover, in the name of abstract ideology, they enforced regressive economic policies that created a gulf between rulers and subjects and produced poverty, pollution, and misery. These policies ensured that the people's demand for freedom and self-determination would not only stay alive but return with a vengeance, once the fear of immediate violence was taken away. In other words, freedom and self-determination are real motives of political action, and people need and want them before they want supranational organization. One of the long-term effects of Communist rule in central Europe from 1945 to 1989 was to deny, delay, and finally exacerbate the demand so that it exploded with all the more vigor in the winter of 1989 and spring of 1990.

The assertion that unification is taking place because East Germany sees freedom as best secured through German unification goes against an influential view found largely, but by no means only, on the German and international left. According to this view, the drive for unification is either sinister, masking a revival of aggressive nationalist aspirations, or materialistic—being driven merely by the East Germans' desire to share in West German material prosperity. The view of this essay, making due allowance for the differences of purpose and interest that separate the historian from the statesman, is that of the West German chancellor and leader of the Christian Democratic Union (CDU), Helmut Kohl. The other view is that of the Social Democratic Party (SPD) and its sympathizers. Adherents of the first view see freedom as central; adherents of the second rarely mention freedom, and when they do it is often to disparage it as a figment of conservative imagination.

The British historian Richard Evans expressed the second view concisely when he asked: "Does the new and seemingly unstoppable drive to reunify Germany in our own day mark the resumption of a submerged but ultimately ineradicable tradition of German national feeling and identity? Or does it merely register a stampede by the East Germans, their consumerist appetites whetted by years of watching West German television advertisements?"[1] For Evans, those who called for political liberty in Germany, whether in 1848 or 1989, were merely calling for a higher standard of living and more consumer goods. Like many left intellectuals, he cannot conceive a desire for liberty that is anything other than a mask for simple greed. Others on the left might admit that freedom is important but then add in the same breath that true liberty is to be achieved through economic equality of a kind unavailable in contemporary West Germany or, according to them, in the sort of unified Germany that is now likely to emerge. Behind this conflict of views lie deep disagreements about the course of German history, the responsibility for Germany's problems, and the lessons to be drawn for today.

To examine these disagreements, which are at the core of the politics of unification, certain aspects of the leftist reading of German history must be considered. The left's vision of Germany is important because Germany has been, and may yet be again, the key asset in the struggle for hegemony in Europe. To an older generation, the purpose of the struggle was to foment revolution, leading to a socialist society. After the Russian Revolution, when the left split into pro-Soviet Marxist-Leninists and democratic socialists, who, while still Marxists, resisted Soviet domination, the nature of the struggle changed as well. The Communists sought total control, regardless of the cost. The more recent generations of democratic socialists within Germany, on the other hand, merely wished to seize social, cultural, and economic power in order to put into practice their agenda of social justice and equality in the belief that democratic socialism would be fairer, more just, and more efficient than capitalism. The collapse of Communist power in central Europe has made the Communist strategy moot. The democratic socialist agenda still lives and plays its important part in the politics of unification.

If Marx was right that men do not know the history they are making, he was wrong in most other matters, notably in claiming that the class struggle was the driving force of history and in prophesying that this struggle would end in a final cataclysm as the exploited majority finally arose to seize power from the exploiters.

The international movement of revolutionary Marxism challenged the forces of liberal democracy for control of the world's most advanced societies. From the vantage point of 1990, it can at last be clearly seen that this challenge has failed politically, economically, and diplomatically. It is less clear that it has entirely failed on the ideological or psychological levels. Many, if not most, Westerners regard Gorbachev as the world's leading statesman. American society, to judge from the poisonous arguments over affirmative action, cultural literacy, and the need to respect the tender sensibilities of innumerable groups, seems headed for ideological warfare at home at precisely the time that committed advocates of democratic capitalism and liberal democracy are scoring their greatest international victories since the late 1940s and 1950s.[2]

The challenge of revolutionary Marxism lasted for about a hundred years, from the 1880s to the late 1980s. For about the first half of that century, Marxism as a movement in European politics possessed intellectual and moral vigor. Marxists developed and organized the labor movements of all European countries, forming social democratic parties as the electoral wing of those movements. But since the Communist-Socialist split, especially in the last half century, Marxism degenerated on the cultural level into academic sectarianism and on the political and strategic levels into little more than a worship of, or in some cases fear of, force — the force in question being the armed might of the Soviet Union. In this way, Marxism infiltrated and influenced the European left as the European social democrats celebrated electoral victories and participation in political power on a scale unimagined by the founders of the labor movements of the 1880s. As a result, leftist politicians and intellectuals routinely interpreted Soviet actions and purposes in the most benign light possible, denied that Soviet power was a threat to Western democracies, and occasionally demonstrated a subservience to Soviet interests that coexisted nicely with skepticism vis-à-vis the United States and concern about American policies and aims.

Nowhere was this tendency clearer than in West Germany, the democratic state created from the three western zones of occupation in 1949. From the beginning, Marxists had regarded control of Germany and its working class as the necessary and sufficient condition of their global victory. Germany was where the philosophy of Marxism was born; it had the best-organized working class and occupied the geopolitical center of Europe. All the more disastrous, therefore, were the four great setbacks to socialist power in Germany. The first was in 1914, when the SPD delegation to the Reichstag supported the government in voting war credits, thereby betraying its commitment to oppose war by all means. The second was in the desperate aftermath of defeat in World War I, when the left wing of the SPD and the newly formed Communist Party of Germany (KPD) tried to seize power by means of workers' and soldiers' councils on the Soviet model and failed in large part because the majority of the SPD allied itself with the army and the center-right — in Marxist terms, surrendering to the class enemy. The third setback was in 1933, when Adolf Hitler and his National Socialists were able to seize power in Germany — partly because the KPD refused to form a common front with the

SPD to oppose him and because many social democrats, with some justice, feared the revolutionary KPD almost as much as they feared the Nazis. The KPD could not conceive that a counterrevolutionary force like the Nazis could hold power for long in Germany and was convinced that the Nazi regime would collapse from its own internal contradictions within a year. That would be the moment for the KPD to reemerge as the only organized political force (all others, including the SPD, having been destroyed by the Nazis) and assume complete control.

Some German Communists refused to support this cynical policy and wanted to put differences with the SPD aside in the interest of resisting National Socialism. Some Soviet scholars today believe that Joseph Stalin, the Soviet dictator, feared that if he had permitted the KPD to join others in a common front against Hitler, the result would have been an independent KPD with native roots in Germany and therefore less amenable to Soviet domination. He therefore deliberately encouraged the KPD to pursue a strategy that guaranteed a Nazi victory, even though he knew that the Nazi regime would not fall apart quickly. Stalin's plan was to wait a few years and then to provoke a war with Germany that he would win. Following this victory he could then impose on Germany a Communist regime entirely of his own choosing.

Instead, Hitler attacked the Soviet Union and was defeated, and Stalin was able to extend his power to only one-third of Germany. This situation, apparent at the moment of cease-fire in May 1945, set up West Germany as the remaining stake in the cold war struggle for Europe.

In this context, the non-Communist left sees the fourth great setback for its cause in Germany, namely, the failure of West Germany to adopt socialism in 1949. According to the SPD, democratic capitalism was imposed on West Germany by Great Britain, America, and their German collaborators led by Konrad Adenauer, the leader of the CDU and first chancellor of West Germany. Had socialism prevailed, they argue, two beneficial consequences would have ensued. First, West Germany would have been a more equal society, with public ownership of the means of production and a genuine purge of the old economic and class interests that, in the Marxist view, were largely responsible for the rise of Hitler. Second, Germany would not have been divided, because Stalin would not have had to fear a capitalist West Germany allied with the United States and possibly bent on revenge for 1945. Stalin would not have had to set up and sustain a Communist East Germany.

Whether socialism in West Germany would have produced the first consequence — a better life for all — is impossible to say. Given what is known of socialist economic policies elsewhere in Europe, it is unlikely that an SPD regime would have encouraged or permitted either the currency reform of 1948 or the intense effort of the 1950s that produced the West German economic miracle. Would the poorest have been better off under the SPD than they were under the CDU? Socialists will say yes, others no. Regarding the second consequence, however, there is more concrete information. In 1952, Stalin proposed free elections in both East and West Germany and effectively offered to end the division of Germany, if the resulting, united German government would remain neutral, which at the time meant staying out of NATO. Since then the SPD has claimed that the offer was meant seriously and that, by rejecting it, Adenauer and the Western allies scotched the best chance they would ever have to unite Germany under tolerable conditions. The left has argued that Adenauer preferred the part of Germany that his party could control to a neutral, united Germany in which the SPD might have a permanent majority. Adenauer's followers and others have retorted that Stalin did not really intend to offer Germans unification under democratic conditions but was merely interested in sowing discord in the Western camp and, if possible, preventing West German membership in NATO. Even if the offer had been serious, a united but neutral Germany would have been an easy victim for Communist subversion and would have fallen under Soviet control sooner or later. If that had happened, Stalin would have accomplished what he failed to do in 1945 when his armies were halted at the Elbe.[3]

The unification that began in 1989 has removed some of the political purpose of the arguments over the 1952 offer, since it turned out that Stalin's offer was not, after all, the "final chance" to end division. The SPD and CDU approaches to the problem, however, remain quite different. Even though the SPD supported the forces of bourgeois order against radical socialist subversion in 1919, the SPD of today is inclined to regret that involvement and to include the events of 1919 in the catalog of opportunities that German socialists failed to seize — or were prevented from seizing — in the struggle for socialism and democracy in Germany. Had the SPD been able to remove the monarchists, militarists, and antidemocrats from the government of the Weimar Republic and forge a truly democratic political culture, the argument goes, Hitler would have never come to power. The SPD, the oldest political party in Germany, regards itself as having a national mission and national responsibility to a degree that is very much at odds with both the internationalist traditions of European socialism and the transnational, Western European focus of the CDU and the the Free Democratic Party (FDP). This conflict between an SPD that is nationally oriented as regards Germany, yet antinationalist in its basic ideology, and a CDU that is postnationalist in European and ideological terms, but at the same time shares the general conservative sympathy for national identity and national interests, colored West German politics on the unification question from the beginning and is as crucial as ever today.

Both before and after the Stalin offer in 1952, the SPD was for unification but strongly anti-Communist. So, of course, was the CDU. The only difference between the SPD and the CDU on the national issue — and the only reason that Stalin's offer caused problems — was that until 1960 the SPD was neutralist and opposed to NATO, and the Stalin offer appeared to promise unification at the price of neutrality. In 1960, the SPD accepted West Germany membership in NATO as the cornerstone of West German foreign policy. At this point, strategic agreement on basic policy between the two major West German parties was complete. It was not to last.

On 13 August 1961, the East German Communist regime began constructing the Berlin Wall and thereby indirectly started a process within the SPD that ultimately led to a complete reversal of its historic position—a reversal that is the immediate root of the SPD's problems in dealing with unification today and the cause of its decisive defeat in the East German election of 18 March 1990. On the very day that the Communists divided Berlin with barbed wire, closing the boundary between West Berlin and East Germany, Willy Brandt, the mayor of West Berlin and the candidate for chancellor of the SPD, decided, as he tells the story, that the SPD would have to change its policy toward East Germany. When the American forces failed to tear down the Berlin Wall, Brandt concluded that there was no longer any hope of unification against the will of the Communist East German government. The way to mitigate the effects of division and keep alive some hope of unification—or at least a future rapprochement—was through negotiations with East Germany and the Soviet Union, not through confrontation and pressure. When Brandt became chancellor of West Germany in 1969, he put this policy into practice, signing treaties with the Soviet Union, Poland, and ultimately East Germany, recognizing the sovereignty of East Germany and its right to control the lives and the fates of its subjects.

The CDU took a different position. From the beginning, Adenauer had maintained that West German democracy could survive the Soviet external threat and domestic instability only through close integration with Western Europe in both NATO and the European Community (EC). He did not, as the left insisted, write off East Germany in order to safeguard West German capitalism. Rather, he thought that unification would mean something only if it took place in a democratic, free-market society and that unification at the price of neutrality could result in a common slavery. Adenauer's response was the "policy of strength," which called for strengthening West German democracy and the West German capitalist economy in alliance with the rest of Western Europe and the United States; at some future date, a strong, stable, prosperous West Germany would, by its very presence and security, undermine the Communist despotism in the east. Communism would not be subverted by the force of arms but by the force of example: ultimately, the East German regime would lose so much of its legitimacy that not even its own brutal armed might could keep it in power.

That is what finally happened in 1989, when Gorbachev mistakenly thought that there were enough idealistic socialists like himself to renew East Germany as a nation without joining the West. In fact, the East Germans used their first opportunity to put into practice exactly what Adenauer had expected of them a generation earlier.

If the policy of strength was in fact successful, there are a number of ironies in the politics of unification. The first irony is that very few even in the CDU any longer believed that the policy of strength was working or had ever worked. In 1985, Michael Stürmer, a historian and publicist with close ties to the chancellor, stated that the Federal Republic should support the inner stability of the GDR even at the cost of "a certain degree of morally ambiguous complicity." Undoubtedly Stürmer, whose reputation on the left is that of a militant and militaristic nationalist, regrets those words today. They nevertheless indicate just how far even conservative and allegedly hard-line Germans were prepared to accept the official Socialist Unity Party (SED) vision of the German Democratic Republic (GDR) as an essential element of the postwar European order.[4]

The SPD abandoned anticommunism and confrontation in the 1960s. From 1969 on, it pursued the policy that Egon Bahr, one of its chief foreign-policy spokespersons, called "change through rapprochement." In concrete terms, this policy granted legitimacy to East Germany and its Communist regime, tolerating its human-rights abuses and other oppressive measures and bribing it with considerable gifts and other transfers to permit a minimum of human contacts between Germans in the two parts of Germany. By the early 1980s, Brandt and other SPD leaders were denying furiously that they had any intention of supplanting or undermining East Germany, that they regarded it as a permanent element in European politics and a guarantee of stability. They based this respect and concern for East Germany on the revisionist tradition of East German studies that came into its own after Brandt became chancellor in 1969. The revisionists rejected the notion of East Germany as an illegitimate tyranny and based their studies of East German society on the SED's own ideological claims and values. For most of the 1970s, Peter Christian Ludz, the leading revisionist, was the leading figure behind the West German government's official annual reports on East Germany and the German Question. In his view, the only legitimate method in analyzing East Germany was to "measure the realities against the theoretical postulates of Marxism-Leninism as propagated by the SED."[5]

Brandt's original idea of mitigating the effects of division and seeking unification in the long term through appeasement of East Germany in the short term had become distorted into a policy of permanent support. In the mid-1980s, the SPD engaged in a series of close, fraternal talks with the Socialist Unity Party (SED), the new name taken by the Communist party in the Soviet zone in 1946. This offended not just the CDU but also many older social democrats as well as dissidents in East Germany, who remembered that the SED had destroyed the SPD in the Soviet zone in 1946 and was for many years the bitterest enemy of social democracy in Germany. In the 1980s, the SPD also insisted that unification would never and should never take place and that West Germany should therefore remove the passage in its Basic Law calling on all Germans to "complete the unity of Germany in freedom." In short, from being prounification and anti-Communist in the 1950s, the bulk of the SPD had become thoroughly antiunification and pro-Communist by 1989. Only the remnants of the old right wing of the party held to a firmer policy on the national question and rejected the meek subservience of their fellows to the arrogant claims of the SED. They had, however, been effectively marginalized in the party since the early 1970s.

It has been necessary to speak at some length about the SPD's past and its attitude toward unification, because only the SPD faced a challenge to thirty years of policy and to its growing pro-GDR orientation in the events of 1989; matters were far simpler for the CDU. In the 1950s, the CDU under Adenauer was the party of democratic capitalism and the free market. The CDU wanted freedom and prosperity for all Germans and rejected calls for unification that would in fact lead to bondage and poverty. In the 1960s, Adenauer's successors developed the policy principle that has guided the CDU ever since and today guides Helmut Kohl and his government in managing the unification process. The CDU, they said, would work toward a "European peace order" within which the German people could exercise their right to self-determination. Like Adenauer, they did not see unification as an abstract goal separate from its political context but wanted a meaningful unification of democratically governed Germans in an integrated Europe. Only such a unification would guarantee peace.

The unification of Germany began on 4 May 1989, when Hungary opened its border to Austria. This gap in the Iron Curtain was an invitation to East Germans to pass through Hungary and reach West Germany. By late summer, thousands were doing so. Thousands more went to Prague, where they occupied the West German embassy, demanding the right to enter West Germany through Czechoslovakia. At that point, the SED in East Berlin seems to have made a crucial decision, which turned out to be the beginning of its downfall. It decided to let not only the East Germans already in Prague but all others who so desired to go to West Germany through Czechoslovakia. Evidently, Honecker and the SED chiefs hoped that only a limited number would take this opportunity. By siphoning off these discontented elements, they thought, they would simultaneously improve their image in the West, satisfy domestic pressure, and preserve their own power.

It is instructive to remember the SPD position at this time. Until the summer of 1989, the SPD continued its high-level contacts and talks with the SED on the basis of full moral equivalence. The SPD, it appeared, had accepted the SED as brother socialists, with whom West German social democrats shared a commitment to peace, stability, and human freedom. As more and more East Germans demonstrated their hatred of the dictatorship, the SPD began distancing itself from the SED. In late summer, Bahr launched a new slogan: "change through distance." Suddenly, the SED was no longer a fully legitimate interlocutor. Bahr's new slogan, unlike his 1963 slogan of "change through rapprochement," was not destined for a long life. Nevertheless, it is worth recalling, since it demonstrated more clearly than many long arguments that the single factor determining the SPD's long relationship with the SED was the fact of Communist power. As long as that power was secure, the SED could intimidate the SPD into the most grotesque and demeaning forms of appeasement. Once that power was seen to be crumbling, the SPD washed its hands of its strange friends as fast as it knew how.

In early October, the SED, under Soviet pressure, made a further crucial decision: not to shoot at the hundreds of thousands of demonstrators who were calling for democratic change and reform in the streets of Leipzig and other cities in East Germany. At that point Gorbachev thought that forcing the SED regime to reform would produce a changed East Germany but one still separate from West Germany. He was not entirely irrational in believing this. The demonstrators in October and November 1989 were not calling for unification. They were calling for respect of human rights, freedom of expression, better work incentives, the right to travel — in short, for a democratically governed East Germany. The leading dissident groups, such as New Forum, called for trust between citizens and responsive government while rejecting the *Ellenbogengesellschaft* (what Americans would call a dog-eat-dog society) of West Germany. Analysts in both the East and the West expected that reform followed by free elections would yield overwhelming support for something resembling the left wing of the SPD: egalitarian, welfare-oriented, anticapitalist, and antiunification.

They were disappointed. Having decided not to massacre the demonstrators, the SED found itself forced to remove Erich Honecker from leadership and to open the Berlin Wall. The people's response was to continue mass emigration, now directly from East to West Germany, and to begin publicly demanding unification. When the Vopos (East German police) did not shoot in Leipzig on 6 October, the people lost what was left of their fear. In the tumultuous weeks that followed, the center of political action in East Germany shifted from the antiunification, socialist groups like New Forum to the much broader, cruder, more popular, and more insistent forces that favored unification and hated the very name of socialism. By January 1990, political parties had formed in East Germany to contest the elections in March. Already the leaders of New Forum and similar groups were heard complaining in some bewilderment that the inhabitants of East Germany did not seem to share their enthusiasm for an independent, reformed nation, for that elusive "third way" of German socialism that would be neither brutally capitalist nor brutally Communist. They did not understand or would not admit that the people knew SED rule to be brutal, stupid, and regressive, whereas West German society, for all its faults, was not that bad; furthermore, only members of the technical and humanistic intelligentsia would benefit from a reformed socialist East Germany, because they would be its ruling class. Other groups in East Germany had nothing at all to gain and much to lose from following such a path. For the vast majority of the people, who were neither members of the SED nomenklatura nor the would-be managers of an enlightened socialist state, unification with West Germany under democratic capitalism offered the obvious — and the only — way toward a better life.

Helmut Kohl, throughout his political career, has suffered from the same problem faced by many other conservative politicians, especially his spiritual mentor, Konrad Adenauer: because the intelligentsia, including most journalists and others who write about and explain politics, are leftist, they have consistently underestimated him. They were surprised when he won the chairmanship of the CDU in 1973, surprised when he won the election in his home state of the Rhineland-Palatinate in 1976, astonished when he led the CDU to within 300,000 votes of an absolute majority that same year, and flabbergasted when he became chancellor in 1982 and confirmed the Bundestag's choice in the national election of January 1983. Whatever one's political ideals and convictions, then, one must admit that Kohl is probably the most skilled and sophisticated German chancellor since Adenauer. His only rival for this position is Helmut Schmidt. On the level of global politics,

Schmidt's grasp was possibly superior to Kohl's. Yet Schmidt displayed significant weaknesses as party leader and in domestic politics. He ignored his radical left wing until it had the party apparatus firmly in its grasp and was therefore subsequently unable to command its support for his own policies. This fatally lowered his credibility in the eyes of his coalition partners in the Free Democratic Party (FDP), who could no longer assume that Schmidt spoke for the SPD. The social-liberal coalition split in 1982 mainly because the FDP knew that Schmidt was no longer able to deliver SPD support for a balanced fiscal policy.

Kohl's skill is stressed to emphasize his extraordinary achievements in early 1990, which contributed decisively to the victory of the East German CDU, despite the fact that most East Germans began the election campaign with a great deal of distrust of the CDU-East, which had been a puppet of the SED for forty years. At the same time, Kohl and his aides did all the preparatory work for West Germany on the treaty of economic unification in order to put it into final form by mid-May and to allow the economic integration of the two Germanys to take place on 1 July 1990. The treaty of economic unification is the single state treaty with a sovereign East Germany that the CDU not only initiated but also actively supported. This would be ironic but for the obvious fact that the treaty of 1972, in which Brandt's SPD government recognized East Germany, had confirmed and supported the power of an illegitimate, dictatorial regime that was denying the rights of its subjects, whereas the 1990 treaty is the first step toward dismantling all that remains of that regime and its legacy—the division of Germany.

At first, the SPD in both East and West Germany presented the events of late 1989—the opening of the Berlin Wall and the democratization of East Germany—as evidence that its policy, especially that of Willy Brandt, was correct. Reform was taking place in East Germany, proving that the SPD's friendly approach was right. However, critics quickly began pointing out that until mid-1989 the SPD had been eager to bolster the hegemony of the Communist party, which had clearly been the single greatest obstacle to reform. As late as September 1989, the former chancellor and SPD chairman, Helmut Schmidt, declared: "An outbreak in the GDR would endanger the reform process in Eastern Europe. The German question will not be solved until the next century." Peter Schneider quoted this sentence in an article that must rank as the most devastating critique of the German left's hostility to reform in central Europe and its complicity with the region's Communist rulers. He went on to comment: "The implicit recommendation to the citizens of the GDR was: 'Keep quiet!' . . . A *tour d'horizon* reveals that the left in recent years again and again belittled the desire for liberty of citizens in the countries beyond the Wall." Worse: the German left, including the SPD, denied what it knew to be true about the human and ecological disasters of Communist states.[6]

With a record like that, how could the SPD take credit for changes that it had actively opposed by its moral, diplomatic, and political support of the SED? According to Peter Schneider, the only way would have been for the SPD and the German left in general to admit that they had been wrong in supporting the Communist regimes and in opposing the dissidents. This level of honesty, however, was too much to ask of the SPD. At its extraordinary party congress in December

1989, the leadership called unification "the fulfillment of an ancient social democratic dream." True, if one ignored the history of the party and its policies for the preceding twenty years. The party program of 1989, which was supposed to be the comprehensive statement of SPD principles and policies for the next thirty years, contained not a word about this supposed "social democratic dream."[7]

Following the East German elections, the SPD began insisting that unification was happening too quickly, was going to cost West Germans too much, would jeopardize the social benefits allegedly enjoyed by East Germans, and would open the door to rampant capitalism in both parts of Germany. The SPD also revised its definition of the SED. Until late 1989, the Germany Communists were fellow socialists; after January 1990, they were once again "communists," with whom true socialists had little in common. Kurt Schumacher, the ferociously anti-Communist SPD leader in the early postwar years, would have smiled grimly at this hasty, somewhat dishonest, and vastly overdue correction of the record.

Looking ahead to the West German national election in December 1990, the SPD adopted a two-track strategy. First, it continued to raise questions in West Germany over the possible costs of unification — a strategy that bore some success in the state elections in Lower Saxony, where the CDU lost its tenuous hold on power in May 1990. Second, the SPD argued that if unification took place, it should be as part of a general process of giving united Germany a new constitution to replace the Basic Law; this new constitution was to include clauses guaranteeing the right to work, partial employee control of business, and protection of the environment, as that phrase is interpreted by socialists. This constitutional argument was designed to sound a note of moderation and common sense — as opposed to what the SPD denounced as the CDU's overhasty plan to have East Germany apply for unification with West Germany under clause 23 of the 1949 Basic Law, which explicitly foresaw such a procedure.

Until September 1989, when thousands of East Germans began occupying the West German embassy in Prague, demanding the right to go west, few if any politicians in West Germany had expected unification, much less had predicted that the process would begin within weeks. The difference between the two major parties was that the SPD no longer officially wanted unification and the CDU did, although the Christian Democrats had no practical policy to achieve it. For over two decades, many people — including members of the CDU — regarded the party's official policy of seeking unification in a "European peace order" as mere lip service to an outdated ideal. Most people thought East Germany was there to stay; it might be more or less oppressive, more or less open to human contacts, but it was not going to disappear.

Nevertheless, the fact remained that the CDU had never given up the hope for unity, though it had become quite abstract, whereas the SPD had. This made it much easier for the CDU and Kohl to slide into the process that began in East Germany in the fall of 1989 and made it awkward for the SPD. The real historical irony in this is that the SPD began as the party of unification, whereas the CDU, in many people's eyes, was the party of division because it favored integration with Western Europe. By pursuing détente with East Germany and courting the

SED, the social democratic leaders had repudiated their claim to be credible defenders of the national interest in unity. Their historic error was to believe that, by repudiating that claim, they were protecting a more important interest in European peace and stability. As it turned out, they were protecting neither peace nor stability but granting approval to the SED's long and bitter war against its victims, the citizens of East Germany. When the crumbling SED regime opened the Berlin Wall on 9 November, the SPD mayor of West Berlin, Wolfgang Momper, insisted: "This is no reunification. It is merely a chance to see one another again." He was expressing the typical view of his party at the time, a view that rapidly changed in the following weeks until, by January 1990, the SPD had joined the unification front that included all parties except the Greens.

A final irony in the politics of unification is that by rejecting unification and supporting the SED the SPD may well have ruined its own chances to be the dominant party in united Germany. The SPD was traditionally the strongest party in the regions that became East Germany in 1949, and as the party of unity and of the working class the SPD would have had a natural majority in any free elections held in East Germany at least through the 1970s. What people regarded as the SPD's abject servility toward the SED bosses — its betrayal of its supposedly sacred democratic principles — destroyed its moral and political standing and led to the defeat in the East German elections in March 1990.

By mid-1990, unification had already taken place on the ground but not at the level of constitutions and institutions, of grand politics, alliances, strategy, and international relations. Many were concerned that the costs of unification would cause inflation and uncertainty in West Germany as well as unemployment and fear of the future in East Germany. Others were afraid that a united Germany — against the desires of its people — would cause fear and worry in the rest of Europe. Yet others were using these concerns to put obstacles in the path of unification. For all these reasons, the path ahead was unclear. But it was clear that a revolution had been taking place in central European politics, culture, and society since mid-1989 and that neither Europe nor the world would ever be the same again.

NOTES

1. *Times Literary Supplement*, review of James J. Sheehan, *German History 1770–1866*, 4–10 May 1990, 463.

2. For an excellent case study of a key episode in America's new cultural civil war, see Aaron Wildavsky, "Robert Bork and the Crime of Inequality," *Public Interest*, no. 98 (Winter 1990), 98–117.

3. The arguments over Stalin's offer have grown hotter as time has passed. See Rolf Steininger, "Freie, gesamtdeutsche Wahlen am 16. November 1952?" in *Die Republik der fünfziger Jahre*, ed. Jurgen Weber (Munich: Olzog, 1989), 88–111.

4. In *Rheinischer Merkur*, 24 Aug. 1985, quoted and commented on by Wolfgang Seiffert, *Das ganze Deutschland. Perspektiven der Wiedervereinigung* (Munich: Piper, 1986), 213.

5. Quoted, with many other outrageous statements by leading Western scholars of East Germany, by Jens Hacker, "Vom Stalinismus zum nationalen Selbstvertrauen?" in *Die Welt*, 17 Mar. 1990.

6. "Man kann sogar ein Erdbeben verpassen," *Die Zeit*, 4 May 1990, 14.

7. Quoted by Hacker.

Alternative Soviet Futures and the New Europe

NILS H. WESSELL

Because the new Europe would be inconceivable without a radical transformation of the Soviet Union's domestic and foreign policies, any systematic assessment of the future of Europe must begin with some consideration of the likely — or, at least, possible — direction of future developments in the Soviet Union. Such an analysis is no longer hampered by the paranoid secrecy that shrouded the Kremlin for generations. But it poses a daunting challenge to the forecasting of the future of a once-rigid society undergoing an unprecedented rupture of social controls. This thaw has spawned the resurgence of political movements that are incompatible. To make matters worse, these antagonistic tendencies are gathering force in a society where the dominant political culture for centuries has honored ideological hairsplitting, conspiracy, and purge over voluntary consensus, mutual goodwill, and political coalition building. The last three characteristics are indispensable to peaceful democratic development and, incidentally, helpful to the analyst crafting a judicious linear projection.

Alexis de Tocqueville, and later Crane Brinton, observed that the moment of maximum danger for a repressive regime is when it begins to mend its ways. Its self-confidence shaken and its internal cohesion disintegrating, the regime boldly embarks on reforms that unleash long pent-up hopes that are not easily controlled, since they greatly exceed the regime's new limits to reform. At the same time, reform undermines the regime's hard-earned reputation for brutally repressing spontaneous political activity — a reputation that is the psychological bedrock of its hold on power.

While it may be premature to conclude that the Soviet regime has lost confidence in itself, it has certainly lost its internal cohesion. Moreover, it has haltingly begun to reform itself, giving vent to new social movements. While this process

The views expressed in this essay are the author's and do not necessarily reflect those of the U.S. Information Agency or the United States government.

unfolded, most of the world was preoccupied with the fate of Soviet President Mikhail S. Gorbachev. But Soviet citizens themselves have largely lost interest in the personal fate of Gorbachev and have shifted their attention to the broader political, economic, and social issues that confront the Soviet system. In doing so, they should lead Western observers in the same direction. However historic Gorbachev's role in instigating the reform of his country's political culture and institutions, the broad social forces that he unleashed—both favoring reform and opposing it—have acquired a life of their own. The crazy quilt of popular demands for restructuring the political system is superimposed on similarly diverse views on economic reform and explosive demands by the ethnic minorities that make up nearly half the Soviet population. The result is rather like the effect achieved by overlaying a dozen clear plastic maps, the contours of which do not align.

Gorbachev's reactionary foes may be excused for questioning his actions. After twenty years of domestic tranquillity, what was so urgent that he had to bring the country to what he himself has called the brink of civil war? Unlike Western observers, his opponents in the KGB, military, and party can scarcely be buoyed by the thought that progress toward greater freedom and democratization may both resolve the crisis and justify its growing costs.

Gorbachev has sparked a process of upheaval normally associated only with wartime leaders or successful revolutionaries. Such an achievement alone justified *Time* magazine's selection of Gorbachev as Man of the Decade—the 1980s, not the 1990s. One can imagine that if *Time* had been publishing in the 1860s, Czar Alexander II would have vied for this honor with the American president, Abraham Lincoln. The Czar Liberator was also assassinated, the victim of a terrorist attack. If the pairings may be excused, the fates of Lincoln and Alexander II, Hitler and Khrushchev, Napoleon and de Gaulle suggest the variety of personal dangers that Gorbachev faces. All of these leaders effected deep institutional change at home and abroad, usually against fierce resistance.

The contemporary analyst would have erred if he had ignored the ways in which the political, economic, and social system was reacting to the changes of which the leader was the harbinger, with the exception of Hitler. In short, the social forces that brought the leader to power outlived him, and the same is likely to be true of Gorbachev. What are these forces? And what do they suggest about alternative futures for the Soviet political system and for the future of Europe?

Social Forces

By now even the casual Western observer is familiar with the seven principal social forces in the Soviet Union:

1. The Moscow and Leningrad intelligentsia initially supported Gorbachev warmly but have become increasingly disillusioned, partly because their expectations were too high and partly because Gorbachev is no Jeffersonian democrat. In any event, they will remain ineffectual unless their agitation and propaganda

change traditional Russian preferences for authoritarian political values. The intelligentsia will affect the future to the extent that they democratize the Duma-like Congress of People's Deputies and the Supreme Soviet. To be influential, these legislative organs must infringe on the now constitutionally protected powers of the executive authority. It may be that no coup has yet been organized against Gorbachev partly because of the deterrent effect of a somewhat mobilized public opinion. But even as the intelligentsia are able to mobilize large crowds to demonstrate in favor of greater democracy, they are unlikely to be effective against a coup if a coterie of party, KGB, and military rivals screws its courage to the sticking place.

2. The emerging entrepreneurial class is likely to provide support for radical economic reform. This support will be important not because Soviet entrepreneurs are numerous or influential but because they will be the de facto implementers of any reform that frees up market forces. If they do their job, guided by Adam Smith's Invisible Hand, they can ultimately make Gorbachev look good. It is in their hands to demonstrate the superiority of capitalism over communism, but only if Soviet economic policymakers give them a chance. Gorbachev must first find the courage to act on the implicit message of the sign held up by an East German demonstrator in 1989 in Leipzig: "What the War Did Not Destroy, Socialism Did."

3. The nomenklatura of party, state, trade union, and collective-farm officials is threatened by glasnost and perestroika where it hurts: their jobs. The term nomenklatura refers to a list of positions that may be filled only with the approval of the next higher level of party officials. Like so much else in the Soviet Union, this system may be obsolescent. If the party's authority is being undermined at all levels, who is to approve high-level appointments in trade unions, collective farms, newspapers, and the myriad institutions long under the party's control? The nomenklatura's jobs would ultimately be threatened by democratization. In the meantime, their jobs have been made excruciatingly difficult. An American federal bureaucrat, annoyed by burdensome requests under the Freedom of Information Act (1966, amended in 1974), can only imagine the scope of the nomenklatura's exasperation. Their long-accustomed Berlin Wall of protection against public scrutiny is tumbling down. For many years, of course, they have been able to go to the front of the line for a new apartment or an automobile. But the luxury of doing business in secret has been the ultimate perquisite. Like the emerging entrepreneurs, members of the nomenklatura are relatively few in number, but they have great operational influence. Just as Gorbachev has not yet taken significant measures to free up the economy, they have done little to remove him from power. Perhaps this is the implicit bargain that has thus far ensured the stability of the existing political arrangement: so long as Gorbachev only tinkers with the political superstructure, the owners of the means of production will merely drag their feet.

4. The army and the KGB leadership, of course, are part of the nomenklatura. For the first four years of Gorbachev's tenure, the KGB and the military were said to have been key backers of both Gorbachev and reform. Operating in the real

world, the KGB was said to understand the full dimensions of the economy's collapse. It realized the magnitude of popular discontent because of its intelligence and informer networks. The army was said to fear technological obsolescence unless vigorous reform was undertaken.

Nevertheless, army and KGB leaders must be deeply disturbed by events since the fall of 1989. The KGB has lost irreplaceable assets in Eastern Europe. It cannot possibly keep track of domestic threats to stability. It cannot even ensure the inviolability of Soviet borders. Meanwhile, the army is in strategic retreat. Not only has the Soviet Union lost its allies in Eastern Europe, but the Soviet army is being expelled from the territory of its traditional enemy, Germany. The United States defeat in Vietnam scarcely altered the balance of power in comparison with the impact of the Soviet Union's ongoing defeat in Eastern Europe. Even more ominously, the Soviet army has been given the task of suppressing domestic rebellions, a role that few armies prize.

5. Workers, the classic blue-collar *rabochie*, have always been poor in Russia. Deprived of their most elementary rights under communism, they are now fulfilling Marx's prophecy of their fate under capitalism. Their immiserization under perestroika recalls the Soviet anecdote about how socialism is the transitional stage between capitalism and . . . capitalism. For three generations the hard core of physical laborers was sustained by their belief in Leninist myths concerning the role of the working class led by its vanguard, the Communist party and concerning imperialist encirclement and all the related Marxist-Leninist gobbledygook that the Western peace movement took seriously. But Communist ideology has lately been demystified. As recent polls and elections in Poland, Hungary, Czechoslovakia, and East Germany have shown, only 10 percent of the people in those countries believed the myths propagated by their regimes and fostered by left-wingers in the West. (In the relative backwaters of Romania and Bulgaria, the myths have persisted while the comrades donned sheep's clothing.)

Their ideological illusions punctured by glasnost, Soviet workers will also be the likely victims of any real economic reform. In Leonid I. Brezhnev's era of stagnation—which may yet be looked back on as a golden age—worker discontent would not have made any difference, but times have changed. Reforming regimes tend to revive long-dormant institutions, which in time assert themselves and undermine the legitimacy of the regime that resuscitated them. In prerevolutionary France, for example, the ancien regime revived the Estates-General and the parlements. Today, Gorbachev seems intent on encouraging the revival of quasi-independent trade unions. Labor unrest in the coal mines of Siberia and the Don Basin suggests that he is already getting more than he bargained for. The long passivity of Soviet workers is ending just as their rations are being cut.

6. The peasantry remains a largely unknown factor. Until the last decade, Soviet leaders were usually peasant in social origin. They may have indicated "worker" on their party documents, but most of them or their parents had just left the land. As Richard Pipes has argued, they reflected the worst traditions of the Russian

village: suspicious of outsiders and inclined to resolve disputes by force rather than by the law, which had traditionally enserfed them.

Peasants were once such an overwhelming majority of the Russian population that Lenin thought that he had to promise them land to engage them in the cause of an urban proletarian revolution; they now account for less than 20 percent of the Soviet population. Nevertheless, the solution to the Soviet food problem is in their hands. The problem is that peasants were cannon fodder in World War I, had their harvest taken by force during the Civil War, were uprooted by collectivization and decimated by proletarian hooligans and famine, and were treated as subhuman by the Wehrmacht and SS. Since World War II, they have been subjected to ruthless economic exploitation. Now these peasants are expected to believe in a scrap of paper that asserts their right to hold leases to their land in perpetuity. The new thinkers even promise that they may pass this land on to their sons and daughters. In return for this piece of paper, the Soviet government expects them to work as hard as an American farmer whose family has owned the land since the Homestead Act of 1862. Gorbachev has yet to recognize this problem. Lawyers rarely understand farmers.

Although the intermittent rural uprisings of the eighteenth century seem unlikely to recur today, the peasants wield the same kind of indirect power that their urban counterparts exert: they can refuse to work. By doing so, they may yet force the regime to go beyond the convoluted half-measures that it calls agricultural reform. Without a free market in agricultural products, perestroika cannot succeed. If perestroika fails to improve the food supply, urban workers will not work. The regime, in short, is in a box, and the peasant sits idly on top of it.

7. If all this were not enough, the most volatile social forces have yet to be mentioned. The national minorities of the Soviet Union (usually majorities in their own republics) are no longer ignored by everyone but Western specialists. The first independent surveys of public opinion in the Baltic republics reveal, not surprisingly, that Estonians and Lithuanians desire independence, want the Communists expelled from power, and favor cuts in military spending. In the Caucasus, local national majorities want the Russians to stay only to the extent that they may be useful in teaching their ethnic rivals a lesson. In Central Asia, Uzbeks and Turks have taken to the streets, aroused by primitive resentments of each other (and Russians). In Moldavia the republic Supreme Soviet has declared Russians to be "occupiers" and threatened them with the loss of their jobs if they do not learn the Moldavian language by 1994. This brief account merely scratches the surface of the ineradicable ethnic antagonisms that only the intimidating interlude of Stalinism succeeded in suppressing. Even more serious, the antagonists are armed. In light of the role of indigenous nationalities in supplying the Soviet army's manpower (and in guarding the armories), one official Soviet estimate that over 15 million unregistered guns are in private hands may be understated. This circumstance may explain the charge by General Igor N. Rodionov — commander of the military forces that killed over a dozen Georgians with gas and sharpened

shovels in April 1989 — that the situation in the country was worse than in 1937, at the peak of Stalin's blood purge.

For all its complexity, the situation in the Soviet Union over the last few years could be summarized by the observation that even as Gorbachev continued to win almost every important political battle in the Kremlin, he was increasingly losing his ability to govern the country. What of the future? Will the Soviet Union survive in a form that is both Soviet and a union?

Writing about alternative futures can be a way to evade difficult questions, an evasion that may become more palatable to the reader who recalls the forecasting record of Sovietologists. Stock-market forecasters observe this maxim: forecast a number if you must; forecast a year if you must; but never forecast a year *and* a number. Although Sovietologists, unlike stock-market forecasters, may predict a year without having to predict a number, the results have not been any more consistently satisfactory. With this caveat, one can discount several scenarios for which there is precedent in recent Russian history. A return to Stalinism is unlikely, if only because the scale of human destruction would be immense and the incidence of paranoia among Soviet leaders required for such a return to systematized barbarism is currently lacking. Still, one conceivable Soviet future is essentially Stalinist from an institutional standpoint, that is, a big centralized government suffocating the creative energies of a remarkably talented population on the (not entirely) specious pretext that the alternative is social anarchy.

A second future would not have needed mentioning until the 1989 revolutions in Eastern Europe: a *February* (not October) *Revolution*. Such a popular revolution, violent or peaceful, would lead to a change of personalities and a change of social regime. Despite the willingness of hundreds of thousands of Baltic peoples to link up in a "Hands Across the Baltic" demonstration and similar numbers of Russians in the capital to turn out for prodemocracy rallies, Gorbachev has been careful not to shoot the demonstrators as the czar did on Bloody Sunday in 1905, touching off the chaos that would lead to the Revolution. Nor is Gorbachev irresolute. Some Soviets may see him as an "idle chatterer," but Soviet Foreign Minister Andrey Gromyko's now-forgotten reference to Gorbachev is almost certainly closer to the mark. In his speech nominating Gorbachev for general secretary on Konstantin Chernenko's death, Gromyko acknowledged Gorbachev's nice smile but added that the prospective general secretary had teeth of iron.[1]

Even as Gorbachev's reforms in domestic and foreign policy are rightfully applauded, analysts should bear in mind several of his other decisions: to purge virtually all of his political opponents from office (even if some sneak back by election); to create an institutional presidency, substantially freeing himself of the Communist party, as Stalin did; to occupy Baku and subdue the nationalist Azerbaijan Popular Front by force while keeping the foreign press out; and to conduct a military war of nerves in the Baltic to slow down, if not reverse, the movement toward national independence. Gorbachev is no Alexander Kerensky.

A third improbable scenario is the one that most popular commentary has assumed will be the ultimate outcome after some trial and error: Gorbachev succeeds. This scenario is improbable for two reasons. First, no one knows—perhaps not even Gorbachev—what he is really trying to accomplish. On the one hand, he has substantially discredited the Communist party, legitimized factional politics within it, encouraged a freer press, allowed greater leeway to national republics, and permitted more democratic elections than at any time since voters rejected the Bolsheviks in the post–October 1917 elections to the Constituent Assembly that Lenin disbanded at bayonet point. On the other hand, Gorbachev has frequently declared himself a Marxist-Leninist, has been assailed by Andrey Sakharov's widow, Elena Bonner, as antidemocratic and illiberal, and has for over two decades been married to a woman who taught Marxist-Leninist ideology to a generation of hapless Soviet students at Moscow State University.

Second, if Gorbachev's objective is to save socialism and make it more efficient, this scenario is completely unrealistic. Marxist socialism has been tried in more than a dozen countries since 1917, and it failed everywhere—a remarkable record for a theory that claims to be scientific. One exception to this rule over the last two decades was supposed to have been East Germany. Apparently, no one informed the East Germans that they were the model of socialism's success. In fact, of course, they were told ad nauseam, a self-congratulatory drumbeat that only discredited the Communist regime further.

Three other scenarios may be more plausible than the ones just discussed: (1) St. Petersburg Spring, (2) Return to Normalcy, and (3) Coup d'Etat.

Scenario 1: St. Petersburg Spring

In the St. Petersburg Spring scenario, "socialism with a human face"—the slogan of Czechoslovak Communist reformers during the Prague Spring of 1968—has been overtaken by free elections. The model is not Communist reformer Alexander Dubcek but the anti-Communist Václav Havel—a man of letters, not a man of scientific communism. While it may be hard to imagine such a development in Russia, which was largely untouched by the Enlightenment, it is worth noting that Havel's symbolic counterpart in the Soviet Union, the late Andrey Sakharov, was reported in one Soviet poll to have enjoyed a higher degree of popularity than Gorbachev. To the extent that Gorbachev persists in advocating free elections, the more likely he is one day to suffer from the same phenomenon recorded so graphically in recent elections in Eastern Europe: the people do not like what Communist leaders stand for.

In this decidedly optimistic future, genuine democracy and civil liberties take root. They are accompanied, as they have been historically, by economic freedom—the abandonment of Marx as well as Lenin, jettisoning socialism as well as the Communist party. Prices are freely determined by the market, factories are privatized, and the central plan is thrown onto Marx's junkheap of history.

Most critically, this scenario means the disintegration of the territorial integrity of the country. "Soviets without Communists" was the popular slogan of the Bolsheviks' opponents in Petrograd and Kronstadt in 1921. Seventy years later, after partly free elections, Communists are in the minority in the Moscow, Leningrad, and Kiev city soviets. In this scenario, they are in the minority nationally and have surrendered the state apparatus: the Soviet Union is no longer Communist. Nor is it much of a union, since the inevitable consequence of democracy is secession. Elections, survey research, and recent events make it clear that no democratically elected government in the Baltic will freely choose to remain a part of the Soviet Union. Rising ethnic tensions elsewhere, even if directed against some nationality other than Russians, are likely to lead to similar separatist sentiment as Moscow's troops become occupiers in the eyes of at least one of the warring nationalities.

With respect to foreign and defense policy, the St. Petersburg Spring translates into a real end to the cold war. The European security environment is transformed as the Soviet Union unilaterally dissolves the institutional remnants of the Warsaw Pact and seeks membership in the North Atlantic Treaty Organization (NATO) as a sign of its commitment to Western democratic values and a common European home. Can anyone imagine that the new Soviet president, Andrey Sakharov's political heir, will have serious differences of principle or fundamental conflicts of interest with the United States? Would such a government spend billions of dollars to prop up Fidel Castro in Cuba, Mengistu Haile Marian in Ethiopia, and Najibullah Ahmadzai in Afghanistan? After all, it took only a few weeks in Czechoslovakia for President Havel to ban the export of Semtex, the explosive preferred by Libyan-sponsored terrorists, and close down the Czech terrorist training camps that Claire Sterling correctly identified even as her critics dismissed the idea that the Soviet Union would ever countenance terrorism.

Nevertheless, there may be flaws within this scenario. Ethnic rivalries inside the Soviet Union, where they are Gorbachev's problem, will become armed conflicts between small nation-states in search of great-power protection. In January 1990 the Shiite Azeris in the Azerbaijan enclave of Nakhichevan, located within the Armenian republic and bordering Iran, called on both Turkey and Iran to support their declaration of secession from the Soviet Union. In this alternative future, when the Brezhnev doctrine has no currency, will Turkey, a NATO member, remain indifferent to the fate of Turkic-speaking people in Azerbaijan and Soviet Central Asia? After all, while 44 million Turks are living in Turkey, 42 million Turkic-speaking people live in the Soviet Union. Or will Iran continue indefinitely to be deterred from coming to the assistance of coreligionists along its borders who are no longer under Muscovite protection? These examples of "internal" ethnic conflicts becoming sources of international conflict could be multiplied many times over, including several potential tinderboxes in what is now the European part of the USSR, central Europe, and the Balkans.

In short, a post-Communist Eastern Europe and Soviet Union will almost certainly prove more unstable than the cold war, which produced forty years of uninterrupted peace in Europe. In fact, the decline of communism may require an alliance or collective security system far more politically ambitious than NATO. Since effective diplomacy rests on power, which requires something more than economic sanctions to back it up, the need for conventional military forces may actually increase. Such forces may be under the command of NATO, an expanded NATO, or a successor to the alliance. While the need for these forces may increase, it is unlikely they would have to be nuclear-based or as numerous as present conventional deployments.

Scenario 2: Return to Normalcy

Frederick Lewis Allen, in 1931, wrote a breezy but influential book called *Only Yesterday* on American society in the 1920s, the era that he called the "Return to Normalcy." Warren G. Harding, Calvin Coolidge, and the early Herbert Hoover presided reassuringly over nearly a decade of prosperity.

In the Soviet Union a return to normalcy means something quite different: a return to stagnation — late Hoover economically, Harding ethically. Usually identified with Brezhnev, this period arguably extends back in time to Stalin's last years and the hare-brained schemes that followed it. The common thread linking Stalin's last years, the Khrushchev era, and Brezhnev's tenure is the emphasis on what Soviet economists call the extensive rather than intensive model of economic growth, in which money and people are used to expand gross output instead of employing brains, technology, and a system of individual incentives to boost the quality of production.

In effect, under a Return to Normalcy the economy would be run in a manner envisaged during Yuri V. Andropov's brief tenure. Instead of freeing up market forces, labor discipline would be imposed to improve productivity. The result would be uninspiring but not fatal, a kind of muddling through in which Soviet technological innovation would continue to lag. Everyone who showed up for work would have a job, particularly the nomenklatura. In this scenario there is no unemployment, no visible inflation, no need to pay high prices at a co-op, and no need to watch someone with initiative get rich. No more demonstrations, no more ingrates spitting on the socialist motherland, and no more youths aping outlandish foreign fads in music and dress. No more parliamentary windbags, quarreling with one another and casting aspersions on Vladimir Ilyich. In short, socialist heaven.

The nationalities, however, could ask for more. They will be kept by force within the embrace of the motherland if the early Gorbachev is subsequently judged a right-wing deviationist, perhaps by the later Gorbachev. None of this reversion to the norm could be accomplished without shedding blood, but the reimposition of order does not necessarily require a full-scale Stalinist bloodbath or genocide. So long as the KGB's Second Chief Directorate (Internal Security) and Directorate to Defend the Constitution keep their informer networks up-to-date, one or two exemplary suppressions of nationalism may be sufficient. But they would have to be more impressive than the relatively modest level of killings in Baku in January 1990 (ninety-three by one early count) and in Tbilisi in April 1989 (nineteen by the USSR Supreme Soviet's count).

In foreign and defense policy, a Return to Normalcy will prove a disappointment to hard-core Brezhnevites. The Warsaw Pact cannot be reconstituted, short of multiple invasions that today might encounter organized resistance not merely by unarmed civilians but by organized national armies. This correlation of forces suggests that for Moscow the crucial threshold for the Baltic or other independence movements may be the first signs of the organization of national armies in the republics. Indeed, at the height of Moscow's war of nerves with Lithuania in March 1990, Gorbachev instructed President Vytautus Landsbergis to "report fulfillment within two days" of Moscow's order to halt creation of territorial defense units.

For Europe and the United States, normalcy is not a bad outcome. NATO would still be needed, and in light of Soviet military action to suppress rebellious nationalities, the Western public would likely support NATO out of sense of prudence. But the offensive military threat by Soviet forces no longer stationed west of Brest would have greatly diminished.

Scenario 3: Coup d'Etat

In this scenario, the KGB or the Soviet military remove their nemesis from power by assassination rather than by election. Gorbachev goes the way of Edward Gierek, who was replaced peacefully as Polish party secretary by Stanislaw Kania, head of the secret police, who was then replaced by General Wojciech Jaruzelski. The orthodox Communist opponents of Gorbachev are finally heard from. While each new, quasi-free election makes a coup less likely, the dialectically inclined will argue the opposite: the worse things get—that is, the more elections and the more chaos—the more likely that disaffected elements in the KGB and military will act. But the countervailing fact is that with every new election legitimizing non-Communist political organizations, it becomes more awkward for would-be plotters.

The domestic and foreign-policy consequences of such a coup are extremely difficult to predict. In the aftermath, the KGB has a strong organizational interest in suppressing all kinds of threats to domestic tranquility, not the least among the national minorities. By the same token, the military, earlier under siege even more severely than during Khrushchev's campaign to cut its manpower and its budget, moves to reverse present policies threatening not only their active-duty manpower but also their forward deployments. The social anarchy set loose by Gorbachev's policies has also compromised its ability to call up reserves without the complaints of mothers being taken more seriously than national-security requirements, as happened when irate mothers forced a reversal of the call-up of thousands of reservists to occupy Azerbaijan in January 1990. "Soviet Army—Don't Shoot Your Own People," read one protestor's placard. Nor will the military have to endure a lot of post-Afghanistan mud being thrown at them in public.

It is difficult to imagine such a successor regime's agreeing to forgo its military assets in the Baltic, particularly ones critical for early detection of a strategic attack on Moscow. And how will the Soviet military be able to defend East Prussia without Soviet ground forces transiting Lithuania?

As for the economy in this scenario, the military-KGB regime overthrowing Gorbachev will have no interest in overseeing experiments in creating market forces autonomous of political authority. Nor are they likely to foster the integration of the Soviet economy into the world economic system, on which it would be dependent. Control over Soviet foreign economic relations will be recentralized to prevent what Henry Kissinger in the 1970s hoped would be the creation of a web of vested economic interests in the Soviet Union in favor of détente with the United States.

The new regime's determination to root out the sources of Gorbachevism will require, in the manner of its Chinese comrades, a calculated assault against Western values and influences. In foreign policy, this implies an abrupt retreat from cooperative problem solving and arms-control agreements mandating intrusive verification means. It will also mean abandoning the now-threatening myth of a common European home. Aleksander Yakovlev, leading ideologue of Right Deviationism and earlier exiled as ambassador to Canada, is banished once again to North America, perhaps to Quebec instead of Ottawa.

From the standpoint of European security, this is the least favorable outcome. It will involve clandestine efforts to oust one or more democratic regimes in central Europe, possibly under the convenient cover of armed ethnic clashes in the region. The traditional Soviet bugbear of German revanchism, rendered more plausible by the existence of a strong unified German state, is likely to be revived as a justification for overthrowing the leader whose "weakness" (the charge against Alexander Dubcek) allowed reunification of Russia's most dangerous enemy. If this coup takes place before NATO's disintegration, the complete collapse of the alliance may be forestalled. But if it occurs after NATO's demise, its reconstitution is unlikely and European security may face its greatest challenge of the century as a divided Europe faces a resurgent adversary no longer hemmed in by a Western commitment to containment.

NOTE

1. The Gorbachev era of glasnost began with the deletion of this reference from the official transcript of Gromyko's speech. See Dusko Doder, *Shadows and Whispers* (New York: Random House, 1986), 266–67.

NATO's Future Role:
A European View

DAVID ROBERTSON

No discussion of the North Atlantic Treaty Organization (NATO) today can ignore two vital points about that alliance. First, a point far too long ignored, NATO is only one of the plethora of intersecting multinational agreements and organizations in Europe. Second, many of the reasons that NATO has been popular in Europe have little or nothing to do with either its overt purposes or America's interests. Only by discussing the other institutions and the latent functions of NATO can one hope to come to an understanding of its possible futures. Thus, much of this essay involves talking about things other than NATO as we have known it.

For all European members, NATO has always had a set of functions over and above its overt role of providing collective defense against an invasion by the Warsaw Treaty Organization (WTO). Some of these functions are common to many or most members but of special interest to a few. So, for example, NATO has been valued as a way of keeping the United States actively involved in European security, and especially in ensuring nuclear "coupling." Though all members can be seen to share this interest, it has, perhaps, been of most importance to West Germany.

For some countries, NATO has served as a legitimation for having military forces at all. The smaller members — the Netherlands and Belgium are good examples — would find it hard to justify to their own voters a military posture much greater than that of a border guard were they not part of an integrated military alliance. In much the same way, the commitment to NATO has been the only focus of defense consensus in British politics for more than a decade, allowing governments to continue spending a disproportionate part of gross national product (GNP) on defense, compared with their European allies. For the United Kingdom and even more for France, NATO's ready forces and the guaranteed American reinforcements have provided a shield behind which defense postures have been developed that have little to do with direct territorial defense. In both cases, money has been available for strategic nuclear arms and for an "out of theater" intervention capacity that could not have been spared had either country been forced to provide fully for its own conventional defense against a Soviet threat. In both cases, NATO has allowed defense policies aimed more at retaining "major" (though not, of course, "super") power status than at specific military goals.

To a much lesser degree, NATO has also provided for Europe what it has, perhaps principally, provided for the United States — membership in a semiofficial, general Western ideological force in world politics. On the whole, European members have preferred to see NATO as a purely regional defense pact, but to the extent that they have, collectively or separately, wished to join their voices to the "defense of Western values," NATO has been the only game in town. None of these functions satisfied by NATO have very much to do with the specific threat posed by the WTO or by the USSR itself. NATO has always been, certainly in law, and to a varying extent in practice, a "political" union as well as a military alliance. Indeed, at its origin it was primarily political and but for the Korean War might have taken much longer to develop the historically unique military structure it is best known for. This political role is now being stressed far more than in the past, both by diplomats and bureaucrats in Brussels and by some member governments. It is important to remember two things, however, as a background to any discussion of a primarily "political" future for NATO. First, as opposed to the Supreme Headquarters, Allied Powers Europe (SHAPE), NATO is a very small organization, and on the whole it has been subservient to the supreme allied commander, Europe (SACEUR) and his military staff in the development of policy and strategy. As it currently exists, NATO is ill-equipped to play much of a role in international politics. Second, the idea of NATO membership as membership in a political alliance where foreign policy is determined probably has no political legitimacy for the electorates of its member states. This is not to say that it could not develop such a role in the public eye but simply that at the moment voters throughout the sixteen states only know of it as a specifically military protection against one specified threat. It must be an open question to what extent voters in Italy, France, the United Kingdom, or America, to mention just four members, would accept that their governments should develop broad foreign policies along the lines of consensus-seeking in NATO. In the United States, the United Kingdom, and France, important neoisolationist feelings have, perhaps, been kept in check only by the traditional threat perception of the Soviet Union. Furthermore, the United Kingdom, France, and Italy are members of a rival supranational body, the European Community (EC), which has long striven to be the institution for the development of an integrated European foreign policy.

Nonetheless, institutions seldom if ever abolish themselves because their function has ceased to be necessary — they simply adopt new functions, suffering what organizational sociology calls "goal displacement." For several reasons it seems that NATO will not go the way of the Central Treaty Organization (CENTO), which was abolished, and is likely indeed to remain more important and vital than the South East Asia Treaty Organization (SEATO). The strongest reason to expect NATO to continue in some form or other is a negative one. Everyone accepts that Europe needs some form of supranational security organization for reasons that will be examined shortly. At the same time, there is little confidence in Europe that brand-new institutions can be created and even less confidence in other existing institutions. As Flora Lewis pointed out, reporting on a recent international conference where this author was present, there was widespread skepticism about "building institutions on a concept."[1] The utter failure of the League of Nations has not been forgotten in Europe, and even with American membership it would have been an essentially European institution. The next two sections explore both the reasons for assuming Europe needs some sort of international security organization and arguments against all other bodies except NATO. The final section sketches the likely future role and nature of NATO itself.

Why Does Europe Need Anything?

Although most practitioners of European security take it for granted that some supranational body must look after the continent's future security, the question that heads this section is eminently fair. Although other world regions do have security organizations, like the Organization of American States (OAS), their records are not such as to inspire confidence in their utility. Furthermore, Europe has, after all, survived for a long time without any formal organization. Either the balance of power worked — as it did for many years — or it failed. It is impossible to believe that any form of regional supranational organization could have prevented the Franco-Prussian War or World War I, and all international bodies failed in World War II. More directly, it can be argued that although World War I did not turn out to be the "war to end wars," World War II did. But the cold war was also a war, and the West "won" it. The thesis is quite popular that liberal states cannot make war on other liberal states, and the future of Europe is a future of liberal states. If any of these arguments are true, there would seem to be little point in continuing an obviously irrelevant military alliance like NATO. Any future organizations would more usefully be developed on juridical lines for the resolution of conflicts that, if not resolved, would still not lead to war.

One reason these arguments are not accepted by Western European governments, or indeed by any of the superpowers, is that the historical record is not thought to justify such optimism. At the same time, predictions of the behavior of the newly free Eastern European states, and to some extent contemporary events in them, are thought by many to herald serious instability. Essentially two issues crop up when the need for a security oversight body in Europe is pressed. The more commonly mentioned problem, at least in public, is that of minorities. It seems to be generally believed that minority issues in Eastern Europe risk being destabilizing to so serious an extent that war might break out. Those who hold this view are not very good at citing concrete evidence, but recent problems in Romania and between Hungary and Romania are usually presented. At the same time, the problem of "German" minorities in Poland are combined with the entirely separate question of the Soviet Union's Baltic provinces to suggest that borders may be in serious question in the near future of Europe.

It might usefully be noted that the Conference on Security and Cooperation in Europe (CSCE) talks have failed to deal with the minorities question since 1977 largely because Western European states refused to have such issues tabled. At no stage has anyone believed that these countries would come to blows because of minorities. It cannot, of course, be disputed that the economic problems of Eastern Europe are so severe and the expectations placed on the developing democracies so high that their political futures may be at risk. In particular, it must be true that an authoritarian regime could arise in, say, Hungary and such a regime might play on nationalistic attitudes in a dangerous way. But how dangerous would even such an event be for Europe as a whole? Is it even remotely plausible that war could erupt in Europe because of an assassination of or by Hungarians, Serbs, Slavs, Czechs, Poles, or Austrians? If the minorities problem is the reason for requiring a new security regime in Europe, it requires a deep conviction about an improbable scenario.

The more powerful worry is referred to politely as the German Question. NATO, or something like it, must stay in being to constrain a unified Germany from . . . ? That is where the intellectual, as opposed to the political, question arises. One of the more interesting phenomena of this entire debate is the way in which Americans and some Western Europeans attempt to persuade the USSR that keeping Germany in NATO is in the USSR's interest. The entire thesis rests on what some might think an oversimple historical thesis. Germany, according to some, is apparently fated frequently to be overcome by a desire to conquer Europe. Consequently, the USSR should prefer to have 16 million Germans and their army—supplied by the USSR—transferred to an alliance that has for forty years opposed the USSR on the ground that it will somehow control this periodic quest. Applied to any other historical scenario, such a *simpliste* view of social history could not be acceptable from a sophomore. Absent some very unusual factors, the idea that a country can become more secure by transferring a previous ally to an opposing alliance, rather than requiring its neutrality, is difficult to credit. These special arguments for a continued membership of a United Germany in NATO will be discussed in the next section. At this point it is enough to recognize a widespread, if incoherent, fear of German expansion throughout Europe.

Though the Soviet Union's initial preference may have been for neutrality, the USSR has neither given up the thought of an alternative European security structure nor opposed NATO's existence itself. The fear can be seen to express itself in most of Eastern Europe by a clearly stated desire that NATO should not be disbanded. In Poland there is an ambiguity on the question of continued deployment of Soviet troops in their territory not found elsewhere in the East that is directly caused by Poland's fear that it may need military support against Germany. Western Europe's fears are less of future military threats than about the new Germany's economic power. Though it should be remembered that until recently most Western European leaders were prepared to insist openly that Germany should not be unified, not, as the Germans themselves claimed, that it could not be. Even here "NATO or something" is seen as the answer by ensuring that German politics develops with a strong sense of obligation to pan-European interests. Chancellor Helmut Kohl's own phrase well describes the hopes and fears that Germany should seek "not a German Europe, but a European Germany." Whether the retention of armed military alliances has any logical connection to solving these fears of economic dominance is arguable, but there is a strong tendency at the moment to load extra tasks on existing institutions rather than build new ones.

There are other pressures for some supranational security arrangement in the new undivided Europe. Some are technical, the principal one being the monitoring of arms-control agreements. This is likely to be a major undertaking, especially for the Conventional Forces in Europe (CFE) and any successor arrangement. The hope is clear that future arms races between any pair of countries, especially the potentially more unstable Eastern European states, will be constrained. One argument is that each pact needs the other—a WTO complaint about rearmament in, say, Turkey and Greece would allow NATO to pressure these two NATO members, and similarly the WTO would hope that NATO would complain about, say, Hungary and Romania.

Though there is much optimism about arms control, nuclear and otherwise, between the superpowers and among European states, there are two imbalances that arms control cannot rectify. Both pertain to the fact that when everything is signed and sealed, Russia, if not the Soviet Union, will remain an enormously powerful country. However successful the Strategic Arms Reduction Talks (START) negotiations are, neither START nor any successor talks can completely denuclearize Europe. The Soviet Union will remain a nuclear power, and unless the United Kingdom and France can somehow be brought to extend their deterrence over the whole of Europe, an ultimate reliance will have to continue to be placed on the American strategic arsenal. The second asymmetry is at the conventional level, between the Soviet Union and European powers. It may be possible to integrate a general European military force powerful enough to stand off a Soviet intrusion, but frankly this is unlikely. If the combined forces of the United Kingdom, France, and West Germany were not enough during the cold war, the addition of very poor Eastern European countries to such an alliance seems of little utility. Of course, the scenario has changed enormously. We no longer think of a standing start invasion from the intra-German border. Instead, we would have to contemplate a much more "traditional" war where, after a long mobilization, a Soviet army had to brush away Polish and Czechoslovakian forces and march hundreds of kilometers before it engaged in military defenses of the economic plums of Europe. Nonetheless, there is nothing in history to suggest that this could not happen: American forces would again have to go "over there." But that would be back to the old scenario—they would not be in Europe and might not even have a standing obligation to go to Europe's aid. In the absence of a security organization that tied United States forces in place to the defense of Europe, it is quite possible that any American effort, for political as well as logistic reasons, would be much too late. It must be noted that this argument is not based on any contention of superpower ideological rivalry, does not imply the continuation of the cold war, and is independent of any guesses about Gorbachev's political longevity. It simply assumes that war has not been disinvented and that perfectly traditional balance-of-power international relations would retain the Soviet Union as an inadequately "balanced" power in Europe. In a nutshell, history is not over, as some American thinkers believe. Rather, the cold war is over, and traditional European history may start up again. One feature of traditional European history is precisely the existence of Russia as a country simultaneously economically backward and militarily strong. In the past this apparent antithesis was possible because of its huge, if badly equipped and trained, peasant army. Now it is possible because nuclear weapons, once developed, are cheap and the USSR will still have a quantitative edge sufficient to overcome any technological edge Europe alone has.

It is fair to suggest that Europe is as insecure about its ability to look after itself as it is about its military preparedness. Europeans are probably right to feel such self-doubt, and the prevalence of the fear of Germany is a telling indicator. The truth is that the historical record tells as much about other nations' failures as it does of anything specifically Germanic. The period cited is from the Austro-Prussian War to World War II (1866–1939). The crude version places the blame for the Austro-Prussian War, the Franco-Prussian war of 1870, and both world wars on Germany, and it insists these are appropriate analogies from which lessons may be learned. But what lessons, exactly? The Austro-Prussian War and to some extent the Franco-Prussian War were nation-building wars, such as all other European countries had fought. Furthermore, a large part of the blame for the Franco-Prussian war falls on the French government, which almost welcomed it and partly brought it about by its own diplomatic intrusions in foreign politics. World War I was a long-expected (and by many quite desired) outcome of Anglo-German rivalries and a general instability. World War II must, of course, forever be seen as an unprovoked aggression. But it was, and not only in retrospect was seen to be, partly caused by the 1919 Versailles Treaty. It may be that the ineradicable structure of European nations with their power inequalities, imperfectable ethnic boundaries, and vulnerabilities to external economic influences desperately calls for some guiding and restraining institutions. But why NATO?

Why Does Europe Need NATO?

Europe is not exactly lacking for supranational organizations and institutions, though the West is clearly more institutionalized than the East. On the military side are NATO and the Warsaw Pact, with sixteen and seven members respectively. There are the two essentially economic alliances — the European Community (EC), with twelve full members, and its rival, the Council for Mutual Economic Assistance (CMEA), whose twelve members include Cuba and Vietnam. For more general integration in the West there is the Western European Union (WEU), effectively a subset of Euro-NATO and the much more broadly defined Council of Europe, whose nineteen members include not only Scandinavia but also several Mediterranean countries. In addition to these is the Conference on Security and Cooperation in Europe (CSCE), the result of the Helsinki accords, with its thirty-five members covering the whole of Europe (except Albania, which refused membership) as well as the United States, Canada, and the USSR. Under CSCE, various negotiations, reporting meetings, and arms-control efforts go on.

CSCE was responsible for the failed Mutual and Balanced Force Reductions (MBFR) talks, the imminently successful CFE, and the potentially successful Chemical Warfare Treaty. Its periodic review meetings since 1977 have varied in success, but increasingly progress has been made. It is the most widely canvased alternative to NATO as a security organization that could, possibly, cope with the predicted strains in the European nation-state system. CSCE has two major advantages over most alternatives. The first is its membership — it covers all of Europe and it involves the United States. Since American involvement in any forum for overseeing European security is deemed necessary by most European politicians, this is fairly crucial. The second advantage is that it already exists, that it has a fair and increasing record of success, and consequently that most governments have experience, skilled diplomats, and a fair understanding of how any issue will play there. It also has a broad mandate, covering human-rights issues as well as economic development in addition to its primary arms-control responsibility.

The counterargument to CSCE is that it is underinstitutionalized. It has no real permanent secretariat, no machinery for day-to-day contact, and, above all, no policy-making power. This latter fact is borne out most strongly by the way that all decisions must be by consensus. Consensus was hard enough to achieve in the days when there were three "bloc" actors — NATO, the WTO, and a disparate group known as the Neutral and Non-Aligned (NNA) bloc. The NNA nations had little in common but served as facilitators. In the expected new European disposition there would be no such simplification of negotiations, certainly not if NATO evaporated in importance. Even more important than this consensus aspect is the brute fact that CSCE is not a military organization. It has no standing military force and no mandate to organize one. Nor is it a treaty organization that imposes any costs or obligations on its members.

If CSCE seems an unlikely organization to handle crises, indeed has no conflict-resolution mechanism at all, can any other organization expect to replace NATO? As far as economic integration goes, the European Community is the obvious candidate. Far more than any other organization, bar NATO, it is experienced, integrated, and deeply institutionalized, with a clear-cut mandate and a high degree of legitimacy among its member populations. No other body begins to be a rival to lead the economic development of the East. Nor has any other body the experience, though not altogether successful, of hammering out consensual policy even in foreign-policy matters. Finally, the EC has to be significant on the question of German unification, because East Germany, once integrated into the West, will automatically become a member. (But this in itself poses problems. East Germany will in fact get membership in the EC ahead of other European countries that have been applying for some time, including Austria and Turkey.)

The strikes against the EC as a future guarantor of European security are two-fold. The first, and simplest, is that it has no military organization, indeed no policy connection to security matters at all, even in the "nice" areas like arms control. That might be dealt with relatively easily, because it is a highly institutionalized and technically competent organization, but such a development would inevitably raise the bugbear of the EC — the question of sovereignty. After all, there was once a plan to build a military equivalent to the European Economic Community (EEC), to be known as the European Defense Community (EDC), which would have had its own entirely integrated European army. Indeed, it was the failure of the EDC plan that finally secured NATO's initially slightly shaky foundations.

The major problem of the EC is ironically its own success. The EC at the foundation of the communities was motivated by the same sort of general hopes for peace through any form of integration that could be managed. It started with the European Coal and Steel Community (ECSC), precisely to exercise some restraint on primary war-making potential. But the EC has become an extremely successful economic club, one in which membership is judged entirely by its economic benefit. It does very well for its members, and 1992 will make it even more worth while to be a member. For this very reason the EC is extremely reluctant to open itself up to indigent nations. It is not, if it ever was, an altruistic international welfare agency and would be unwilling to increase the burdens it has accepted with Greek, and to a lesser extent Portuguese, membership. Any idea of the EC's taking on a European coordination role, still less a European security role, except in a way that would show clear profit to its existing members is dubious. Indeed, Austria, Turkey, and Norway[2] may have their membership delayed precisely because some Eastern economies may be more attractive. But no general extension of its mantle is remotely thinkable.

The Council of Europe is probably the most plausible candidate among existing institutions in many ways. Its membership is large and geographically extensive. For example, with its Mediterranean membership (which includes Cyprus and Malta as well as Greece and Turkey), it could address the interests of those Eastern European countries with a concern for Southern Europe effectively. Furthermore, it has shown political teeth in defense of democracy; both Greece and Turkey have been required to leave at times because of their politics, and support for democratization is going to be as vital as economic and military support in the near future. The council has strong functioning institutions and a competent civil service. One of its institutions, the European Court of Human Rights (ECHR), has built real legitimacy among member governments, most of which now accept its jurisdiction even if with limitations. The concern for "human rights" is an increasingly important part of the CSCE process, and CSCE is struggling to find some enforcement machinery. Frequently, "the minorities question" is cited as a principal source of instability in Eastern Europe. Adopting the European Convention on Human Rights and accepting the jurisdiction of the ECHR would be a natural and administratively easy step. Already several Eastern countries, including the USSR, have asked to be given at least observer status.

The Council of Europe has no existing military role, structure, policy, or force.

If this argument is to be fatal, then by definition only NATO or NATO and WTO can serve the purpose of European security. Of all organizations, however, the council could most easily graft on to itself a military structure. Like both the EC and NATO, its guiding body is a Committee of Ministers, and a subcommittee of defense ministers could relatively easily organize and control a force something like NATO. Similar to NATO but somewhat more effectively, it has a parliamentary body of delegates from national parliaments that could exercise a remote control. There is one enormous problem with the Council of Europe. The United States and Canada are not members, and neither is the Soviet Union . . . yet. In principle, there is no reason why they should not become members, on the same grounds that they are members of CSCE, which, after all, stands for the Conference on Security and Cooperation in Europe. Yet there might be concern about diluting the focus of membership. And, indeed, America might well find the role of the ECHR irksome, especially if, to help Eastern Europe and the USSR, moves were made to increase the court's jurisdiction. An important sideline presents itself here. One powerful aspect of the jurisdiction of the court is that it allows a citizen of a member state to take his government to the court and allows other governments to take a country to the court on behalf of one of its citizens. Weaker but similar provisions apply before the EC's court, the European Court of Justice (ECJ), under article 177 of the Treaty of Rome. It may be that involvement in Europe will cost North America a loss of sovereignty that it would hate, much as North America preaches it as ideal for Europe.

Assume, though, that the United States does join the Council of Europe and that the council develops some form of military structure. Could it then replace NATO? The answer, alas, seems to be no. There would still be two, related, problems. We cannot ignore the simple fact that no general mutual-support agreement can have a major target. Yet, as argued earlier, the Soviet Union must remain the major threat, however distant or merely potential, that such a security organization faces. The very nature of collective security arrangements is that they are "collectively" neutral. All that is most useful about the Council of Europe would suffer were it not to take the Soviet Union as the principal, though not sole, "designated enemy." One can put this in a phrase one analyst used in discussing the suggestion that Germany be neutral: "Neutral against whom?" The truth is that apart from the historical anomalies of Switzerland and Sweden, neutrality in Europe means indifference to the outcome of specific conflicts.

The second, though related, problem of the Council of Europe is the nuclear issue. Ultimately, and despite all good intentions on everyone's part, there is the historical fact of the Soviet nuclear arsenal. European countries, even the United States given "honorary European" status, cannot be expected to dedicate their nuclear arsenals to a new body or to a body like the Council of Europe with new powers. Without some nuclear basis, no European force can protect against this long-term, vague, merely potential threat of a disruption of any European balance of power. This is the case for NATO. It is entirely negative. It relies on no positive quality of NATO but on the inherent weakness of all alternatives. NATO has only three virtues: (1) it already involves the United States and Canada; (2) it is already a nuclear alliance — indeed it is, though it hates to admit this, primarily a nuclear alliance; and (3) the military organizational structure of NATO has a special value for the stability of central Europe.

The third point is the additional vital aspect of NATO. As it has developed over forty years, NATO is a very odd alliance. It is odd, indeed probably unique, because of its integrated standing army. NATO forces are not a number of allied armies operating together but under the direction of their own commanders. Instead, they are contingents of a multinational force operating, and for the most part training, under the direction of a single commander in chief and by the direction of an integrated multinational staff. Although Britain, France, and obviously the United States keep some part of their national military force outside this control, the vast bulk of Euro-NATO, and all West German military forces operate, train, and are socialized, as part of this collective entity. The operative phrase here is *and all West German.* As long as Germany is part of NATO, its military strength is harnesed and committed to joint operations as part of a single NATO drive for European security. All of West Germany's defense efforts are directed in this way, from doctrine and training to staff roles and, above all, procurement and interoperability. As long as this is so, Europe cannot really fear the new Germany's individualism or any theoretical revanchism. This is NATO's unique gift to Europe, and it is this that a neutral Germany would threaten. If Germany cannot effectively operate absent its NATO colleagues, the USSR has little to fear and therefore little reason to react. The nuclear role of NATO also counts enormously, of course. But one reason it counts is that there is no reason for Germany to develop its own nuclear forces as long as it is part of a nuclear alliance. Independent Germany, with a still potentially hostile and nuclear-armed USSR, might find the temptation to revoke its commitment to the Nuclear Non-Proliferation Treaty too much to withstand.

These arguments for NATO are not good arguments. They do nothing to overcome the obviously preferable desire for genuine and egalitarian collective security. They are simply real-world arguments that cannot be overcome. NATO alone offers a way of dealing with the potential threats of both the Soviet Union and Germany, and doing so by uniting the United States to Europe. This does not mean there are no major problems about the future shape of NATO, and there is no guarantee that NATO can or will, even if it could, solve these problems.

But What Must NATO Look Like?

Even if NATO is "the last and best hope," there are formidable problems and no guarantee it can solve them. The problems can be broken into three aspects: Who are the members? What is the political justification? What is the operational doctrine and force structure? The membership question follows from the change of role. NATO cannot continue to be a defense of Western Europe against Eastern Europe or the WTO. There no longer is an Eastern bloc, and the WTO has collapsed. If Europe needs a stabilizing security arrangement, these unstable Eastern European states must be involved. The Soviet threat may be the reason that NATO is uniquely suited, but the other concerns cannot be avoided. Nor can containing a remotely possible German threat justify the unchanged existence of NATO. Europe would hardly be stabilized by a competition between two or three security needs, and a NATO that refused to redefine itself would serve no purpose whatsoever. So countries like Hungary, Czechoslovakia, and Poland will have to have some association with NATO, or it will be quite unable to solve boundary or minorities disputes. Legally, there is no problem. The treaty setting up NATO guarantees any member state the support of all the others if attacked by anyone. Legally, also, any state may apply for membership in NATO. Even if these other states do not join NATO, they cannot be seen as the enemy, and some provision will have to be made for NATO troops to deploy and exercise in what has previously been WTO territory. If the Soviet threat is felt by its immediate European neighbors that are not members of the alliance, just how is NATO supposed to help them? No NATO member would have any obligation currently to provide military force. Any decision to do so would be legally akin to the "out of theater" operations that have been so politically contentious in NATO's history. An appeal by, say, Hungary for aid against a Romanian invasion could no more be addressed to NATO than could an appeal for help from Nigeria. Unless something is done about this identity problem, NATO cannot be credibly seen as playing a role in general European stability. But as something has to play this role, NATO could at best be a rival security organization.

The problem of political justification is obviously tied in with the membership question, but it also raises important domestic political questions. NATO is perceived by its electorates as a defense against a specific threat. On all sides the electorates are told that the threat is diminishing. NATO members spend 3 to 6 percent of their GNP on their defense budgets, and for most of these countries NATO represents the vast bulk of defense expenditures. It cannot simply be assumed that, because the defense and foreign-affairs elites see the necessity for NATO both as a long-run defense against future Soviet ambitions and as a stabilizing force for Europe, they will be able to carry on with no change. Some efforts will have to be made to sell the new definition of NATO, and these efforts will necessarily be embroiled in local party electoral competition. In other words, the political supporters of a continued and redefined NATO will have to make a serious effort to sell the new role, and the success of this sales drive is by no means guaranteed. The obvious problem is defining the threat in such a way that a population is willing to pay to defend against it. A way must be found to avoid creating a diplomatically unpleasant atmosphere that itself militates against increasing détente. There is no obvious solution to the problem.

The most challenging of all the problems involves the force-structure and military-doctrine aspects of reinventing NATO. For forty years, NATO has been committed to a linear defense of Western Europe, with heavy and relatively immobile divisions. These divisions have been trained, equipped, and organized for a static and passive defense, combined with a high-technology deep interdiction strategy. Currently, they are totally unsuitable for moving forward deep into Eastern Europe to meet a Soviet invasion and even less well organized for intervention in trouble spots. As it is likely that NATO members will also be more interested in out-of-theater operations, especially in the Mediterranean and Indian oceans, yet a further restructuring will be required. It is important to remember that light and highly mobile forces are not necessarily cheaper than the forces that NATO has built up, and they will have to be bought and trained. Exactly what they are to train for is in itself a major and unresolved problem. So is the question of command structure and the relationship between different national contingents. The current organization of NATO's integrated military, with the various commands, international staff, national staff, and so on is totally dedicated to defending against an enemy that no longer exists. Whether NATO needs to restructure, as opposed to destructuring, is a separate question. "Destructuring" means going back to the historically more usual form of defensive alliance, where each national military force goes its own way but accepts a commitment to join an ad hoc expeditionary force at times of crisis. This in itself raises the question of deployment; normal alliances have no forward deployment but arrive at the scene, usually rather too late, once the geography of the conflict has been defined. It NATO does that, it will be less able to act as a general stabilizing force — but where should it deploy? This brings us full circle to the question of membership.

None of the problems can be solved here. This essay has attempted to show that NATO probably is, marginally, the best foundation for a new European security order but that unless it is radically redefined it will not be able to act, even marginally, in this role.

NOTES

1. *New York Times*, "Verification Is Where to Start," 7 Apr. 1990. The meeting in question was a conference held by the Institute for East-West Security Studies, attended by strategic analysts, politicians, and bureaucrats from most of Western and Eastern Europe, as well as from the USSR and the United States.

2. Norway is contemplating an application, but the required national referendum has not yet taken place.

NATO's Future Role:
An American View

ROBERT L. PFALTZGRAFF, JR.

The role to be played by the United States in Europe and in a transatlantic relationship in the 1990s represents a logical extension of interests that have long shaped American policy. In geopolitical terms, it is in the United States's vital interest to ensure the emergence and preservation in Europe of as many independent states as possible and, by inference, to prevent any one nation or combination of powers from establishing a hegemony. For the 1990s, the possibility that such a condition will prevail appears to be remote indeed. Instead, the United States confronts a Europe in which the rate of change includes the breakup of the political order imposed on Eastern Europe by Joseph Stalin's advancing armies and party cadres at the end of World War II.

In sharp contrast, the Europe of the final decade of this century features the widely discussed phenomenon of Europe 1992. Together, the increasing fragmentation of Eastern Europe and the further unification of Western Europe pose for the United States a series of important opportunities as well as challenges in the 1990s. From the American perspective, a transatlantic security framework has represented the indispensable basis for the creation of Europe as it now exists. Without the security umbrella furnished by the United States for the past two generations, it is difficult to imagine that the Western portion of Europe could have achieved its unprecedented levels of prosperity and taken major strides toward economic unity embodied in the European Community (EC). At the beginning of the 1990s, therefore, abundant evidence exists that the North Atlantic Treaty Organization represents for the United States and its NATO allies a remarkable phenomenon.

It was NATO that both symbolized and made tangible the American transatlantic commitment. The alliance provided for the formulation of a military strategy based on capabilities for the deterrence of a Soviet attack against Western Europe. Whether or not the Soviet Union ever intended to use military force to conquer Western Europe has been a matter of debate. Such a question can never be fully answered. The fact is that the Soviet Union did not launch a military strike westward even though Moscow's geographic location and conventional-force preponderance made such an attack appear both feasible and probable in the minds of many on both sides of the Atlantic since NATO was founded. In joining the alliance the United States committed itself to employ its ultimate means of destruction in order to deter a Soviet attack mounted against another member. Such a commitment was unprecedented. It is unlikely that it would be repeated if NATO ceased to exist, for the risks entailed by any power in providing a nuclear guarantee have grown enormously since the alliance was formed.

No less important to Western security was the role played by NATO in establishing the framework within which West Germany could be rearmed. Without West Germany there would have been no NATO forward defense, let alone one that provided for a conventional threshold. If the alliance had achieved nothing more than a multilateral consensus about the type and level of West German defense forces, it would have been of major and enduring importance for this reason alone. Together with the European Community, NATO formed part of the architecture by which West Germany was harnessed to a broader Western grouping of states. The close bilateral relationships that evolved between West Germany and France and between West Germany and the United States were decisively shaped by the multilateral institutions represented by NATO and the EC. Without NATO, it would probably have been impossible to achieve a mutually satisfactory basis for German rearmament, just as in the absence of the European Community, German economic dynamism would have probably rekindled the not-so-latent fears of neighboring European states. It is instructive to recall that, from the beginning of the post–World War II European integration movement, a motivating factor has been the perceived need to find an institutional basis within which to embed Germany. In the 1990s such a need will continue to buttress support for the EC, as its other members ponder the role to be played by Western Europe, particularly by the Federal Republic of Germany, in shaping the process of political and economic change in Eastern Europe.

Such an assessment of NATO in retrospective terms is indispensable in setting the overall context for the alliance in the 1990s. Whatever the importance of NATO as a security framework for linking the United States with its European allies and for bringing West Germany into a multilateral decision-making process for mutual defense, the fact remains that the alliance was created more than two generations ago under circumstances that now seem almost unimaginable to emerging leadership groups on both sides of the Atlantic. The history of international alliances is such that when the conditions that existed when they were formed undergo a fundamental change, interest in and support for their arrangements declines. The history of NATO contains numerous episodes in which the alliance has experienced crises of one kind or another. Its fortunes have waxed and waned with the rise and decline of perceived threats from the East. Each of the decades of NATO's existence has featured successive periods of East-West tension and détente. If the threat posed by the Soviet Union has now been finally dissipated, it would follow that NATO has served its purpose and should be dissolved if it cannot be altered to fulfill the needs of a new era. If the Soviet Union is, or is becoming, so preoccupied with internal problems that its military forces cannot be regarded as either a political or a military threat, the logical inference is that NATO is an unnecessary relic of a bygone era. If the purpose of the alliance was to provide for the common defense of its members, the dismantling of Communist regimes in Eastern Europe, and possible sharp reductions in Soviet military power, then the realization of these goals would appear to constitute ample grounds for its dissolution. Such arguments can be expected to be made with increasing frequency and intensity on both sides of the Atlantic, especially in the United States, all the more so in the absence of a strategic vision of the role of Europe in a global security concept on which to base American policy and power.

NATO was the product of an era of major defense needs marked by increasing expenditures in support of alliance commitments on the part of its members, despite continuing debates within the alliance about burden-sharing. For this reason, sharp cuts in defense expenditures, hastened by the expectation or actual achievement of a drastically diminished Soviet threat, would have as their logical counterpart a commensurate reduction in the importance attached to NATO by its members. Although Secretary of State James A. Baker III has called for the refurbishment of NATO as part of a "new architecture for a new era," it is appropriate to ask whether such an invocation represents only an exercise in nostalgia or forms part of a process in which the United States somehow cushions the impact of change toward an as yet undefined future structure by respectful deference to the known symbols of the past. Conceptually, the question is not what is an appropriate strategy for NATO in the 1990s but what are the principal security issues confronting the United States and its NATO allies in a new decade and, furthermore, what are the appropriate frameworks, with or without NATO, for their resolution.

Since the alliance was founded on the fundamental premise that a transatlantic security commitment was needed from the United States, it was deemed to be essential that the United States have an active and visible presence in Europe as a prerequisite for political and military stability. When NATO was founded, there was no mutually agreeable basis for a postwar political settlement like that achieved, for better or worse, in the aftermath of Europe's previous conflicts. In place of a new concept of Europe, there arose the two blocs sharply delineated between East and West. Historically, periods of conflict have been understandably characterized by opposing alliances, just as the diminution of conflict has been accompanied or followed by the weakening or dissolution of alliance groupings. Just as the former condition characterized the circumstances under which NATO was formed, it follows that a diminution or disappearance of the threat and its replacement by an agreed peaceful order would herald the arrival of a more multipolar political configuration in and beyond Europe.

Although NATO was formed to provide a necessary basis for a continuing American security commitment to Europe, for much of its history the alliance has been based on the perceived need to maintain defense as a prerequisite for an improved relationship with the East. As NATO approached its twentieth anniversary in 1969, the Harmel committee prepared a report designed to establish its major tasks for the decade ahead. The maintenance of a robust military capability was considered essential if NATO and its members were to engage in détente diplomacy with the East. Although the ultimate outcome of such efforts, peace through strength, logically lies in the achievement of the overall World War II settlement that eluded the powers at the end of World War II, no such ambitious goal was explicitly stated. Instead, the Harmel report settled for the far more modest goal of gradually improving relations with the Soviet Union, based on minor modifications in the political status quo, including the implicit assumption that Communist regimes would remain in power in Eastern Europe. As recently as 1989, on the occasion of NATO's fortieth anniversary and a generation after the Harmel report, the question of a Harmel II exercise was put forward in unofficial NATO forums and discussions at the transatlantic level. Had such a committee been formed, its work would easily have been overtaken by the rapidly unfolding events that followed the commemoration of NATO's fortieth anniversary in April 1989 and which have transformed Eastern Europe and caused the reevaluation of defense priorities in NATO capitals.

In retrospect, the basic conceptual approach to security followed by the United States and its NATO allies, including the overall thrust of the Harmel report, has been vindicated by the transformation that has swept away the Communist regimes of Eastern Europe. It is conceivable that the *de facto* political settlement that is now evolving more than two generations after the end of World War II includes an Eastern Europe whose internal political configuration and foreign policies will bear a resemblance to Finland. The specter that haunts Europe is not the once-feared Finlandization of Western Europe but the encouraging prospect that such a status is well on the way toward achievement in Eastern Europe. Such a settlement bears a close resemblance to what was undoubtedly envisaged at the ill-fated Yalta Conference of 1945, whose communiqué had included a call for free elections in Eastern Europe, particularly in Poland. As President Franklin D. Roosevelt summed up in his address to Congress just after returning from the Crimea: "Our objective was to help create a strong, independent, and prosperous nation, with a government ultimately to be selected by the Polish people themselves." Such words would have been expressed by Poland's Solidarity-led government.

To be sure, Yalta with all of its bitter legacy is history, to be recalled only when there are remarkable similarities in certain respects between the stated goals of Yalta and the events that are transforming the region. It was at Yalta that the wartime leaders, so Churchill and Roosevelt believed, had framed the basis for a postwar political settlement. It has apparently taken nearly half a century for the Soviet Union to reverse Stalin's interpretation of Yalta: "Whoever occupies a territory also imposes on it his own social system. Everyone imposes his own system as far as his army can reach. It cannot be otherwise." It was, of course, the sharply clashing and differing images of Europe's postwar order between Stalin's forced imposition of Communist regimes in Eastern Europe controlled by Moscow and Western expectations of open, democratic political systems and market-oriented economies, together with Soviet political pressures against Western Europe and elsewhere, that led to the onset of the cold war.

Political agreements, including peace treaties at the end of major conflicts, are inevitably based on the prevailing circumstances of the time. Such accords normally codify an existing order, including the relative positions of the key actors. The Yalta experience is of interest, from the perspective of the 1990s, not only because it recalls the aspirations of the West for Eastern Europe in the closing days of World War II but also because it furnishes vivid evidence of the limitations of formal agreements not firmly grounded in political realities. What is unfolding in Eastern Europe, in sharp contrast to Yalta, provides the conditions for a settlement that was impossible in the years following World War II. The lesson of Yalta was that no political settlement could be achieved without agreement by all of the major powers. Similarly, no agreement on the future of Europe on mutually satisfactory terms in the 1990s can be reached without the United States and its NATO allies, particularly West Germany. Because the alliance furnishes the framework for an American defense commitment to Europe and for West Germany's participation in the defense of Europe, it follows that the alliance forms a necessary ingredient in any political settlement that will codify the momentous events that are transforming the Eastern European landscape. Although Western Europe has gained an unprecedented level of prosperity with the prospect for greater economic integration in the 1990s, by itself it remains unable to reach agreement with the Soviet Union on Europe's future. Even if Western Europe were able to do so, there would be a compelling argument, based both on past sacrifice and vital interest, for the United States to play the fullest possible role. What distinguishes the 1990s from 1945, of course, is the extent to which the settlement that formalizes the events now unfolding in Europe will include not only the victors of World War II but, as a central element, a resurgent Western Europe, of which West Germany forms a leading part. The result of World War II was the dismemberment of the German state; the 1990s are likely to feature, in some form, a reconstituted Germany, or at least rapidly expanding links between the two Germanys that emerged from the postwar political division of Europe. From an object of the European security problem, Germany has become a full and necessary direct participant in its solution.

Fundamental to a NATO strategy for the 1990s, then, is the achievement of the ultimate goal for which the alliance was formed: the creation of a political order on terms acceptable to as many of its members as possible. Specifically, this means negotiating a settlement of issues that were the legacy of World War II and its aftermath, of which the German Question is of central importance. From the outset, in the minds of the founders of the Federal Republic of Germany, particularly the thinking of Konrad Adenauer, West German membership in the institutions of Western unity, including NATO and the EC, was the necessary basis for eventual progress toward reunification. The opening of the inter-German border in November 1989, together with the hope of further progress toward some form of reunification, provides in itself the partial fulfillment of Adenauer's vision. However and in what precise form the two German states achieve a new relationship, it is impossible to envisage progress broadly acceptable to other interested parties outside a multilateral framework. Aside from the legal basis on which the four occupying powers remain in Berlin, all of West Germany's alliance partners have a legitimate stake, and therefore major interest, in the future form that a unified German state would assume. Just as it would be inappropriate for the victors of World War II today, as contrasted with the Yalta period, to reach a settlement of the German Question and related issues to the exclusion of other European states as directly interested parties, it would be unacceptable to develop a solution on a strictly German-Soviet basis, with all the bitter memories of Rapallo and the Molotov-Ribbentrop Pact that would thereby be resuscitated in the minds of Germany's neighbors and across the Atlantic as well. In either case an agreement so reached would be in the interest of neither the parties included nor those excluded. If neither a strictly German nor a European framework is adequate for addressing such issues because of the crucially important role of the United States, what remains is the transatlantic relationship, of which NATO is the embodiment. Just as the alliance provided the mechanism for consensus formation with respect to West German rearmament in the 1950s, so has NATO a crucially important role to play in developing an agreed Western basis for the future of Germany in the years just ahead.

A closely related question is arms control and European security. The ongoing negotiations to achieve a conventional balance at lower levels of armaments embodied in the Conventional Forces in Europe (CFE) process include NATO and Warsaw Pact members and in the case of the parallel Confidence and Stability Building Measures (CSBMs) those states and additional European parties as well. It is inconceivable that stability at an agreed political-military level could be achieved outside NATO. The alliance provides the framework within which the present Western negotiating position for CFE is set forth. The consequences of separately negotiated levels of armaments between members of NATO and the Soviet Union, as an alternative to a common alliance position, need hardly be elaborated. Such an approach would hold the potential for disaster. By the same token, arms-control agreements form an essential basis for any future relationship of greater stability across the present inter-German border. Hence, the abiding and growing West German commitment to arms control as a basis for the creation of what is termed a new European *friedensordnung* (peace order) within which the process of German reunification could proceed.

Discussions of the potential roles for NATO in the 1990s, including pronouncements by the Bush administration, have featured the idea of the alliance as an organization providing a basis of reconciling force-structure requirements with arms-control policy. Just as the negotiation of arms-control accords for European security on a strictly bilateral basis would be detrimental to the West as a whole, it would be a deficiency of strategic thought to develop arms-control positions if the alliance fails to agree on an approach to force levels and strategy. If one assumes, as seems probable, a continuing and rapid evolution in the European security setting, it follows that defense doctrines and force structures that are the legacy of the past forty years will be outdated and therefore eventually discarded. NATO and its members face the unfortunate prospect that decisions about security needs will be dictated more by budgetary considerations than strategic logic. Even with a CFE treaty, NATO members will be tempted to press for unilateral cuts as part of an exercise of defense burden-shedding. The result could be a force posture that fails both to meet the criteria for NATO's existing strategy of flexible response and to embody the necessary elements of an alternative concept based on a form of "defensive defense." The creation of a force structure that is responsive to the needs of Europe and other directly interested parties, primarily the United States, will be difficult under the best of circumstances. Without NATO, the task of formulating a defense concept for the West as a basis for equilibrium, however defined, would be next to impossible. By the same token, the failure to formulate an acceptable concept in place of flexible response has the effect of denying NATO and its members the essential framework both for designing appropriate force structures and for achieving necessary arms-control priorities — of knowing what to include and what to exclude from an ongoing arms-control process. For example, what is to be the appropriate mix between nuclear and conventional components of a deterrence concept for Europe in the 1990s? If nuclear weapons have any role to play, what types of systems should be retained or modernized, and who is to possess them? If nuclear weapons are of at least residual importance to an emerging European political-military equilibrium, the question becomes one of the organizational basis for such deployments.

In the absence of a European defense entity, no framework outside NATO is available for this purpose. Therefore, an American nuclear commitment, or coupling, at the transatlantic level — however amended for the 1990s — would seem to be inconceivable if NATO were to be dissolved. Similarly, CFE negotiations resulting in a first-phase agreement and its implementation, according to NATO agreement, will be followed by negotiations on an accord limiting short-range nuclear systems that are land based with ranges below 500 kilometers. Such talks will necessarily have NATO as a focal point. Although such systems are principally deployed on the territory of the Federal Republic of Germany, they have been deemed to be a crucially important component of NATO strategy. Presumably, in the absence of an agreed alliance defensive concept for the 1990s and beyond, the formulation of an arms-control policy for short-range nuclear systems would be devoid of strategic logic. In short, the tasks that lie before NATO in developing an acceptable defense concept and force structure as a basis for arms-control policy, will be of major and continuing importance in the years ahead.

Conceptually, the role of NATO arms control can be divided into two phases, the first of which would be, as described above, directly associated with the actual negotiation of agreements based on the formation of adequate force structures. The second would encompass the implementation of such agreements, including especially questions of verification. Because Soviet compliance is an issue of direct importance to the West as a whole, with obvious implications for the future configuration of the defense capabilities of NATO members, the alliance as such has a vital and continuing interest in arms-control agreements both in their formulation and implementation phases. It is likely that verification teams would be drawn from most, if not all, NATO members and that compliance issues would be properly the object of discussion at an alliance level. Because the process of arms-control negotiations will be ongoing, given a projection of present trends in Europe, these two phases will intermingle — negotiations and verification as, for example, the implementation of a Phase I CFE treaty would be followed by short-range negotiations and the likelihood of further talks on conventional forces. How such negotiations in which diverse parties, interests, and perspectives would be undertaken in a coherent fashion without the multilateral framework provided by NATO is difficult to imagine.

In the structure of the emerging Europe of the 1990s and beyond, the EC is expected to play a role of increasing importance. To the extent that economic issues gain in salience over defense, the EC will more and more overshadow NATO. Such an assumption has undoubtedly formed the basis for proposals for institutional links between NATO and the EC. Together with arms-control agreements, economic relationships are seen as the principal mechanisms for strengthening relations in a once-divided Europe. If security policy encompasses defense and arms control as well as economics (including trade and investment) it follows that NATO and the EC have roles that will increasingly intersect and overlap. Hence the basis exists for some form of increasing association between them, or at least encompassing those states whose membership extends to both organizations. This is not to suggest, however, that NATO should assume major economic functions. Its experience outside the defense realm would not augur well for such a role, even though article 2 of the North Atlantic Treaty makes provision for such an extension of the alliance to essentially nonmilitary tasks. Ideally, however, a Western strategy for Eastern Europe would contain as an essential ingredient an integrated approach not only to defense and arms control, as noted above, but would also address the basic elements of economic policy. Under the circumstances that are likely to prevail, there will be extensive bilateral economic relationships, including, as should be the case, a heavy emphasis on private-sector initiatives designed to build and strengthen market economies. Institutions at the European or Atlantic levels can best assist such a process by minimal interference within a strategic framework whose goal is the extension of political pluralism and private-sector economic initiatives in place of discredited Communist systems in Eastern Europe. NATO and EC agreement at the highest level about such an integrated strategy would constitute a major contribution to such a process. Periodic efforts to consider issues directly related to such a strategy could be undertaken, perhaps at and below the level of joint meetings of the Ministerial Councils of both organizations.

Much of the discussion of future roles for NATO focuses on the prospect that it will become more fully and overtly a political organization in the 1990s. As a military alliance, NATO has always performed an important pivotal role that has included the development of agreement on such key issues as relations with the East (Harmel report), the topics and levels of defense contributions by its members, the strategy for deterrence (since the 1967 flexible response), the sharing of defense burdens, the coordination of arms-control policy (Mutual and Balanced Force Reductions and Conventional Forces in Europe) — and, with far more limited success, common approaches to "out-of-area" issues. Each of these categories has occasioned debate that has often led to major political divisiveness among its members but eventually produced a level of agreement sufficient to permit the alliance to achieve its basic objective.

Central to NATO's political role has been the politics of the defense issues for which the alliance was founded. To the extent that such security questions are no longer to preoccupy its members, it could be anticipated that NATO as both a military and political organization will decline in importance, unless of course new issues arise at the transatlantic level. However, the immediate task for NATO, as proposed here, lies in the codification and management of the Western approaches to the security issues arising from the rapidly changing European scene. It is an axiom of alliance relations that, once the threat for which the grouping was created subsides, the coalition fragments or disintegrates altogether. It is equally true that, until the settlement is achieved that fulfills the original purposes of NATO, it would seem premature to write its political obituary. In the early 1990s, major strides are being taken toward that goal, although much remains to be done.

The periodic reduction in the threat for which NATO was created has brought to the forefront latent differences among its members at various times in its history. The 1980s were especially notable in this respect. The alliance faced not only the divisive and protracted controversy brought about by the decision to deploy intermediate-range missiles but also other areas of difference, such as Central America and relations with the Soviet Union. On both sides of the Atlantic, the emergence of new groups and generational change have led inevitably to a questioning of the relevance of NATO to the needs of the 1990s. The increased focus of United States policy on security issues outside Europe, an inevitable consequence of a reduction in tensions on the Continent, would necessarily be reflected in American perspectives toward the alliance. The withdrawal of United States forces from Europe, within or in addition to agreed reductions in CFE, is likely to diminish American interest further in the alliance. If the issues of the 1990s become increasingly those of economics, together with concern about the EC as a trading bloc, the United States will suggest that if its European allies want an economic "Fortress Europe" they can defend it militarily. To the extent, then, that economic and political-military issues become more extensively linked — a likely result of a diminished military threat — the need for a comprehensive policy approach to such questions at the transatlantic level will grow in importance. At the same time, the possibility that economic issues, such as protectionism, will supersede defense in saliency will also be enhanced, further diminishing the perceived importance of NATO in the minds of many on both sides of the Atlantic.

All of the foregoing analyses presume a sharply reduced threat from the East and stability following the changes that are transforming the European political landscape. However, even a passing acquaintance with history yields the insight that such epochs are likely to contain the ingredients of great instability. Political change is the product of the breakdown of a particular political order and its eventual replacement. The process by which a new set of political relationships comes into being is often violent and uncertain in its evolution. The stability of the past two generations in Europe represented the outcome of the upheavals of the first decades of this century. The Soviet Union and Eastern bloc that Leonid Brezhnev bequeathed to the present Soviet leadership is now a relic of history. The forces that have been unleashed by the obvious failures of Communist systems have yet fully to run their course. Having pressed for reform in the Soviet Union and in Eastern Europe in order to save communism itself, the Soviet Union confronts the specter of change on its borders that has swept away regimes whose principal claim to legitimacy lay in the power of the bayonet. It is unlikely that the Soviet Union can withstand the forces that are sweeping away Communist regimes elsewhere, except by the force of arms. As Western Europe prospers, the Soviet Union sinks into further political turmoil and economic chaos.

The Soviet Union seeks Western assistance to help rebuild its tattered economy. The extent of Moscow's need is evident in Mikhail S. Gorbachev's apparent willingness (or need) to tolerate, if not promote, political and economic changes in Eastern Europe and the Soviet Union that he had resisted at an earlier time. Demands for independence by its minority nationalities shake the Soviet Union, and conflicts that lay dormant under Soviet hegemony have resurfaced in Eastern Europe. Yet Soviet military power remains intact. For the first time in history, a potentially unstable regime — a military superpower — is in possession of the ultimate means of destruction. Although no one knows to what lengths it would go to retain its own position, the fate of the Romanian Communist leadership cannot have escaped the Soviet nomenklatura. Such a European security environment is hardly a basis for euphoria or for the assumption that, after forty years of cold-war turbulence, Europe has now entered a placid security setting in which military power will have no role.

What, then, is the architecture for a new era that features greater opportunity for the West, but also greater uncertainty, than the past two generations? Just as the United States and its allies moved cautiously toward the development of the multilateral frameworks that have so well protected their basic interests since World War II, the United States is likely to improvise and adapt to unfolding circumstances in the years ahead. For this reason, the precise roles to be played by NATO cannot be easily discerned. But NATO will probably remain indispensable as insurance, as a security umbrella, in a Europe in which change and stability are not necessarily coincident properties. However powerful economically, Europe is not organized politically to provide fully for its own defense. For its part, to the extent that the United States continues to regard itself as a world power with the elements of a global strategy, Europe, especially in light of the sweeping changes taking place there, forms an indispensable ingredient. The United States has a vital interest in Europe, particularly in its peaceful evolution under conditions of economic growth and political independence. NATO's role remains that of an organization designed to ensure a continuing European political-military equilibrium and to provide a framework, or security shield, within which the unfolding links to the East accelerated by the failure of communism as an ideology and as a political and economic system can be most fully developed. Moreover, NATO is important as a political-military framework within which Western consensus can be reached about the terms and forum that German reunification will take.

The transatlantic relationship of the 1990s will feature a Western European economic core of increasing power built on the foundations of the EC. The extent to which its members will enhance their political cohesiveness remains to be seen. The Federal Republic of Germany will emerge as a power of increasing importance with growing links to Eastern Europe. Germany's neighbors, especially France, will try to strengthen the EC as a framework within which to continue to harness German energy, strength, and dynamism. From the French perspective, therefore, the Franco-German relationship will be of increasing importance in the 1990s. The EC will be preoccupied not only with its own integration as a basis for managing relations among its members and accommodating possible new entrants, such as Norway and perhaps even Austria and Turkey, but also with the development of associations with a substantial number of additional states, including not only European Free Trade Association (EFTA) members but also economically reforming countries to the east, especially Poland, Hungary, and Czechoslovakia. Ideally, the transatlantic economic architecture for the 1990s would include a broadening of the European Community to provide for links with North America, just as the United States interest lies in the development of transatlantic and transpacific free-trade areas linking democratic states with market economies. Such a formation would build on the political and economic successes of the past two generations. It would mobilize and increase the resources available to fuel processes of change, not only in the East but also in other regions of the world. Such an economic relationship at the transatlantic level would provide the economic counterpart to the security framework provided by NATO, while diminishing the prospect for divisive economic disputes whose outcome would be to the advantage of none of the contending parties. Together the alliance and a broadening set of transatlantic economic relationships linking the EC and North America would provide an architecture for the years leading into the third millennium worthy of the transatlantic accomplishments of the past two generations.

The Atlantic Community: A Grand Illusion

MICHAEL VLAHOS

The term *Atlantic Community* — taken here as a defining title — has marked a reality built on an illusion: a proud and necessary illusion, but an illusion nonetheless. Although an artifice, it became the jewel in the crown of the postwar world. If other coronets have failed or fallen short — such as the image of the West, the free world, and the United Nations — the Atlantic Community remained unshakeable, true, and forever. But it was only a myth.

That statement, of course, is a kind of heresy, a label often applied to new and uncomfortable truths as a way of stifling dissent against the orthodox "truth." How, then, can one discuss a proposition whose validity is denied? The problem is compounded by employing *Atlantic Community* as a political code word covering several deeper foundations on which the postwar world was built. Uncovering them may be as difficult as it is uncomfortable. One can begin by asking how the orthodox might respond to a more general acceptance of the Atlantic Community as myth. The believers, one imagines, would respond: "So what if it was myth? It worked. And it was a necessary myth; it kept us going. Why not keep a good thing going? And why criticize its effectiveness as myth?" A myth that people believe for forty years is arguably no longer an illusion but the new reality: two Atlantic worlds intertwined. As such, it remains the only model for any united democratic world order to come. This argument could be styled "the good thing for the West" argument. The alliance survived for many years because of the Soviet threat. The truth is not that both sides are coming together but moving apart: the real system today is not transatlantic but pan-European: the European Community (EC). And the evolution of global democratic values does not depend on a grand democratic military coalition as upholder and model. The end of the Atlantic Community as a military alliance would not mean the end of a good thing but the natural transformation of a good, formalized, militarized kinship system into a loose, extended post–cold war family.

Adding force to the orthodox world view is the "bad track record of the bad old days" argument — the pessimists' response to the contention that the Atlantic

Community is a grand illusion. Who, they ask, would wish for the days when bickering European states launched two world wars? There are, however, two aspects to this argument. One is that only the Atlantic Community—however artificial a concept—keeps a nasty set of feral European instincts at bay. This premise dismisses any chance for European unity without American might. The other aspect sees even a united Europe as essentially weak. The East is weak now, but another great Eurasian force could breathe down the delicate, white-skinned Euro-neck. A fractious Europe will always need the United States. "The bad track record of the bad old days" might kindly be called the pit-bull theory of history. It is time to clear American memory banks of this notion. Germans no longer goose-step, French do not sing while firing from a Parisian barricade, and Britons no longer rule the waves. The old national premises have died hard, even cruelly, at the hand of history, and its momentum is now toward consolidation, if not confederation. The question is not whether to unify Europe but how soon and to what extent. The "European" Community is rising from the Atlantic Community's ashes.

Both of these arguments condescend to Europe, implying a racist, though contradictory, stereotyping of Western Europeans. That may not be the best way to promote an Atlantic Community from the vantage point of European interests and sensibilities, but the arguments persist on both sides of the Atlantic.

No one who has bought into the NATO, transatlantic social establishment will ever admit that it is a cultural sham. Call it illusion, call it myth, and the response will be: "What, disparage the West? Barbarian! Isolationist rube!"

Part of the problem is social. The Atlantic Community came closest to reality as an elite club: an extension of the Washington postwar political establishment, which harbors a natural resistance to ceding both career and comforts. Members of the elite who admit that the emperor has no clothes stand to lose the international conferences, the diplo-perks, the exchanges, the plum berths, the titles, and the glossy promo mags from Brussels. Then there are institutional problems to any confession. Calling the Atlantic Community a grand illusion announces the end of the North Atlantic Treaty Organization (NATO), or at the very least its continuing existence as a merely symbolic peerage. The Atlantic Community was the premise that gave NATO its moral and emotional claim on European and American citizens. Without the Soviet threat, after all, one might still concoct other, "out-of-area" justifications for NATO. Without the Atlantic Community, however, there is no natural association for a collective response to threats. Hence the range of replies from Halford McKinder's historicism to ad hominem attacks. But it must be reiterated: the Atlantic Community is an illusion.

The second aspect of MacKinder's argument, which some Americans have called "Eurowimps versus Eurasians," is also a nineteenth-century figment best forgotten. In truth, there is no Eurasian land-mass pivot point of history. The Soviets are in a historical slide. What they may become is significantly different from what they have been. And can the United States conjure up substitute threats? China? India? A new caliphate or Central Asian horde? Hardly. Europe is becoming a world power in its own right. The question is not whether Europe can defend itself in Eurasia but whether the EC will effectively be Eurasia.

There is still another weary but socially relentless argument. Why put everyone out? The party is over, but continued political association is good for all; that is what NATO is becoming anyway. The lonely heretic is admonished: "Why be a chump? Why let others call you a barbarian rube and drop you from the invitation list to the most socially correct discussion groups? Why fight a lingering natural death, both for NATO and the Atlantic Community?"

Keeping the illusion of the Atlantic Community alive will prejudice American interests in the new world now emerging. The erosion of the Soviet Union is not the only driving aspect of world change. Europe is rapidly integrating, and the United States is on the cusp of a profound era of reinterpretation. In other words, they are evolving apart, again going their separate ways. The Soviet slide has accelerated this natural process. What is happening in Western Europe is real fraternity; the sibling European Community revealing true family ties. By contrast, they also reveal the Atlantic Community for what it was: a live-in relationship; more than a fling — like 1918–19 — but something less than a marriage; perhaps a conjugal partnership — intimate and intense and demanding but without enduring bonds. Because it was never a marriage, there need be no divorce. The partners can remain friends, but the talk of a closer union is over.

This metaphor helps explain the actual terms of the European-American relationship during the postwar world. Rather than trying to force the blood-kin symbolism, it shows how two separate culture areas came together and made common cause and why at last they should come — quite amicably — to part. The end of the old order is part of a larger global process of change leading to a new world system — a new reality, with different premises and different ways of relating. One set of altered terms will be those between North America and the EC. This new structure will not demand, nor will it ultimately allow, the perpetuation of the myth of an Atlantic Community, save in hortatory declarations of common interest. This world will be shaped by competition between three world powers: North America, the EC, and Japan. Their altered relationship will not permit the sentimental myth of a transatlantic community. Those who will try to perpetuate it are, in fact, those who created it in the first place, and the postwar establishment has no interest in disestablishing the myth that has sustained it.

But that postwar establishment is aging and out of touch with change in America, as well as in Europe. This is the real reason for disbanding the Atlantic Community. The United States needs to renew and rebuild itself as a society. The postwar establishment has sought to maximize American global power, and therefore tasks its energies and judges its policy results on the basis of strategic-military arrangements. The establishment is neither interested in nor attuned to the coming reinterpretation of American values and political vision. Its archons inside the beltway do not see this country as other people see it, corrupt and coming apart and sorely in need of a renewing vision. They are operators, not visionaries. But they have nothing to operate now that is relevant to the nation's future needs. They want to preserve alliances that preserve American military chieftainship, created originally for a protracted military struggle.

The United States needs a working agenda for a world where competition is already fundamentally altered from a dying postwar reality. The NATO social infrastructure within the political establishment is pursuing a sentimental policy where one illusion (the Atlantic Community or the West) defends another, even more cherished (the United States as the West's warrior chieftain), as in the supreme allied commander, Europe (SACEUR); its "superpower." Policies pursued primarily to preserve this illusion may ultimately hurt American economic competitiveness against both the EC and Japan. That is not to say that the United States will necessarily trade substance for a continuing illusion but that it will still focus on the wrong problem and the wrong reality. Americans need to shift their focus to the future competition.

Discarding the grand illusion is part of a necessary process of exiting one world and entering another. America's purpose in the new world will be different from that of its previous great global mission. And Europeans need to confront their own course. Forcing them to pay homage to the United States through the continuing mantle of NATO only postpones the inevitable for them as well, and they have many issues to face in confederating. The conflict with Iraq may have shifted this course of evolution in the summer of 1990. Europe is "behind" the United States, and internationalism is resurgent. Even the moribund United Nations seems to have been reborn. Yet this, too, is but the passing fancy of a historical transition, an illusion cut from the newsreel footage of the two world wars, screened as proof that the United States is still supreme commander and Europe its loyal cadets. Some go even further and insist that America is now the world's "omnipower."

It is only fair to suggest that the Atlantic Community has been an essential — perhaps the essential — code word for the United States postwar paradigm. Its gathering desperation is quite visible now in the shrill insistence that all of its members are democracies, that democracies do not fight democracies, that trade intimacy makes real conflicts of interest impossible, and that societies sharing an RRE (Renaissance, Reformation, Enlightenment) heritage must share everything else. The time has come to remove the mask. But how can one address issues dominated by the narrow language of the Atlantic Community's postwar orthodoxy? One way is to pose three basic questions as to why two separate regions chose to make common cause and declare a common identity and why they then should part: (1) How could the Atlantic Community be an illusion if all its members are Western democracies? Does this not mean a basic commonality of attitude and behavior, deeper and more enduring than any state-to-state ties? (2) If the two sides are in fact separate culture areas, why do Americans continue to insist that the United States and Europe be seen as a cultural fraternity? Why not just leave it at the level of political alliance? (3) Why do Europeans persist in nurturing the illusion of an Atlantic Community? As they integrate economically and politically, why hesitate in charting their own way?

Two Separate Culture Areas

The World as a place of many realities. Culture defines reality. This notion contradicts the prevailing belief in "objective reality," which cannot be perceived save through culture's prism, which bends reality to its own needs. Even the physical environment is remade, and redefined, to suit the culture. How people think and behave is a function of culture — their reality — and all else is bent to fit it. Are Americans and Europeans, then, part of the same culture? Yes and, more important to this discussion, no. Yes, in that Americans in the main trace their lineage to Europe and can thus maintain that the transatlantic phenomenon is a naturally "Western" cultural reality. The working, cultural "truth," however, shows two distinct, highly differentiated culture areas, that have in fact made common cause (along with Japan, an entirely alien culture) for fifty years without converging. They are now going their separate ways again.

Just what is a culture area? It is an extended family of related societies that share membership in an encompassing cultural reality. With rare exceptions like Japan, most national societies are a part of a larger cultural reality. They come to this kind of macroidentification through an extended historical process of culture-area evolution. Consider Western Europe's evolution first. The barbarian successor-societies of the former Western Roman Empire had pulled together at the end of the eighth century. Their coalescence was abetted by isolation from the Byzantine Oikoumene (or commonwealth, which was developing on its own as a culture area) and the containment by caliphate, Viking, and Magyar. Europe in effect turned inward. The pulse of trade and industry pulled member states even closer. War quickened the pulse of cultural intercourse, accelerating the movements both of goods and people.

War has had an unappreciated melding effect on the evolution of the European culture area. For Europe, war often forced the physical intermingling of cultures. War has also served as a celebratory ritual shared by societies within the culture area: continual battle actually defined Europe as Europe. The European tradition used war as the benchmark for social standing and rank within the "civilized community." Intramural fights helped sharpen national identities increasingly dependent on the support of adversaries and allies. National identity, in other words, was awarded from within the cultural system. Contrast this process to the cultural function of wars fought by European states outside their culture area. Whatever the European army engaged, it shared with all others the reinforcing vision of civilization versus barbarism. This was a different use of war as celebration: the opponents were true aliens, and the heroic mythology of these desert and jungle combats was to underscore the blood ties of European tribes against the savage stranger. The most cherished images of a Europe united emerged from these forays into strange lands, whether at Acre in 1189 or Peking in 1900. Europe is a culture area that evolved from a historic isolation that etched its boundaries. Of course, the European culture area today is much larger than the original medieval core.

The Turkish retreat from the Balkans began a return of the lost Greek-Eastern world to the European fold. With the collapse of Lenin and Marx, the rest of the old Byzantine-Slavic commonwealth now seeks admittance. It is ironic that an antitheist religion would protect for some generations the remaining lands of the patriarchate from Rome. What is taking place today is the final triumph of West over East in a split that began in the eighth century.

Another split historically dividing the European culture area is North-South. After initial centuries of isolation, Europe diverged along northern and Mediterranean paths. Mediterranean Europe in the sixteenth century mingled with the Islamic culture area, and that world of which Fernand Braudel writes was very different from the dour and driven North. Europe's division was heightened by religious fissuring with Reformation, Counter-Reformation, and the Thirty Years' War. For a long time, there were two Europes. They were not joined until the twentieth century, and the fusion is yet incomplete.

However widely the markers of the European culture area are set today, the vital center — the animus — is still eighth century in scope. It is the boundary of the European Community: Britain, France, Germany, Italy, and the Low Countries form the core. Among these, the Protestant North dominates. Catholic South and orthodox East even now can be seen slowly sloughing their traditional value systems. The Germanic center of the reemerging culture area called Europe may seem merely economic, but the premises and pull of the society its economy created means that Germany, however much it resists, exerts a kind of missionary strength, whereby the long-term outcome of a confederated economy will be a further homogenization of the European belief system — and its very values — with Germany again at the center.

How different the United States! Originally a beachhead of European civilization, the twin shocks of breaking from Britain and watching an America-inspired revolution in France turn sick and corrupt, in effect wrenched it away from the European culture area. It pursued a separate cultural evolution, a separate descent channel. The result is a society — now embracing Canada and soon to include Mexico — that has become a North American culture area. It has some remote blood relations with Europe, and Americans share with Europeans the same badges and appurtenances of daily life. But there the cultural connection ends.

America and Europe: existential opposites. Europe evolved from tribal rooting in the defining land and pulled together over millennia, only to come together in recent decades. America is self-defined and self-conscious: an identity proclaiming its own creation. And above all, America is an idea . . . an idea that sought its own ark. Not that European societies simply mark turf devoid of defining ideas. Europe is really the home of ideology; but ideology is the grist of groups; it separates the modern clans of class. And the great European ideas — like Liberté, Egalité, and Fraternité — are today more often preserved in cherished mythic niches tied to major events and their romantic evocation: the burning political shibboleth of 1789, for example, has become the familiar, even denatured, symbolic vehicle identifying the nation: but the slogan does not animate — as it once did — the French agenda and the French soul.

America, however, continues to live by the original political content of its defining ideas. It is not a place, a lineage, or even a language. Ideas are not a badge but the thing itself. The way Americans relate to one another as a polity is what makes them Americans: one might even say that they have come to ritualize the workings of their polity as a kind of secular religion, with the Constitution as its sacred text. Battles over "the intent of the founders" have much the same passion as early Christian hermeneutics: the nature of its democratic compact is as critical to America's survival as the nature of God was to fifth-century Romans. Americans have no existential tribal roots but are bound by their shared allegiance to common ideas, no matter how bitterly they contend over their interpretation.

Americans are also self-defined: defined as different from all other polities in origin and intent (if not the result, often a democratic outcome that they directly influenced by their actions) and different in working practice. Not only do they think of America as the modern birthplace of democracy; they think of their own democratic relationship as unique by virtue of its very self-consciousness. Anyone who comes to America becomes an American just as the very first immigrants did — by self-proclamation. The United States is the only self-created world culture, and its initial uniqueness sets it apart from the tribal foundations of membership throughout the rest of human society. A Manichaean world view is also a natural by-product of being a society in opposition to all others.

All of this is critical to understanding the cultural divide between America and Europe. It is far less important that the original settlers of the new World came from Europe than that their collective determination both to shrug off the premises on which their societies of origin were built and to embrace new and fundamentally opposing premises.

The United States was at first a sanctuary for immigrants: from Puritans to Mennonites to Huguenots to Galician Jews; but what began as a flight to survive became transformed over time into a conviction of mission to proselytize American values. Fleeing tyranny to preserve a way of life is arguably the work of first-generation immigrants only. The values of struggle and conviction in one's own way fade into a more collective sense of an American agenda with succeeding generations. As new Americans assimilate through the generations, they bring powerful antityrant, antistatist attitudes into the mainstream mélange of the American idea. In other words, the American ethos is reinforced by self-selective immigrants who are unusually receptive to an idea built on individual cultural determination. It is therefore more important to trace American social evolution than it is to trace American roots. Roots are a kind of necessary nostalgia in a society built on continual group uprooting. But it is the thing that brought the uprooting, and the thing sought — America — that defines.

Americans evolved far from their European roots over three centuries. Consider Great Britain, the European society closest to America's. Churchill's quip on two societies divided by a common language masks a powerful truth: even a shared language does not imply a shared agenda or a shared vision. Britain's class system, its dependence on the monarch for national legitimacy, and its intrusive, all-powerful state are only broad indicators of a society and polity — a national ruling idea divergent from Americans' sense of "democracy." The United States evolved from a shared common point in 1763 to another place: Americans live in a different world from Britons. It does not matter that some elitist Yankees watch British Broadcasting Company costume dramas (although the attitudes of United States elites toward Europe is a crucial part of the historical episode called the Atlantic Community), nor that Britons view reruns of "Dallas." These interests express cultural affinity, the same affinity that allows an Englishwoman to marry and migrate to America more easily than a Sinhalese. Affinity translates into powerful cultural nostalgia, however, and can give political alliance the patina of real emotional commitment. But the shared interests that drive an alliance must preexist. For Britain and the United States, these links have existed almost without interruption since 1815. As Britain declined after 1900, it ceased to be a competitor in the American mind, while popular social Darwinian theories of Anglo-American blood-fraternity laid the basis for an enduring alliance highly inflected by mass nostalgia. The myth making of two world wars has kept the tie tight.

The same cannot be said for the rest of Europe. In fact, Britain is the wonderful exception, hardly sufficient to support a theory of alliance as cultural nostalgia. Of all European societies, Britain is America's most intimate relation. It might even have chosen membership in the North American culture area, but in the last few years it finally committed to European integration. Differences in values and ruling ideas between Britain and America are all the more pronounced between the United States and other European societies. These cultural moats were masked after 1945, as American cultural imperatives were accepted and displayed by dependent Europeans.

Reemergent Europe is increasingly charting its own course. America may play commercially in the world of the EC, but it cannot be a part of that world because of separate ruling ideas whose separation is only obscured by the shared appearance of "democratic institutions." European societies share ruling premises not only of tribal identity but also of state control, elite orchestration, and community intrusion; America holds to a vision of authority vested in the individual citizen, of a society dependent on civic virtue instead of state virtue, where the rights and relationships of individuals and groups are in a constant process of balancing and reinterpretation. Europeans see America as chaotic and brutal; Americans see Europe — especially its dominant Protestant North — as the triumph of the overbearing and oppressive, if "all-caring," state.

As American and European interests increasingly diverge through the 1990s, notions of cultural fraternity will fade. The manufactured nostalgia on which the Atlantic Community was nurtured, the fraternity of Western Civilization shoulder-to-shoulder against Communist barbarism, will not survive to sustain it much longer.

Prospects for a Purely Political Alliance

Europe: threat and promise. Americans do not learn their own history. When they look back, it is most likely through the lens of myth, packaged as lively docudrama (even the Public Broadcasting System series on the Civil War falls into this pattern). And serious retrospection in Washington rarely goes further back than 1945. As a result, Americans miss broader currents and continuities in how their country has approached the world. What ultimately may be a historical aberrance — the postwar era — is thus seen as the only normal and permanent basis for American foreign policy. Of course, this era has been dominated by the metaphor of the Atlantic Community. But that metaphor itself grew out of a rather tortured United States–European relationship, a weave tangled, torn, and intertwined. With the winter of 1945, however, the United States dropped references to the old transatlantic tapestry. It described the "new" world after 1945 as though it had passed a historical watershed. As nuclear weapons made all former notions of war and strategy "obsolete," so America's new world role and the new world situation erased all traditional truths about American foreign policy and American interests. The United States could never go back to anything like the world before the war; therefore, its history was of little use now. Indeed, it assumed the great Punic struggle it called the "containment" of communism would allow it no choice for generations to come.

America tried to bury the inherited legacies of two culture areas by announcing them one — an Atlantic Community. By 1950, with Western Europe saved from communism at the polls and Germany on the road to reform, if not spiritual ablution, the United States could support this slogan with a noble alliance, a shared monetary and trading system, and an appearance of political unanimity as sister democracies.

What happened to the old, defining American vision of Europe? Before 1945 it had a powerful role through the balance of the American experience. By 1950 it was almost unmentionable. But it still lived. Codified by George Washington's Farewell Address, America relied on Europe for a crucial element of negative self-definition. It was the place from which most Americans had fled, and the force that had made them flee was that dark tyranny against which they contended. Europe was the ancient source of threat and the present danger as well. Although Americans had sought a new world as sanctuary, they acknowledged that there was no ultimate escape from the dark idea that European tyranny represented. This dual tension — seeking to deny Europe's impact on American lives while creating an alternative force for good that would eventually overthrow it — is still the driving dynamic of American foreign policy. Americans shift between active world engagement and domestic introspection, using the image of Europe — as a threat or a promise — better to define themselves. Europe was primarily, and naturally, seen more as a military threat through the nineteenth century; the United States did not have the national strength to think of contending there. In the twentieth century, however, it has used Europe more complexly. In World War I it made "German militarism" the totem for all the world's evil, focused on a single people. Other European states were redescribed in America's image as little "Eaglets": the result of Jefferson's picture of spreading the American good news. Woodrow Wilson touted Czechoslovakia and Poland as evidence of Europe's reform. It is important to remember, however, that it was easy to engender a kind of democratic paternalism in American hearts and minds for such defenseless countries. The naked power plays and greed of Britain and France at Versailles shocked Wilson, and Sidney Fay's *Origins of the World War* helped to evoke a majority American response by the 1930s: they were all to blame. After all, were they not simply the same old, cynical European powers, playing their imperial games with the lives of their people?

American sympathies went out to Czechoslovakia, and one might argue that the crucial connection in turning emotionally against Hitler was the picture of Munchkins enslaved by a great-power wicked witch. Joseph Stalin's postwar trampling of these states locked in American emotional commitment to containment after 1945. This may help explain part of the continuing pull of an Atlantic Community. Defeated or brought down (like Britain) as they were from great-power glory, Americans enjoyed the vision of their country guarding a weakened and defenseless Western Europe. While Americans reveled in protecting and reshaping Western Europe, they kept alive the image of a European threat as well. But, instead of German militarism or Nazism — threats dependent on a single individual or institution — the United States had an entire concept against which to contend. It was an idea, moreover, that embraced the core of modern European philosophy: elegant theories that had now gone terribly wrong. It must have been a secret delight for Americans to fight a primitive force arising from the most enlightened European thought: it was a vindication of the American idea as Europeans sought succor from the United States against the demons they themselves had created. The critical element of America's image of Europe, then, is a cultural threat. Europe's military threat was simply the vehicle of its idea, which could finally be defeated only through the substitution of the American idea and its free embrace by Europe.

The European "spirit of the age" and America. The visible sense of Europe as a threat came in the form of its autocratic ways and institutions: realpolitik, imperialism, militarism, and state control over society. The latent conflict — flaring up from time to time in American politics — was between the American and European ideas. Europe dominated the world scene through the nineteenth century, and what historians call "the spirit of the age" exerted a powerful influence on "Americanism" and the path taken by the United States's culture area.

The impact was felt from two directions in European thought: the statist and the revolutionary. Statist concepts tended to find a receptive audience among some American elite groups. Theories like social Darwinism tended to justify the efforts of American elites to use class and caste to preserve their lock on politics and American life. Naturally, European notions of social revolution were introduced by some immigrants into the lexicon of American groups seeking to expand their political power. Bolshevism and communism were only recent importations in a growing process of European ideological pollination.

The highly limited ability of European ideology to take root in America is one crucial measure of culture-area identity. The main impact, in fact, of European thought on American politics has been to underscore and intensify Americanism, by painting European theories as subversive attacks by the evil stranger. Whether English Cavalier-aristocrats infecting the South (the caricature of abolitionists), or wild-eyed Irish incendiaries, or German anarchists, or Lower East Side "Reds," European ideas were often used as weapons in domestic political struggles of one group or coalition against another. The subliminal fear that Americans arguably still harbor of European ideas continues to drive a hope that the willing substitution achieved in 1945 — that of Europeans displacing their own ideology for America's — will not be reversed. An analysis of European-American cultural intercourse since 1945 would explain why this fear still persists.

Europeans retained their world view and their embedded view of America. In the period of America's greatest cultural efflorescence — from, say, 1945 to 1965 — Europeans accepted a kind of reverse historical process, whereby an American spirit of the age infected Europe. This was the time of Mercedes with fins, of French entrancement with Jacqueline Kennedy. Americans were cool, and so was David Brubeck and his music. Paris worshipped Jerry Lewis as the god of comedy, and American rock and roll was truly king among European youth. Americans reveled in these times: the ultimate wish fulfillment in their national myth, the American passage complete. And it was not simply that Europe had exchanged its philosophic foundation — its existential postulates — for America's. They nurtured an even more powerful American dream: that of a global culture molded in the American image.

The United States and global culture. The American world view is skewed by two disabling fallacies: that America is the seedbed of an integrated human society and that this united world culture will emerge only through this country's intercession. This national mission transcends foreign-policy swings; in fact, it has infused all American approaches to the world. When the country was young and weak, taming the New World wilderness, it was building the alternative society: the model, the City on the Hill. When it was a bit stronger, it dictated to European powers how they might conduct themselves in the Western Hemisphere. Stronger still, it intervened to save them from themselves. Weakened by depression, it tried to keep its distance from their growing corruption and strife; when it saw no choice, the United States intervened again. So great was its victory that it accepted what then seemed the denouement to the American story, the last stage in fulfilling its original charge.

The postwar world was all about creating a universal world system of mutually enjoined democratic societies. A powerful if unspoken assumption was that a world of like-minded polities was latent, waiting to be born: a world of shared social values that would become a United States global culture. This was the true metaphor of the postwar world. The American spirit of the age was one of cultural conversion, and the grand strategy of containment simply an instrument to get from here to there. In this context, the Soviet Union and Western Europe played critical roles in the passion play that Americans still mistakenly call the cold war. The Soviets took on the old mask of European tyranny, that hallowed lineage going back to George III and the Jacobin terror, updated by Prussian militarism, fascism, and Nazism. They served stalwartly for forty years as the demon force to the American archangel of democracy.

Western Europe, especially Germany, took up the role of Europe reformed. The United States did not treat Western Europe as a strategic beachhead or a critical industrial-economic bastion critical to the survival of an American empire; it did much more than that, and asked much more of Europeans. It is a testament to the afterglow of the American victory, to paranoid-aggressive Soviet behavior, and to the new and passionate immediacy of "atomic war" that they came so far along with the United States.

Americans asked Europeans — and their ruling establishments, which have always looked on the United States as barbarous -- to become like them. As suggested earlier, they willingly complied for about twenty years. This response was an extraordinary act of cultural submission. Europeans were not simply accepting an American spirit of the age; they were abdicating a historical process: giving up their ownership to the dominant world spirit of the age. At that time, Europeans spoke of a historical shift in the world-power balance from the heart of Europe to its former margins, East and West. The truth was more bitter: the surrender of cultural identity to America.

Then why do Americans continue to insist on a transatlantic cultural identity? The simple answer is that many in the postwar political establishment, entrenched in Washington, still cling to a cultural convergence on United States terms. They ignore the reemergence of Europe and other culture areas, ignore the bitter experience of the 1970s when America's chosen institution of world enlightenment — the UN — was debased by the Third World, and they ignore their own history, whose great mission foundered in the hot forests of Indochina. It is understandable, it is natural; perhaps it is even inevitable. But it is sad.

Europeans started quietly casting off the American baggage in the mid-1960s. Just one example of Europe's cultural shrugging off things American: the fins disappeared from Mercedes and, by the 1980s, traditional Teutonic arrogance came to mark that car's appeal in the United States. Young American elites, the "yuppies," wanted nothing more than to pass as Europeans. General Motors surrendered in 1984 when it swathed its standard celebrity sedan with special styling cues and called it Euro-sport. The Atlantic Community is no longer the banner for an American global culture — especially in the manner of the "Crusade in Europe." It has become a new code word for transatlantic elites, who have always played in the American social mix and yet who have suggested an offshore presence, a mere strand of American cultural life. American attitudes toward Europe in 1990 almost seem to reflect a nineteenth-century ambivalence. Nativists raise the specter of a united Germany or of a "Fortress Europe," while East-coast elites enamored of European style and statism keep talking about the Atlantic Community. But today's terminology differs from the code words of the postwar world. Then the Atlantic Community was about the American mission, an American global culture. Since the collapse of the Soviet threat, the only real, passionate connection between Europe and the United States hinges on elite social-political groups in America. That those groups continue for a time to define the official line—as the Bush administration does—on the United States and Europe means that the redolent shibboleth, the Atlantic Community, will continue as well in America's political vocabulary. For a time.

Why the Myth Goes On

How the Atlantic Community benefits Europe. Like Japan, Western European countries learned early how to use their dependent status to their advantage. When liberated by the United States, they were defeated societies, and this helplessness created an important American emotional attachment. Long after their rebuilding, the United States continued to look on Western Europe as a place that would always need American protection. This perception, once locked in, buffered European states from an American backlash as they grew stronger and more demanding. They could hardly be real competitors without military power. This situation meant that European countries could demand concessions on a number of economic issues—the pipeline was one of the most salient—and the United States would cave in without necessarily feeling like a loser. Furthermore, the United States needed them to remain in the garb of dependents in order to perpetuate its vision of an American global culture, in which they were the "Vanguard Eaglets." European countries—except France—discovered early on that the United States would give in on less-central economic issues so long as they yielded on strategic issues. This relationship is too cozy to break up prematurely. Before the Soviet crack-up, with seemingly long decades ahead of twilight struggle and a conveniently (for France) divided Germany, Europe 1992 looked like a perfect way to ensure that the United States would continue to foot the bill for European security while acceding to all regulatory and tariff demands from a united European economic polity. Now in a world dominated by three powers—North America, the EC, and Japan—the free ride is over: both military and economic. But Europeans cannot be blamed if they try to keep their postwar advantage at least until Europe 1992 is a reality.

Lingering insecurities. The problem with four decades of dependency is terminating it. Soviet weakness does not mean an abrupt end to NATO. One might even argue—perversely, perhaps—that the Soviet threat was subordinate to the sense of order, the security blanket that the United States presence had created. German unification and Eastern uncertainties keep Europeans clinging to its American legions. And other United States cohorts are actively protecting European vital interests in the Persian Gulf, with typically token European contributions offered in return. In other words, the military payoff of the Atlantic Community, for Europeans, is still a good deal. But is their current popular feeling an existential truth or is it, like the belief in a permanent East-West struggle, an expectation that people want to preserve? After all, the era of the great United States–Soviet stand-off lasted more than forty years. These transient, post–cold war world times, however, are no more than a historical transition. The ending phase is just about over; yet the new primary relationships between great powers — and just as critically, their terms of relationship — are not yet fully visible. It makes sense for Europeans to hold on to old-world institutions a bit longer.

The breaking up. The Atlantic Community as myth drew its power from three premises: United States leadership, the Soviet threat, and mutuality of European and American interests. It has been argued here that a fourth premise — cultural fraternity — was inspired propaganda, a way of weaving the three core assumptions into a single popular image that was, essentially, politically inarguable. That embracing image of cultural fraternity has been hard put to persevere without the Soviet threat. Ultimately, the Manichaean Soviet premise inspired the assumption both of inevitable United States leadership and of an indivisible transatlantic "interest."

United States leadership evolved beyond simple security; it grew into a comforting framework in which old European woes need never be revisited. This was always described *sotto voce*, however, as a historical bonus by-product. In the future, with an EC framework already working in some areas as a substitute for NATO, political gymnastics will be required to explain why American armored divisions are needed to adjudicate tiffs and teapot tempests between mature, long-allied societies.

Mutual interests, such as embedded trade and tourism, of course, will continue to exist. The Soviet threat, however, created a sense of even deeper, submagna fusing of European and American interests. The Soviet threat, and its barbarian mask shaped from European ideas, gave force to the belief that the preservation of civilization itself was America's fundamental mutual interest. From this premise it was but a step to the erection above ground of a great, colorful proscenium of cultural fraternity. This transformed the urgent need of the historical moment (which, after all, lasted forty years) into an instant legacy of shared values, habits, and goals. Again, without the threat the rest rings hollow, like the bitter aftertaste of a stump speech. If the old "postwar" alliance of NATO and Japan opens up into three centers — North America, the EC, and Japan — one can imagine three diverging, if not yet opposed, agendas as well. Though the EC phenomenon is far from achieving political confederation, it is much closer to initiating economic integration. And through integration Europe will focus more on itself. Soon, its great internal market will begin to vie with the great North American Free Trade Zone.

The Bush administration is apprehensive that the new Europe will go its own way. Robert Zoelick, an adviser to Secretary of State James A. Baker III, set out the fears of the Washington establishment when he suggested in a 21 September 1990 speech that Europe could develop in three different directions. One, which he called "insular," described an EC "absorbed" with the process of Europe's economic integration. Another, which he disparaged as "itinerant," imagines a Europe "that will engage around the world, but autonomous, without much interest in new, durable alliance ties for this new era." *Autonomous* is the code word. Obviously, these are the bad European futures. The third direction — the good future —

would be, of course, the "international": the United States–Europe–Japan free world alliance persisting forever, with of course United States leadership. And he called on the myth of the Atlantic Community to buttress his argument. He used the badge of "Euro-America," which "grows from the common roots of the Renaissance, the Reformation, and the Enlightenment." Ancestral roots, as many American blacks have discovered on setting foot in Senegal or Nigeria, does not equal cultural identity. If that were true, then the United States would have shared the same inevitable basis for alliance with Germany in 1935.

The truth is that the American political establishment wants to perpetuate the world it knew and still loves. The burden of the argument presented here is not that the Atlantic Community was bad but simply that it cannot be maintained much longer as a working — or even coherent — basis for American foreign policy and national strategy. The United States can maintain political arrangements and friendly associations with the EC or individual European countries, but it cannot impose leadership on its historical-nostalgic terms. If Europe and its peoples could continue into the indefinite future as a collection of weak and timid states, incapable of asserting their own course — desperately pleading for America to stay and protect them — there would be no reason to take issue with the useful creation that was the Atlantic Community. But America has not yet taken the time to reflect truly on world change. This means that it has not confronted the ramifications of the Soviet slide and the emergence of the EC and Germany. This means also that it has not examined — let alone accepted — the impact of political shifts now impending in its own society.

The United States is now living in an inherited condition. It entered the world situation it now occupies with many advantages, not the least of which was the virtual collapse of its great adversary. But the movement of change was merely initiated with the Soviets' fall. Simply announcing a new world order is not the same as forging it. Creating a successor world system would require the same kind of assertion that gave America its authority in 1945. To make an Atlantic Community II—"Euro-America"—would require a historical forcing function, a dramaturgy through which heroic American leadership would sweep Europe and Japan into a new compact . . . with the United States on top. The opportunity and the means to do that exist as this is written, in the Persian Gulf. Yet the American impulse so far has been to avoid seizing it, to avoid even recognizing that seizing this strategic opportunity is necessary to renew the vision of United States world leadership. Moreover, failure to achieve America's stated goals in the gulf would arguably achieve the opposite result. Anything less than the coronation of a great victory would mean not just a defeat but a quick end of the last lingering element of the postwar world: the United States as warrior chieftain. And with it would go the basis for an Atlantic Community.

From Containment toward Federation

ROBERT STRAUSZ-HUPE

"In international politics it is easier to predict what will happen than to make sense out of what has happened."—X

Since the 1940s, the quintessential purpose of American foreign policy has been to prevent Soviet power from upsetting the international status quo wrought by World War II. This policy of containment was suggested by events long before it received its name and the accolade of the burgeoning community of foreign-policy and national-security intellectuals. Although the urgencies that gave rise to the containment policies have long been forgotten, the *Foreign Affairs* article in 1947 that gave the concept its philosophical gloss retains its luster as the most celebrated footnote of modern history.[1]

The makers of these policies were pragmatic politicians, not intellectuals steeped in the history and theory of international politics. Their decisions responded to what they conceived to be the Soviet challenges of the day—Stalin's attempts to intimidate Turkey and subvert Greece and Iran and then the siege of West Berlin, capping the subjection of the peoples of central and Eastern Europe to Communist rule. With hardly any precedents, American policymakers had to improvise much of the order they sought to wrest from the chaos of postwar Europe. They did remarkably well; Western Europe, rather than going Communist, achieved unprecedented prosperity under democracy—corroborating Talleyrand's statement that, in foreign affairs, only the provisional endures.

Nothing in the charter of the North Atlantic Treaty Organization (NATO), the prime instrument of containment, pledges the allies to maintaining an everlasting armed confrontation. Quite to the contrary, beginning in 1967 (with the "Harmel Exercise," so named after the then Belgian foreign minister and chairman of NATO's high-level planning group), NATO sought to prevent the cold war from heating up, if not end it altogether some day. If anything has remained constant about NATO, it has been this double-track approach to the problem of East-West relations. Thus, from the outset, the doctrine of containment implied that the Soviets, barred from seeking relief from internal pressures by expansion abroad, would eventually come to the conference table and seek to advance their interests by diplomacy rather than by open or clandestine aggression. As it turned out, this was the winning strategy. The Soviet Union did come to the conference table. After a forty-year military standoff, the glaring insufficiencies of the Communist socio-economic system and growing popular discontent have forced the Soviet leaders to launch reforms at home and to pursue détente abroad.

It would have been reasonable to assume that the brilliant success of the containment policies, won by the immense effort and steadfastness of NATO, would please the allied publics and ensure their continued dedication to a policy to which they owed so much. If this has not been the case and if Mikhail S. Gorbachev, rather than the alliance's statesmen, receives the credit in Europe for what is so patently NATO's achievement, then the explanation for this baffling phenomenon must be sought in the Soviet president's brilliant public relations abetted by the divisive debates in NATO's own camp.

A large sector of the American press clamors for faster and more far-reaching concessions to Soviet proposals for arms control and more economic aid to the needy members of the Warsaw Pact. The Bush administration is told to hurry up or lose the unique opportunity offered by an enlightened Soviet leadership; if this, the latest essay in détente, fails — so the critics of the administration's Soviet policies assert — the fault will be ours, stuck as we are in cold war immobility. The critics, wrong as they might be, have gained the ground left undefended by the administration, caught in the unavoidable ambiguities of détente.

At the center of the ongoing debate over how much or how little has changed beneficially in the Communist countries are these two questions: (1) Is it likely that the Soviet system, which controls the state and its repressive organs absolutely, will transform itself into a democratic state? (2) Is it likely that the reform leadership will be able to perform this feat by decrees handed down from the top without engendering a cataclysmic upheaval with incalculable consequences? These questions cannot be answered without a retrospective assessment of the Marxist-Leninist version of communism: Communists are intensely conscious of history — and, incidentally, Americans are not. Gorbachev has brought to his role as reformer an intensely historical mind: Where has communism gone wrong? What is left of it? What has happened to its ideological sources?

Thanks to the revelations of glasnost, the United States is able to glimpse Soviet realities that the Communist strategies of concealment and sheer mendacity have kept covered up for seventy-three years of Communist rule. The Soviet Union has been broke for a long time, and this fact now appears to have been the Soviet Union's best-kept secret until Gorbachev decided to reveal it and try to rid the Soviet system of economic mismanagement. It is not yet clear whether Gorbachev can reform a vast bureaucratic system, serviced by 100 million functionaries, and make it more transparent than a people raised to the discipline of secrecy ever wished it to be.

Perhaps the most important thing Gorbachev has said about himself is that he is a Leninist and that the purpose of his labors is the renaissance of Leninism as an ideological guide to the modern age. If his political philosophy is indeed derived from Leninist theory, it follows that as a matter of course he accepts the core thesis of Leninism: since Germany's defeat in World War I failed to rouse the German proletariat—then the largest and best-organized body of workers—to revolt against the German capitalist state, something had manifestly gone wrong with Karl Marx's dialectics of history. Why had the German workers failed to validate *Das Kapital?* It is here that Lenin came to the rescue of Marxism as amended. In *Imperialism: The Highest Stage of Capitalism,* Lenin stated that the contribution exacted by the Western capitalists from the colonial peoples had prolonged an economic system that otherwise would have fallen under the blows of the "immiserated" proletariat. No "immiseration," no revolution. It was this Leninist "discovery" of the colonial roots of capitalism that rescued Marxist ideology from its German fiasco. Lenin saved Marxism; communism rose to power in Russia, not in Germany—despite the fact that Marx had disqualified Russia as the right place for making the right kind of revolution.

Wars of national liberation have been the response of Leninism to the alleged capitalist exploitation of the colonial peoples, as in the Third World. By striking at the capitalist hinterland, Communist strategy would deprive capitalism of the sources of cheap raw materials and labor that allowed the capitalists to distract the proletariat of the advanced industrial states from the revolutionary mission that Marx assigned to it.

Gorbachev, the self-avowed, good Leninist cannot but subscribe to the Leninist theory of empire and revolution. In none of his voluminous statements has he tried to refute it. In sum, nothing in the ideological stance of the Soviet leadership forcefully avowed and adumbrated implies a fundamental shift in Communist priorities: Marx and Lenin were not in error; the incorrect interpretation and sloppy implementation of the Marxist-Leninist writ have compelled the Communist leaders to yield ground.

A lot of ground has changed hands. But does the retreat of communism from Eastern Europe mark a proportionate gain in all-European security? Even more important, has the power of the Soviet state, notably its military power, been seriously diminished? It does not seem so, despite a great deal of enthusiastic reporting on the end of the Soviet military threat, if not of all confrontations between political powers and, hence, history.

Although historical analogies can become ambiguous in retrospect, they tell a good deal about national character, which is exceedingly slow to change. Some Russian history therefore seems highly relevant to an assessment of the changes that have taken place under Gorbachev and to the United States's defense and foreign policies. Czar Alexander II, "the Liberator," introduced far-reaching reforms that triggered controversies at least as heated as the debates on glasnost and perestroika would be one hundred years later. The czar's assassination led not only to mounting domestic turmoil but also to a foreign war. Nicholas II and many leading Russian statesmen welcomed the war against Japan as an escape from insoluble domestic problems into patriotism and world politics. Although czarist

Russia lost this war, the czar tried to win on the battlefield what he feared to lose in domestic strife—the perpetuation of his autocratic rule.

The overthrow of czarism was not a garden party. It was a long, drawn-out, sanguinary affair beginning with the failed rebellion of a handful of aristocrats in December 1825. Throughout the nineteenth century, it was marked by scores of peasant uprisings, all of them bloodily suppressed; increasingly murderous anarchist convulsions; a series of reforms decreed from the top down; and the dialogue of countless conspirators and the stool pigeons of the secret police. It gathered momentum in 1905 when the domestic and foreign blunders of a demented government cried out for radical changes and seemed to make the fall of the rotten regime inevitable. The regime tottered but managed to remain upright, able to fight in World War I against the premier military power of the age, Imperial Germany. For three years the Russian people went along docilely with a grotesquely incompetent military leadership that exacted hecatombs to no discernible good purpose. In 1917, the regime collapsed under the sheer weight of its failures. The Bolsheviks pushed what was falling and in the process buried the short-lived republic of Kerensky, Russia's only experiment in democracy. From then on, a new set of autocrats, more ruthless than the czars and a shade more efficient in war, has ruled the nation from above, reformed it from above, and drawn their power to reform and to rescind reform from the most elaborate police state in history.

It is unlikely that developments less protracted, less adventitious, and less cataclysmic than those that brought down czarism will rid Russia and the world of the Communist system. In this century, the passage of a country from totalitarian rule to democracy has always been marked by the intervention of forces from outside the respective national system, to wit, by a war that the regime had lost. The modern police state is much too secure to succumb to any internal opposition. In a short while, computerized vigilance will foreclose the few possibilities for dissent under communism, not to speak of resistance to the system. The rulers of the Soviet Union, though they have much to learn from the West about the management of their national patrimony, are advanced in the techniques and control of communications. In brief, though it would seem that the transition of the Soviet Union from despotism—the up-to-date, modern variety—to democracy is the precondition of world peace, it is doubtful that this happy denouement will be brought about soon and without the unrelenting exertions of Western statecraft. Furthermore, Western statecraft, far from consistently pursuing the appropriate policies, has consistently wavered in that pursuit and needs to clarify its choices. In all the great issues of world history, the choices have been scant. In this, the greatest historical issue to date, the West has no choice. It has to get used to living with this prospect as if it had freely chosen it. This is the only illusion that the few free peoples left in the world can safely indulge in.

Gorbachev is a Communist and a Russian, a Communist by intellectual formation and a Russian by birth, speech, and ethnic pride. He is an archetypical Russian as well as an exemplary member of the party. In this respect—patriotism and loyalty to the party—the leaders of the Soviet establishment are cast in the same mold as the czar's bureaucrats, who were unquestionably loyal to the monarchy and deeply patriotic. Indeed, this amalgam of Leninism and Russian nationalism is the strongest bond that holds together the establishment, otherwise split by the struggle for power. Thus the leaders of the Soviet establishment—the only Russians who make decisions that matter—do not and cannot see the issues of war and peace and hence the present and future world order the way that Americans do. This also goes for the degree of force that must be applied to shape the world in the image of the American or the Soviet concept of order. The differences in the United States and Soviet arsenals of nuclear weapons reflect this difference of national attitudes toward the uses of force.

There is a gap between what Gorbachev and his military aides say about the Soviet military establishment and what the United States knows about the strategic capabilities of the Soviet Union. While it is now likely that both Soviet and American conventional forces in Europe will be gradually phased out, there is as yet no indication of a proximate reduction in the number of Soviet strategic missiles, especially systems that are not matched by similar systems in the United States inventory. The Soviet military establishment—the High Command and the high-ranking political watchdogs in uniform—has publicly given Gorbachev its support. This, unfortunately, says next to nothing about the Soviet political leadership's actual control of the military. It takes a large conventional force to capture and hold ground but only a relatively small body of highly trained professionals to start a nuclear war. No one knows exactly how the commanders of the Soviet nuclear forces would respond to a crisis within the Soviet government. Of all the asymmetries of the Soviet and the United States political systems, this is the most imponderable and troubling one. The Western peoples have fought and bled for the control of the military by civilian authority. Without such civilian authority, true democracy is inconceivable.

Neither Gorbachev nor his most ardent apologists at home and abroad have chosen to raise this issue. Until the Soviet Union reveals exactly who has the authority to start a nuclear war, there is a massive discrepancy in the Soviet-American relationship. The one Soviet gesture that would be persuasive that Soviet thinking on peace and war has begun to rhyme with that of the United States would be the deactivation of the Soviet multimegaton batteries deployed against America.

The Soviet Union is the last colonial empire. The central Asian republics are czarist conquests of the late nineteenth century; the Eastern European client states and the German and Polish territories incorporated into the Soviet Union are yesterday's acquisitions. Unlike the people of Europe, the Russian people did not have the benefit of the moral criticism that turned European public opinion against colonialism: Lenin's *Imperialism: The Highest Stage of Capitalism* was addressed to the Western public, not to the most massive colonialists of all—the Russians. Lenin might have meant it that way; but the fact that Russia's colonies were adjacent to the motherland while other countries' colonies were situated overseas may have had something to do with this peculiar fault of vision. Thus the Russian people, unlike the Western imperialists, have not been assailed by a bad conscience that, more than lack of the requisite military means, has killed off the spirit of imperialism and colonialism.

Thus far, the strategy of containment has prevented the domestic crisis of the Soviet system from breaking out beyond its borders into world politics. Containment must still be the overarching goal of the United States in world politics. Much will change in the next century, but the threat of the Soviet Union's flight from domestic failure into foreign war will remain the same for at least another generation. A new generation of Russians might gradually dismantle the Soviet system; and NATO, having done its job, could disband. Though the United States cannot yet see this sea change, it can hope for it. Indeed, it is the only hope.

The intellectual and material contributions to the political stability of the Soviet Union that the United States and its allies now deem desirable need to be tempered by an awareness of how little they can do about it — and how ineffective Western credits and investment have been in fostering democracy in the Soviet Union. The Soviet regime's restraints on individual freedom have stifled the growth of private enterprise in the Soviet Union. Lifting these restraints must precede economic reform — not the other way around. For example, Lenin's New Economic Policy of the 1920s and Khrushchev's revelations in the 1950s elicited substantial investments in Soviet industry from a distinguished list of Western capitalists. Then the critics of these capitalistic contributions to economic growth under Communist management were told that the capitalist input would raise the recipient's average standard of living and sow the seeds of a consumerist society on the sure way to democracy.

If there is any country where the fallacy of this reasoning has been proved again and again, it is the Soviet Union. As for natural and demographic resources — arable soil, proven deposits of minerals, hydrological potential, space available for settlement, and almost 300 million healthy and literate people — the Soviet Union's endowments exceed those of the United States.

Previous attempts at fundamental reforms, as distinguished from reform-for-show, were defeated by a political system guaranteed to eviscerate any and all reforms that would loosen the grip of the Soviet ruling class on the levers of government. This is exactly what an open market of goods and ideas could not help doing. Until this happy event comes to pass, there is no reason for the United States to scuttle its long-standing policies toward the Soviet Union. These policies were prudently conceived: how to do business with a state monopoly rather than individual traders in an open market; and, more important, how to ensure that credits guaranteed and investment made by private United States business will not be diverted by the Soviet rulers to shore up the Communist bureaucracy that has consistently put the power of the state ahead of the economic well-being of the individual citizen. Admittedly, this means subordinating economics to the priority of political interests. Nothing has yet happened in the Soviet Union that would allow the United States to switch priorities.

The most effective — indeed, the essential — aid that the United States can render the forces of democracy in the lands of the Warsaw Pact is to maintain its military and economic strength. That, rather than the fevered search for markets in once inhospitable lands, will foster the rise of democracy and keep the peace in Europe.

So great has been the success of Western statecraft and so irresistible the power of Western values that it is tempting to hail the convulsion in the Communist core countries as the end *tout court* of Soviet power politics. Yet some of the issues arising now from the commotions in central Europe and the Balkans bear a remarkable resemblance to those that fueled ethnic strife and nationalist passions at the beginning of the century and finally dragged the world into war. So close is the resemblance that it seems as if the issues of three generations ago and the issues now arising from the decay of Soviet Russian power are the same. Then the major Western powers could not stand aside. It was the fragmentation and complexity of central European–Balkan politics that upset the calculations of high policy and jostled the great powers into a confrontation they did not want.

Violent as were the shocks imparted by World War I to the international system, hardly any of the major issues it was fought over have been resolved. The failures of the Versailles Treaty and associated treaties were carried over into World War II. In fact, the peoples of these contested lands still see in one another the archetypes of their tragic history. To this day few Poles can be found who want to deal with Russia, Communist or non-Communist; hardly any Hungarian has forgotten Hungary's bid in 1848 and 1849 for freedom or its replay in 1956 and that in both cases it was Russian arms that defeated the Magyars' attempt at national independence. The hard edges of the historical relationships of these peoples have been sharpened rather than blurred by perestroika and glasnost.

The shrinkage of Communist power has triggered centrifugal forces, heretofore repressed, in almost all the states along the rim of the Soviet Union. Most of these states will have to come to grips with the multiethnic issues that, before World War II, made them easy prey of the Nazi-fascist predators. Since then, these divisive issues have increased in numbers and intensity.

The relevancy of federalism to these issues — the classic federalism of the American Founding Fathers enriched by the experience of scores of new nations — is so obvious as to make one wonder how the statesmen of the day could have missed it. It is as if the world is now holding its breath, waiting for the world's leading federation to take the lead in transcending the system of nation-states that can no longer meet the challenges of the postindustrial age.

Before deciding on its policies toward the post–cold war world, the United States needs to reflect again on its place in the world. What makes the United States compellingly attractive as a political and economic model — despite the fact that the governing elites of most countries profess to disdain it? The answer is quite simple: the United States has developed and perfected a political system that checks authority with authority — leaving the executive, the legislature, and the courts as well as innumerable private associations and citizens to do what they do best. The system does not always work to satisfy all the criteria of perfect democracy. Nevertheless, the union of fifty states is philosophically the wisest and operationally the most effective government in place. With the least commotion and fanfare, this system has ensured a high degree of civic contentment of its people.

What is puzzling is America's disregard of its own political experience as a guide to its foreign policy. Perhaps the most grievous error of United States foreign policy after World War II was the failure to lead the West toward federal unity, the very unity that it hailed in the abstract and rejected in fact. In the first years after World War II, the nations of the West would have followed the United States into virtually any experiment in community building. They had no choice but to take their cue from the one great power that had emerged undamaged from the war. Surprisingly, the United States did not bring to bear its considerable leverage — shaped by its victories in Europe, Africa, and Asia — on the state system. Instead, the United States let it be known that it would be pleased if its European allies and friends joined together in supranational unions, such as the European Community and the Western European Union — as long as it need not itself become part of such a supranational union and yield an iota of its sovereignty to it. Consequently, NATO stopped far short of integrating its members politically.

Once again the United States can learn from history. It has the opportunity to sublimate the wartime alliance into a confederal and then — Deo volente — a federal state. But to take advantage of this opportunity, it needs a philosophy and a will born of this philosophy. The philosophy is there to be translated into a program of action. The United States is the heir to a rich tradition of thought ranging from the Federalist Papers to Clarence Streit's Union Now. Indeed, the federal idea has been the one seminal idea that American philosophy has contributed to American foreign policy in this century. Its two applications, the Marshall Plan and NATO — attenuated versions of the Atlantic Union — saved the free world from sharing the lot of the peoples that, upon the defeat of the Nazi and fascist despots, fell under the rule of Communist despotism.

A new Europe is taking shape; American relations to the Europe-to-be must be thought through now. The first, most urgent step to be taken toward a new United States–Europe relationship should be a grand review of the American federal experience and its relevancy to United States foreign policies. If ever there was a time for creative American statesmanship, that time is now.

NOTE

1. X [George F. Kennan], "The Sources of Soviet Conduct," *Foreign Affairs* 25 (July 1947): 566–82.

Index